A SERIOUS CASE OF THE BLUES

A SERIOUS CASE OF
THE BLUES
CHELSEA IN THE 80s

CLIVE BATTY

VSP

Vision Sports Publishing Ltd
2 Coombe Gardens,
London, SW20 0QU

www.visionsp.co.uk

This First Edition Published by
Vision Sports Publishing in 2006

Text © Clive Batty

ISBN 1-905326-02-5

Editor: Jim Drewett

Cover design: David Hicks, **davidhicksdesign@mac.com**
Design and typesetting: Neal Cobourne, **ourkidesign@btinternet.com**

Front cover photograph: Empics
Back cover photograph: John Ingledew, **www.chelseabluesinblackandwhite.com**
Inside pics: John Ingledew, Mark Westwood, Empics, Action Images and Mirrorpix

Proofreading: Brackley Proofreading Services, **brackleyproof@lineone.net**

Printed and bound in the UK by Cromwell Press Ltd, Trowbridge, Wiltshire

A CIP catalogue record for this book is available from the British Library

CONTENTS

A SERIOUS CASE OF THE BLUES
is the follow-up to the best-selling
KINGS OF THE KING'S ROAD

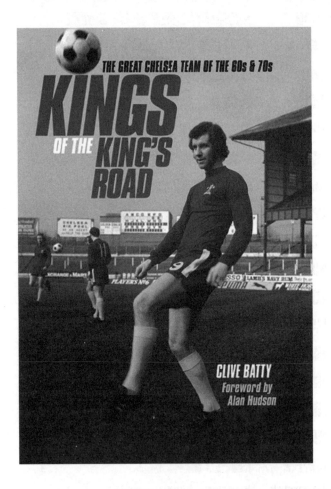

"Playing in this magnificent Chelsea team was unbelievably exciting. The Sixties were in full swing and that was reflected in our style of play – both on and off the pitch. *Kings of the King's Road* is a brilliant re-creation of those incredible times."

ALAN HUDSON, CHELSEA 1969-74

ACKNOWLEDGEMENTS

T his book would have been a much slimmer volume without the contributions of the many Chelsea players who gave so generously of their time. In particular, I would like to thank Peter Bonetti, Ian Britton, John Bumstead, Gary Chivers, Kerry Dixon, Mickey Droy, Steve Finnieston, Ron Harris, John Hollins, Alan Hudson, Tommy Langley, Colin Lee, Ray Lewington, Pat Nevin, Peter Osgood, Colin Pates, Garry Stanley, David Speedie, David Stride, Clive Walker, Graham Wilkins and Clive Wilson.

Cliff Auger, Paul Baker, Scott Buckingham, Roger Cumberbatch, Alan 'Punky Al' Delaprelle, Tim Harrison, Ron Hockings, Robert Howard, John Ingledew, Dave Johnstone, Patrick Kenny, Dave Key, John Kiely, Chris Ryan and Nick Worger provided some fascinating memories for the three chapters focusing on the fans, while Mark Westwood was a tremendous source of stories about the players, many of which found their way into Chapter Eleven, Footballers' Lives.

Thanks are also due to Fred Roll, who donated a collection of Chelsea programmes from the period; Ayoob 'Mo' Atchia, who did some of the research for the book at the British Newspaper Library in Colindale; and Sheila Batty, Mark Colby, Des O'Reilly and Bob Wheeler, all of whom came up with some worthwhile suggestions.

Despite being a passionate Manchester United fan, David Hicks did a great job designing the cover. Jim Drewett, my editor/publisher at VSP, was a constant source of excellent ideas and encouragement, while his business partner Toby Trotman provided enthusiastic backing for the project from the start.

Although all the people mentioned above made valuable contributions, I should like to stress that this interpretation of Chelsea history from 1975-89 is, ultimately, a personal one and that, with the exception of the individual recollections of players and fans, the views expressed within these pages are those of the author alone.

FOREWORD
BY KERRY DIXON

I joined Chelsea from Reading in the summer of 1983. My first impressions of the place were great. The club had been in the doldrums but that didn't really matter to me. I was moving up a level, from the old Third Division to the Second. I was looking to continue my progression, Chelsea was the next step up but without making too big a step at once. I thought I could do something at Chelsea, I had confidence in my own ability and I was thrilled to be joining the club.

I was there, and more new players were coming in. I was looking forward to a decent season, to us doing something, to making some sort of impact. A new chairman, Ken Bates, had come in the year before and with new players arriving as well there was a sense that the club wanted to move forward, but no one knew how that first season would go or what would happen. But we beat Derby 5-0 on the opening day of the season and never looked back.

The fans and the fanbase were what made Chelsea a big club, even though we were in the Second Division. For the big games we were getting 30,000 and, by the end of that first season, almost 40,000 at the Bridge. That wouldn't have happened at Reading. I was aware just how passionate the Chelsea fans were right from the start. I think we only got 15,000 or so for that first game against Derby but the next week at Brighton there were thousands of Blues fans at the Goldstone Ground. I think that's when it hit me how big a club Chelsea was. The support filled the away end behind the goal, there were fans spilling onto the pitch, it was all a bit chaotic – and I remember thinking, "We've got fantastic support here." But I knew that anyway, to a degree, because of the previous history of the club. The fans were great to me. I don't know when it started exactly but at some point during that first season they began chanting my name and for quite a few seasons they used to sing "England's number nine" as well. It was fantastic for your confidence to get that sort of backing, it really gave you a lift.

It snowballed from that good start to the season. We had a new team, new players and fans who'd maybe stopped going were coming back through the gates. We had some wonderful attendances. The thrill of going up was fantastic for everyone. Nobody thought at the start of that year that it would be like that. When it ended in promotion, after we beat Leeds 5-0 at home, it was an incredible feeling. But we were thinking about promotion long before that. We believed that we could do it, because we knew that we were one of the best sides in the league. Promotion was the priority but we went on to win the Second Division title which was an absolute thrill. As for myself, I was quite single-minded: I believed in the team, I believed in myself, I wasn't finding it tough. I believed I could score goals and I had the same belief when we were in the First Division.

Before I signed for Chelsea I had never been to Stamford Bridge. The stadium was very different from how it is today. People might have said it was run down, but I never looked at it like that. You had that big imposing stand, the East stand, and the noise used to come from the Shed and the West stand benches. We used the running track for sprints and a warm-up on the Friday and I loved every minute of being there. As far I was concerned everything about the club was spot on. Compared with Reading, Chelsea had more staff and facilities and it was a definite step up for me.

It's great to see Chelsea now fulfilling the dream that we all had when I first came to the club. Ken Bates had a dream of what Chelsea could be and he pushed it that way. Matthew Harding and lots of other people played their part in helping Chelsea to where they are today, although it took the input of Mr Abramovich to take it to the level where the club is now. Matchdays now are absolutely wonderful at Chelsea. I enjoy every moment of coming to the games at Chelsea and at other grounds when the Blues are away. Top-level European football is one thing I never tasted but I always hoped to be a part of it, and thanks to my commentary role with Big Blue and Smooth FM I've got that involvement in the modern game.

I've known Clive Batty for about five years although I'd seen him around the club well before that. He's a genuine Chelsea fan of many years standing and when asked to contribute to this book I was only too pleased to have an input along with all the other players and fans who have been interviewed. I am sure you, like me, will enjoy reliving the incident-packed seasons covered by the book.

INTRODUCTION
TURBULENT TIMES AT THE BRIDGE

The Eighties were a time when, as Michael Douglas put it in *Wall Street*, greed was good and lunch was for wimps. The avaricious, 'get rich quick' culture was embraced by red-braced yuppies, Filofax-brandishing executives and even lowly council tenants, who were encouraged to buy their homes with the promise of making a killing on the booming property market. The cult Harry Enfield character 'Loadsamoney', while conceived as a satirical figure, summed up the money-obsessed times as he waved a well-stuffed wallet and poured scorn on those on who had missed out on the cash-fuelled party.

London, especially, was awash with readies – although, of course, there were exceptions to the general affluence and prosperity of the times, particularly among the massed ranks of the unemployed who felt the full brunt of the downsizing of manufacturing industry. Ironically, given the millions Roman Abramovich has pumped into the modern Chelsea, one of the most notable pockets of poverty was to be found at Stamford Bridge. Saddled by huge debts and playing in a crumbling, tumbledown stadium, Chelsea FC resembled one of the clapped-out, loss-making nationalised industries Margaret Thatcher and her tax-cutting chums in the Conservative government were keen to sell off to the highest bidder. In the Blues' case that turned out to be Ken Bates, who stumped up a mere pound to buy the club in 1982.

Unlike Abramovich, Bates did not have the wherewithal to be an overnight saviour.

Indeed, almost immediately, the problems facing the white-bearded entrepreneur multiplied when the ownership of Stamford Bridge was transferred to Marler Estates, a property developing company with a sharp eye for the main chance – in this case turning the Blues' ground into a hugely profitable residential complex for braying Sloanes and champagne-quaffing Hooray Henrys. Despite the best attempts of Bates to fight off the threat, for the rest of the decade Chelsea would continue to play at the Bridge with the very real prospect of being permanently evicted from their ancestral home.

"It wasn't a nice feeling knowing that we could lose the ground," says Colin Pates, who was a fixture in the Blues' team throughout the Eighties and captained the side for four years. "But throughout my time at Chelsea we never knew what to expect. There were times when we didn't know if we were going to be paid, for example, but we couldn't let any of that bother us. When things happened we just had to get used to them and get on with our job."

That meant trying to improve Chelsea's lot on the pitch. Sadly, in the early Eighties at least, there was little respite on the field of play from the despair and despondency enveloping SW6, as the Blues' performances veered between the mediocre and the abject. Under-funded and poorly motivated, the team struggled along in the middle reaches of the old Second Division, only occasionally suggesting that a return to the top flight was likely. With the club's name also tarnished by the hooliganism and racism of a section of its fans, these were some of the darkest days in the history of Chelsea FC.

However, this is not a story of unremitting gloom. Chelsea's fortunes did pick up in the mid-Eighties after manager John Neal went on a summer spending spree to overhaul his under-achieving side. The amount he spent, around £500,000, would barely cover Jose Mourinho's seasonal fines bill now, but back in 1983 it bought five players – Kerry Dixon, Pat Nevin, Eddie Niedzwiecki, Nigel Spackman and Joe McLaughlin – who would go on to play leading roles in the Blues' revival. They joined ambitious and committed players like Colin Pates, David Speedie, John Bumstead and Colin Lee who were already at the club; together with the new boys they would take Chelsea back into the First Division after a gap of five years and re-establish the club as a force in the top tier.

It seems incredible now that Kerry Dixon only cost Chelsea £150,000 (plus another £25,000 when he was eventually capped by England) when he joined the Blues from Reading in 1983. A powerful, pacy centre forward with a bullet-like shot and excellent ability in the air, Dixon's impressive scoring feats made him synonymous with Chelsea throughout the Eighties. His final tally of 193 goals for the club worked out at just £907 per goal and, more importantly, guaranteed the blond-haired striker a place in the club's hall of legends just one step below the Blues' all-time leading scorer, Sixties' striker Bobby Tambling.

If Dixon's position in the Chelsea pantheon is assured so too is that of his striker partner for four goal-filled years in the mid-Eighties, David Speedie. Fiery, combative, aggressive and determined, but also a fine, technically accomplished footballer who created as many goals as he scored, 'Speedo' was the perfect foil for Dixon. Together they terrorised defences, first in the Second Division and then in the top flight, and as a pair were instrumental in Chelsea's revival in the middle of the decade.

As, indeed, was the third element in the Blues' attacking triumvirate of that period, winger Pat Nevin. Chelsea's most skilful dribbler since the incomparable Charlie Cooke, Nevin had the uncanny knack of being able to glide past defenders as if they were rooted to the spot. The little Scotsman's ability to jink his way out of a tight spot gave Chelsea an extra dimension, as his admiring manager appreciated. "When the game was tight John Neal would say at half-time, 'Give it to Pat and let him weave his magic spells,'" reveals Colin Lee. "Then Speedo would usually shout out, 'Fuck his magic spells, how many players are there in this team?' But Dave was good for the side because he was a great player and he was a winner. What John Neal did was to bring in more players with a winning mentality. That's what was missing before."

As the Eighties wore on, though, Chelsea were once again winning fewer matches than they were losing. John Neal's side of swashbuckling cavaliers was broken up and remoulded by new boss John Hollins and, following an initially promising season, the Blues began a slow descent which culminated in the pain of relegation in 1988. Yet, continuing the theme of flux and change which characterised the decade, the club was back in the big time the following year, again under a different manager, Bobby Campbell.

From the perspective of the Chelsea of today – English champions, regular Champions League contenders, financially comfortable (to put it mildly) and, as the marketing men would have it, not so much a club as a 'brand' with millions of 'customers' worldwide – the up-and-down experience of the Blues in the Eighties seems, in many ways, more like 50 than 20 years ago. Yet, for many fans who follow the star-studded Blues now, the fluctuating Eighties provided some of the formative years of their Chelsea support and are not easily forgotten. Having seen the club struggle on and off the pitch during a tumultuous decade, these longstanding fans appreciate all the more the new glorious era which is now unfolding under Abramovich and Mourinho.

The late Seventies and Eighties may not have been so trophy-packed for Chelsea but there were, nonetheless, fascinating years. With the help of vivid contributions from players and fans this book, which can either be read as a single volume or as a follow-up to *Kings of the Kings Road: The Great Chelsea team of the 60s & 70s* (also published by Vision Sports Publishing), relives a time of turbulence, uncertainty and no little excitement at the Bridge.

CHAPTER ONE
A CLUB IN CRISIS
1975-76

The summer of 1975 was a wretched time to be a Chelsea supporter. Since the end of the Second World War, with the exception of one season, the Blues had been ever- presents in the top flight. Now, following a depressing campaign culminating in relegation, the club was facing the prospect of life in the old Second Division. To make matters worse a number of players, including long-standing fans' favourites Peter Bonetti and John Hollins, had been let go in the summer, while the financial constraints imposed by the club's massive debts meant that there would be no exciting new signings.

Yet it had all been so different just a few years earlier. In May 1971 thousands of fans had danced the night away in the King's Road, celebrating the Blues' epic European Cup Winners Cup victory over Real Madrid in Athens. Following the club's thrilling triumph in the FA Cup over arch rivals Leeds the year before, Chelsea were established as one of the country's most successful, entertaining and glamorous sides.

At that point the future had looked bright, but a souring of relations between manager Dave Sexton and some of his players, notably creative midfielder Alan Hudson and star striker Peter Osgood, soon led to the premature breaking up of a glittering side which, arguably, had still to reach its full potential. After one final, bitter bust-up with their manager, Osgood and Hudson, to the dismay of their legions of fans in the Shed, had left the club, only to be followed quickly out of the Stamford Bridge exit by Sexton in the autumn of 1974. At the end of the 1974/75 season, with another Seventies hero, Eddie McCreadie, recently installed as manager, the unthinkable happened: Chelsea were relegated.

Instead of fixtures with the top sides at home and in Europe, Blues fans were now contemplating trips to humble footballing outposts such as York, Plymouth and Bristol Rovers. London derbies would no longer be with Tottenham, Arsenal and West Ham but with Fulham, Charlton and Orient. Suddenly, the heady days of the early Seventies, when Chelsea's sparkling football had captivated fans and delighted the press box critics, seemed like a lifetime ago.

A hard-tackling defender in the 1970 FA Cup-winning team, McCreadie might have been expected to build his new side around the nucleus of his old team-mates who remained at the club. Instead, he adopted the same ruthless approach with most of them as he used to take with tricky right-wingers back in his playing days. To the surprise of many, three more stalwarts of the early Seventies team – left-winger Peter Houseman, midfielder John Hollins and goalkeeper Peter Bonetti – left Chelsea during the late spring or summer of 1975, while the remaining survivors of the glory days were left in no doubt by McCreadie that their places in the side were far from guaranteed.

The departures of Hollins and Bonetti, in particular, upset many supporters. Hollins was an energetic, consistent and enthusiastic player who had captained the side during most of the previous season and, as he was to prove over the next eight seasons with QPR and then Arsenal, still had the necessary fitness and ability to play at the highest level. At 33, Bonetti was five years older than Hollins, but hardly in his dotage as a goalkeeper. Moreover, 'The Cat' was a Blues legend and it was a sad day for Chelsea fans when he was allowed to join St Louis All Stars in the North American Soccer League.

McCreadie, though, was determined not to let sentiment cloud his judgement. The older players, he believed, were not going to turn Chelsea's fortunes around and, perhaps remembering how his first Blues manager, fellow Scot Tommy Docherty, had revitalised the club 12 years earlier by promoting players from the junior ranks, McCreadie gave every indication that he, too, would favour youth over experience.

After becoming Chelsea manager in April 1975, one of McCreadie's first decisions had been to appoint 18-year-old central midfielder Ray 'Butch' Wilkins as captain. No player had ever skippered the Blues at such a young age, but Wilkins immediately showed his leadership qualities with a series of mature performances.

A superb passer of the ball over short and long distances, and a regular scorer from long range, Wilkins was very much the jewel in the crown of the dozen or so young players who had either established themselves in the side or were pressing hard for first team recognition. Of this group, Chelsea fans were most familiar with Ian Britton, a pint-sized midfielder with a busy, bustling style and an extraordinary poodle-like haircut; striker Steve Finnieston, a prolific scorer in the youth and reserve teams who had enjoyed a short run in the side during the 1974/75 season; left back John Sparrow, a tidy defender who had been given his debut at the tail end of Dave Sexton's reign; and another defender, Graham Wilkins, Ray's older brother, whose progress had been hampered by a broken leg sustained at Old Trafford in November 1973 in only his third first team outing.

In addition to these players McCreadie could also call upon a quartet of 1970 veterans, Ron 'Chopper' Harris, Charlie Cooke, Ian Hutchinson and John Dempsey; a trio of young strikers in Teddy Maybank, Kenny Swain and Tommy Langley; a useful goalkeeper in John Phillips, backed up by a less experienced understudy, Steve Sherwood; Steve Wicks, a highly-rated teenage centre half; and three up-and-coming midfielders in Ray Lewington, Garry Stanley and Brian Bason.

McCreadie's squad certainly covered the bases in terms of youthful promise and 'been there, done it' experience, but it almost entirely lacked players in their mid-20s who were at the peak of their careers. Only four players fell remotely into this category: defender-cum-midfielder David Hay, the club's record signing, who had arrived at the Bridge from Celtic for £225,000 after a fine World Cup with Scotland in 1974; Bill Garner, a bruising centre forward whose battling style of play made him prone to injury; Mickey Droy, a massive centre half whose towering headed clearances from his own penalty area invariably passed beyond the halfway line; and 21-year-old Gary Locke, a pacy, attack-minded right back who had been voted the club's Player of the Year in 1974.

Having parted company with two more seasoned pros in midfielder Steve Kember and striker Chris Garland in the summer, McCreadie would have liked to have used the money from their transfers to buy replacements. There was never any question of that happening, however. Chelsea's finances were in a terrible state, the result of the ever-increasing cost of the new East stand which had finally opened at the start of the 1974/75 season after a year-long delay. McCreadie wasn't surprised to be told that the transfer kitty was empty: he would have to go with what he had.

Many managers would have used the absence of a transfer budget as an ideal opportunity to get their excuses in early and downplay expectations among the fans of a quick return to the top flight. That, though, was not Eddie's style. "Next season? No sweat. We will win the Second Division," he had confidently predicted in the days following the Blues' relegation.

Wearing a new Umbro blue kit with a fashionably floppy white collar, Chelsea limbered up for the new season with three uneventful games in the Anglo-Scottish Cup against Bristol City, Norwich and Fulham (the tournament was organised along regional lines, with English and Scottish clubs only meeting each other at a later stage). A penalty by former England star Alan Mullery at Craven Cottage ended Chelsea's interest in the competition, but few Blues fans cared: the goal for the season was promotion, not success in some meaningless cup.

Despite their lack of involvement in the transfer market and somewhat unbalanced squad, Chelsea were considered a better bet for a quick return to the First Division than the two teams who had taken the drop with them, Luton Town and Carlisle United. Among the other favourites for promotion were Sunderland, FA Cup winners just two years earlier; Southampton, who, impressively for a Second Division team, could boast two England internationals strikers in Mick Channon and Peter Osgood; and West Brom, whose well-organised team included a young Bryan Robson, 1966 World Cup hero Geoff Hurst, former Chelsea full-back Paddy Mulligan and former Leeds playmaker Johnny Giles, now player/manager at the Hawthorns.

Chelsea were handed a difficult start to the season with trips to Sunderland and West Brom in the opening four days. These games provided a disappointing return of just one point from a 0-0 draw at the Hawthorns, but the campaign appeared to be taking a turn for the better after two consecutive home wins, both by 3-1, over Carlisle and Oxford.

The win against Oxford, on a sunny evening in front of a reasonable crowd of 22,841 at the Bridge, was particularly encouraging as the Blues had to fight back from a goal down. Certainly, *The Times* correspondent, Christopher Warren, seemed impressed by the performance provided by McCreadie's mix of young guns and old stagers.

"Shrugging off their early misfortune, Chelsea played attractive, direct football," he wrote. "They were faster than Oxford, used the width of the lush green pitch sensibly to stretch the visitors' defence, and gave a thoroughly competent and confident display."

The fans had enjoyed the two emphatic home wins but, rather like Chelsea supporters in the modern era, were less pleased by the club's ticket price policy: despite the drop to a lower division, seat prices in certain areas of the ground had gone up by 25 per cent, while ground admission was increased from 50p to 80p (half price for juveniles). The price of the programme also went up by 50 per cent from 10p to 15p, although there was no increase in quality. Quite the contrary, in fact. Among the Chelsea programme collecting fraternity the 1975/76 vintage is generally agreed to be the poorest effort the club has ever produced: 20 black-and-white pages (apart from one colour picture on the cover), five of which consisted of adverts from local businesses, ranging from Alan Hudson's favourite boozer, The Markham Arms ('Great company, great beer, great food') to London Lady Escorts ('Attractive and discreet company – for any occasion').

Still, if the supporters were unhappy with the club's pricing policy, the club had equal cause to be displeased with the behaviour of some of the fans. Three days after the win over Oxford, Chelsea travelled to Kenilworth Road to play Luton. In the closing minutes of the match, their mood darkening by the second as their side slumped to a dismal 3-0 defeat, Chelsea fans invaded the pitch and attacked Luton goalkeeper Keith Barber. The mayhem didn't end there, either: after the match Chelsea fans rampaged through Luton town centre causing thousands of pounds worth of damage and then set fire to a train on their way back to London (see Chapter Four, 'Hello, Hello, We are the Chelsea Boys').

It wasn't the first time the players had seen Chelsea supporters involved in trouble, but the violent events at Luton seemed to unsettle them. The team failed to win one of their next eight matches, crashing out of the League Cup 1-0 at Fourth Division Crewe in the process. Ron Harris, a cult hero on the terraces for his ferocious tackling and unyielding commitment, was the villain on the night, conceding a penalty for handball which Crewe's Gerald Humphreys fired home.

A crushing 4-1 defeat at Southampton in early October, which plunged Chelsea dangerously close to the relegation zone, finally convinced McCreadie that something had to be done about the team's leaky defence – and, specifically, the goalkeeping position. His first choice goalkeeper, John Phillips, had broken a leg in pre-season training and his young deputy, Steve Sherwood, was going through a sticky patch. There was, of course, no money to buy another goalkeeper, but there was another option: a recall for Peter Bonetti.

"When Eddie McCreadie became manager he told me he was going to bring in the young players and so I went to America to see what it was like there," remembers Bonetti. "Then I came back to England to see what the situation was, and maybe look for a club. I was training at Chelsea, initially on a weekly contract, and in no time I was back in the first team: John Phillips was injured and Steve Sherwood wasn't playing so well, so Eddie put me straight back in."

The return of Bonetti, one of the most famous and best-loved players to pull on a Chelsea shirt, gave everyone a lift. 'The Cat' kept a clean sheet on his second 'debut', a 2-0 win at the Bridge over Blackpool, the goals coming from Ray Wilkins and Tommy Langley in the second half. After that, the Blues' schizophrenic season changed course again, this time a run of five wins and two draws propelling them to the outer edges of the promotion race, behind pacesetters Sunderland, Bolton and Bristol City.

During this period, McCreadie's young Blues played a Past Chelsea XI, featuring many of the big names from the double cup-winning side, in a testimonial game for Peter Osgood at Stamford Bridge. A crowd of 25,302, the highest of the season to date, turned up to pay tribute to 'The King of Stamford Bridge' and wallow in blue-tinged nostalgia as old favourites like Keith Weller, Alan Hudson and Tommy 'The Sponge' Baldwin rolled back the years. Another attraction was the sight of George Best, still the biggest star of the era despite a troubled couple of years during which he had left Manchester United under a cloud and threatened to quit the game altogether, demonstrating his sublime dribbling and passing skills as a guest for the Past XI.

In an entertaining match, the 1975 Chelsea team came out on top by 4-3. What struck McCreadie most about the evening, though, was the performance of Best who, while clearly not match fit following his long lay-off, had scored two goals and tormented the Chelsea defence with his close ball control and deft footwork. Seizing the moment, McCreadie suggested to the former European Footballer of the Year that he should consider playing for Chelsea on a pay-per-play basis with his wages being linked to attendances.

The proposal interested Best, who later said, "I had a lot of offers but Chelsea were the only side I would have played for then. They were a good club, a glamorous side and I always admired Charlie Cooke." Unfortunately for McCreadie, the board told him that Best's demands for £1,000 per game were out of Chelsea's league and, as it turned out, the Irishman soon chose to revive his career in the States with Los Angeles Aztecs. Yet it was hard not to think that a wonderful opportunity had been missed – especially as, when Best next returned to the Bridge in Fulham's colours the following season, the match attracted a crowd of over 55,000, Chelsea's biggest for almost six years. With pulling power like that, a grand a game would have been a small price to pay for the most talented British player of his generation.

Two weeks after Osgood's testimonial, the Blues met third-placed Bolton at home in a match which proved to be something of a turning point in their season. Four points behind the Trotters, this was a game Chelsea really needed to win if they were to get involved in the thick, rather than the fringes, of the promotion race. McCreadie, as ever, was in confident mood, telling fans, "There is no doubt that the second half of the season should see us put in a strong challenge for one of the promotion places."

On a grey, early winter afternoon at the Bridge, though, a wily Bolton team including future Premiership managers Sam Allardyce and Peter Reid took the points thanks to a first-half goal by Roy Greaves. Late on, Ray Wilkins had a chance to salvage a draw for the Blues only to see his side-footed penalty brilliantly palmed away by Trotters keeper Barry Siddall. In a tight division, the defeat pushed the Blues back down into mid-table, where they stayed until the end of the season. Home defeats against Oldham (0-3) in January and Orient (0-2) in April were particularly dispiriting occasions for both the fans and players.

"Division Two was completely different," recalls veteran defender John Dempsey, explaining Chelsea's disappointing showing. "You had your Notts Countys, teams like that. It was less playing football, more about the long ball. Kick and rush was the name of the game and we struggled to adapt."

Indeed, the second half of the campaign as a whole was fairly nondescript and only enlivened by a decent run in the FA Cup. After wins over Bristol Rovers (in a replay at Eastville, thanks to a lone Kenny Swain goal) and York City (a match in which the injury-raddled Ian Hutchinson scored his last goal for the club before announcing his retirement from the game on medical advice), the Blues were handed a plum fifth round tie at home to Crystal Palace.

Palace may only have been in the Third Division, but flamboyant manager Malcolm Allison and his enterprising coach Terry Venables had created a real buzz around Selhurst Park. Invariably chomping on a fat cigar and sporting his trademark fedora hat, 'Big Mal' was predicting big things for his young Palace side, which featured the likes of future England Under-21 manager Peter Taylor at left-wing, white-haired former Everton striker Alan Whittle and hardman defender Jim Cannon. Despite their lowly station, the Eagles would not be an easy touch.

The game was one which, it seemed, half of London was desperate to see. Chelsea's average home attendance during the season was less than 19,000, but over 54,000 fans crammed into the Bridge for the third FA Cup meeting between the sides in the last six years (the Blues had won the previous two, in 1970 and 1971). Ever the showman, Allison walked round the Stamford Bridge pitch before the game, waving to his own club's fans and, in a provocative gesture to the Chelsea supporters in the Shed terrace, forecasting a 3-2 win for Palace by holding up three fingers of one hand and two of the other.

Amazingly, 'Big Mal's' predictive powers proved to be spot on as Palace ended the Blues' cup dreams in a five-goal thriller. "It was a big game, and there was a huge crowd," recalls Ron Harris. "We were two down at half-time but we got back to 2-2 with goals by Ray Wilkins and Steve Wicks. Then Peter Taylor curled a free kick round the wall to make it 3-2. It was a big disappointment for us. But, make no mistake, they were a good side, even if they were in the Third Division."

The defeat was galling for the fans, especially as Palace went on to the semi-finals before falling to eventual winners Southampton. It was small consolation that Stamford Bridge was chosen as the venue for the game, bringing some much-needed additional funds into the club coffers. For the younger Chelsea players, too, the sight of the Palace team cavorting in their team bath with a topless Fiona Richmond, a noted porn actress of the time, in a tabloid photo shoot shortly before the semi-final must have produced a nagging sense of what might have been.

All in all, it had been a far from memorable season: 11th place in the league and two unexpected cup defeats by lower league opposition. It hadn't helped that, thanks to a combination of injuries and inconsistent form, McCreadie had been forced to chop and change his team with the result that just three players – Ray Wilkins, Ian Britton and Ron Harris – played in more than 30 league games. Still, on the plus side, young players like Stanley, Swain and Wicks had all gained valuable playing experience which would stand them in good stead for the following year's campaign.

Assuming, that is, Chelsea could survive the close season. Throughout the 1975/76 term fans had known that Chelsea were in financial difficulties – after all, ads in the programme requesting supporters to donate match balls rather gave the game away – but they were largely unaware of the full extent of the club's problems. That all changed in the summer of 1976 when articles appeared in the national press outlining the details of Chelsea's debts.

On 3rd July a headline in the news pages of *The Times* reported that the club's creditors had given Chelsea "a year to put their house in order". There followed a short report of a 70-minute meeting at Stamford Bridge in which, to chairman Brian Mears' delight, the creditors had voted overwhelmingly in favour of a 12-month moratorium on payments. "I'm speechless," a grateful Mears was quoted as saying, "I thank you all for your support to Chelsea."

Yet, it was clear nonetheless that this was a stay of execution rather than a reprieve. The details of the debt made alarming reading for any Chelsea fan. In all, the club owed £3.4 million, equivalent to more than 15 times the fee the Blues had paid for their record signing, David Hay. The bulk of this money was owed to Chelsea's bankers, Barclays (£2,536,240) who had provided loans for the building of the new East stand. A further £403,508 was owed to the stand's builders, W and C French, while other major creditors included the Inland Revenue (£64,000), Customs and Excise (£29,113 VAT owed) and Hammersmith Council (£29,939 owed in rates). The small print even revealed that the Blues still owed Celtic £35,000 for Hay, two years after the player had packed his bags to play in England.

That detail in itself suggested the financial problems had been building for some time, without being properly addressed. Finally, however, it looked as though the Chelsea board was going to be given the professional help it so clearly needed. As part of the moratorium agreement, a committee of six was appointed to serve as advisers to the club over the coming year. One of the six, Martin Spencer, an accountant with Stoy Hayward and Company (a firm acting for some of the creditors), was quoted in *The Times* as saying the Chelsea directors had spent too much time being involved with the football side instead of exploiting commercial opportunities at the club.

Rejecting the opportunity to point out that Stamford Bridge was hosting a money-making Independence Day 'American all-star family show' the very next day, Mears explained that a large part of the mess was down to 'ambition' when the club had been doing well. Unfortunately, he went on, the East stand had taken an extra year to build at a greater cost than anticipated while there had been a "decline in attendances because of the poor form of the team, eventually leading to relegation."

The creditors and their professional representatives, though, were less concerned with Mears' analysis of past failings than with his plans for the future. How exactly, they all wanted to know, did Mears and his fellow board members propose to extricate Chelsea from the appalling mess it was currently in? There was no escaping this key question, and Mears was forced to admit that "very stringent economy measures would have to be made by the club."

The professional staff, he pointed out, had already been reduced from 35 to 28.

Further cuts could be made, Mears suggested, by withdrawing Chelsea from the Football Combination although this would not necessarily mean the end of the reserve team "because we could always move into the midweek league." What Mears was not prepared to countenance, he insisted, was a fire sale of the club's best players. "There is no way we are going to sell players like Butch Wilkins, (Garry) Stanley or (Steve) Wicks," he told the meeting, "because I consider that would be a retrograde step and that is the last thing we want."

When pressed, the Chelsea chairman also admitted that talks had gone on with another unnamed club in regard to sharing the ground. "But it would mean sharing Stamford Bridge and not us moving out," he explained. Another possibility, he added, was the return of greyhound racing to Stamford Bridge – the last races had been held in August 1968 – "because we have to look at anything that is going to attract money to the club."

Cutting costs, greyhound racing , a possible ground share: all these things could help to improve Chelsea's finances. However, the key to turning the club's accounts from red to black was a successful Blues team on the pitch. If only McCreadie's young side could mount a sustained promotion challenge then the 19,000 break-even home attendance figure Mears mentioned to the creditors would be smashed every time the Blues played at the Bridge – the enormous gate for the Palace game had, after all, shown just how many fans would attend matches when the stakes were high enough.

Mears, chairman since 1969, was no fool and realised that a good season, preferably one ending in promotion, would cast a completely different light on Chelsea's seemingly desperate plight. "We have the nucleus of a football team that will do well, although I am not saying that they will win the championship," he stressed to the assembled crowd of solicitors and accountants. "But they are certainly stars of the future."

As if to prove his point, Ray Wilkins made his full international debut for England during the summer of 1976 and collected rave notices for his performance in a 3-2 win over Italy in New York. It was a heavy burden to place on a bunch of teenagers, but Chelsea's short-term future now largely rested on the shoulders of young 'Butch' and his equally youthful team-mates.

CHAPTER TWO
BLUES ON THE MARCH
1976-77

F or a second successive close season Eddie McCreadie spent not a single penny on transfers in the summer of 1976 – hardly surprising given Chelsea's dire financial position. Yet, ever the optimist, the Blues' boss refused to let off-the-pitch problems affect him. Instead, he cleverly turned Chelsea's difficulties to his advantage by issuing a rousing rallying cry to the club's fans. "This club won't die," he told them. "I won't let it die. These players won't let it die." The implication was clear: the staff and players were doing their bit, even agreeing to a small pay cut for the coming season, now it was up to the supporters to show their love for the club by turning up in their thousands and backing the newly-launched 'Cash for Chelsea' fundraising campaign.

Even before the season kicked off there was some good news for the fans: none of the players had been sold to pay off the taxman, the VAT man or to raise some cash for the electricity meter. With various interested clubs hovering like hungry vultures around Ray Wilkins, the Chelsea captain delighted Blues fans by declaring his loyalty to the club. "I was brought up on Chelsea," he said. "It has never even occurred to me to move. My two brothers are here and so are my friends. We've known each other since we were ten years old. We're all Chelsea mad. I wouldn't have felt right about deserting what appeared at the time to be a sinking ship and leaving my mates aboard."

After Chelsea had again warmed up for the season in the Anglo-Scottish Cup, Wilkins led out the Blues for the opening day fixture at Orient in front of 11,456 fans. The side chosen by McCreadie was one of the youngest in Chelsea history. At nearly 35, goalkeeper Peter Bonetti was the oldest member of the team by some distance, but was still as athletic and agile as ever. The back four of Gary Locke, Graham Wilkins, David Hay and Steve Wicks, had an average age of 22 and combined strength and aerial power in the centre with speed and skill on the flanks.

The midfield quartet of Ray Wilkins, Garry Stanley, Ian Britton and Ray Lewington was even more youthful, having an average age of under 21. None of the four were natural wide players, but their differing qualities and attributes nonetheless provided a more than reasonable balance. In the centre of midfield, the red-headed Lewington was a tenacious, hard-tackling ball-winner who could turn defence into attack with a thudding challenge and an accurate short pass. On the right, mop-topped Garry Stanley was a useful all-rounder with a rocket-powered shot, while little Ian Britton was a bundle of energy on the left. Supported by these three hard-working lieutenants, Ray Wilkins was free to roam where he pleased. Sometimes he would drift into the 'hole' behind the attackers where he could either shoot himself or set up an opportunity for a team-mate; at other times, he would drop deeper where his ability to despatch raking 30 or 40 yard passes could be given full expression.

"It didn't matter that none of us were wingers," says Garry Stanley. "On my side, Gary Locke was very quick on the overlap and was an excellent crosser of the ball. Graham Wilkins got forward, too, on the left. There was a lot of rotation in midfield, so I would come inside from the right, for example and Ian Britton would sometimes pop up in the penalty area. Eddie, though, was keen that we all got behind the ball when we lost it."

"It wasn't called that at the time but basically we were playing a diamond formation," adds Ray Lewington, who played the 'holding' role at the base of the diamond. "Eddie McCreadie gave me clear and precise instructions: stay deep, win the ball and give it to Ray Wilkins, who was playing behind the strikers and was hard to pick up. At the time, it was a unique formation – no other teams, not even First Division ones, were playing it."

As a group, the midfield quartet were also instructed by McCreadie to try to win the ball back as early as possible, and this aspect of their game was often worked on in training. "He'd get us playing three against three in grids," recalls Stanley. "That improved our work-rate, so we developed the ability to close opponents down and stop other teams playing. One Chelsea player would go towards a member of the opposition, closely followed by one of his team-mates."

The high tempo, give-and-go, full throttle football McCreadie favoured required two strikers who would not only score goals but could also be relied upon to chase every ball and harry defenders into making mistakes. Having looked at various permutations in the 1975/76 season, McCreadie finally settled on a pairing of Steve 'Jock' Finnieston and

Kenny Swain. An old-fashioned penalty box poacher, Finnieston's goalscoring pedigree was exemplary: 105 goals in three seasons in the youth and reserve teams. Yet McCreadie appeared to have reservations about the Edinburgh-born forward's ability to reproduce that success at first-team level, selecting the blond-haired Teddy Maybank ahead of him for much of the previous season.

"I don't think Eddie fancied me at first or I'm sure I would have got a chance earlier than I did with him," says Steve. "It probably didn't help that I'd had a run-in with him over a new contract. During the close season in 1975 I was getting married and so asked him for another fiver to take me up to £35 a week. When he said 'no' I asked for a transfer. He said, 'You've still got two years on your contract, you're staying at the same money but you're never going to play for the first team.' I thought that was it. I thought I'd be stuck in the reserves for the next two years."

Along with David Hay, Finnieston's strike partner Kenny Swain was the only other non-youth product in the team. A former trainee teacher, Swain had been plucked from then non-league Wycombe by Dave Sexton's assistant, Dario Gradi. A clever, skilful player, Swain wasn't as prolific a scorer as Finnieston but he was more versatile, fitting seamlessly into midfield when needed.

With so many young players in the Chelsea side, it was essential that the players' confidence could be boosted by the team getting a good start. And that's precisely what they did get at Orient, Steve Finnieston shooting home the only goal of the game with just three minutes left. True, it was only one game, but already there was a sense that the Blues' promotion wagon was rolling.

The feeling that this could be Chelsea's year only increased over the next two weeks as the Blues picked up five points from their opening three games and then eased past Sheffield United, just relegated from the First Division, by three goals to one in the second round of the League Cup. "I've been at the club 14 years and have been in great sides – yet this should be the best Chelsea have ever seen," McCreadie gushed after the win over the Blades. "We are an attacking side, that's our strength. They're a bit inconsistent now because of inexperience. In another 18 months there will be no need to make excuses for them."

Chelsea's bright start did not go unnoticed, with Eddie McCreadie picking up the Bell's Second Division Manager of the Month award. During that first month of the season Ron Harris, the one nominated substitute for the opening four games, had not made even the briefest of appearances off the bench. Concerned that 'Chopper' might be losing match sharpness, McCreadie suggested to his former team-mate that he play in the Blues' reserve match against Crystal Palace at Stamford Bridge before joining up with the first team squad for the trip to Millwall.

"The reserve game was a morning kick-off which we won 1-0," recalls Ron. "Then I quickly got changed and went on the team coach to Millwall. I was sub again so I was sitting on the touchline during the first-half when we were 3-0 down. Then 'Jock' Finnieston got injured so I came on at half-time. It ended up staying 3-0. So from not playing at all I played a match and a half on the same day. I was so stiff afterwards it was unbelievable!"

The curse of the Manager of the Month award had struck once more. More worrying for McCreadie than the result was the performance: Chelsea had played poorly at The Den, once again seeming to be affected by the scenes of crowd violence which provided the game's backdrop. Ian Britton admitted as much some years later, saying:

"It was the worst trouble I've ever seen. In the warm-up there were people coming out of the crowd with meat hooks in their heads. I think that's the only time I've been frightened in a game."

That setback, though, proved only temporary as a run of just one defeat in the next 12 games propelled Chelsea to the top of the division, ahead of promotion rivals Bolton, Blackpool, Wolves and Nottingham Forest. McCreadie, much to the delight of the tabloid press which couldn't get enough of the 'Chelsea kids', continued to talk up his team in increasingly positive terms. "This team will be the best in the country in two years," he told the press after a thrilling 4-3 home win over Oldham. "They are capable of great things. They are arrogant in the right way. They believe in themselves."

Nor was this just the usual PR hype managers sometimes utter in the immediate aftermath of an exciting, edge-of-the-seat victory. "Oh no, he really meant it," says Graham Wilkins. "It wasn't just for the public either – he made us feel just as positive. He was a real players' manager and as a motivator he was brilliant. For example, he told me I was an excellent left back even though, really, I was a right back. But, because of Gary Locke, the left back slot was the only one I could get."

"Eddie had this way of making you believe that you were better than you actually were," adds Tommy Langley, who broke into the side later in the season. "When you're young you're very impressionable, so when somebody like Eddie McCreadie turns round and says 'You're the best centre forward in Europe, you're the best midfield player in Europe, there's no one better than you at your age...' you actually start, not to believe it, but there is an element of belief that sinks in. Like Jose Mourinho now, he came in and got all the boys on his side and that was the key that first year."

The ultra-experienced Ron Harris, though, didn't share McCreadie's rose-tinted view of his squad. "Eddie was always talking up the team," says 'Chopper', "but when you go through the side and the midfield of Ray Wilkins, Garry Stanley, Ray Lewington and Ian Britton you couldn't compare them to the likes of Charlie Cooke and Alan Hudson. They were young, they ran around but, without being too critical, they weren't a patch on the players we had before."

Nonetheless, the buzz surrounding the Blues continued as Chelsea came back from behind to beat FA Cup holders Southampton 3-1 at Stamford Bridge with late goals by

Swain, Ray Wilkins and Finnieston. "We have the makings of a very fine team – that's our salvation," beamed a delighted Brian Mears afterwards, while the season's best home attendance to date of 42,654 gave him added cause to smile. In the next home game Garry Stanley hit a spectacular 25-yarder into the top right-hand corner of the Shed end goal as the Blues beat Charlton 2-1 in front of another big crowd. A few days later Stanners' famed shooting powers were on show at White Hart Lane in a 'London hot shot' competition, part of the entertainment organised for Pat Jennings' testimonial. "Malcolm McDonald was representing Arsenal and I think Glenn Hoddle was there too," says Garry. "We had to hit a small board which registered the power of the shot, but we all found it difficult to get our efforts on target. Malcolm McDonald eventually landed one at 98mph, but when I hit the board with my next shot it broke the equipment. I was handed a moral victory."

Later that month, following a 1-1 draw at Nottingham Forest in front of the *Match of the Day* cameras, McCreadie was once more heaping praise on his side: "I thought I knew what my team are capable of, but they surprised even me with beautiful moves which just aren't in the book." The Blues' stylish performance also impressed Forest manager Brian Clough, who afterwards predicted: "Chelsea will walk into the First Division and prove a formidable force when they get there."

The only real disappointment on the pitch during the autumn was the 2-1 defeat at Arsenal which ended the Blues' interest in the League Cup and saw Brian Bason, filling in for the injured Ian Britton, carried off with a broken leg. The game turned out to be Bason's last for Chelsea, as shortly after recuperating from his injury he joined Plymouth.

Off the pitch, though, Chelsea's financial position remained a cause for deep concern. In October the club was forced to announce that, contrary to newspaper reports, it was not in imminent danger of closing because of pressure from the Inland Revenue. Martin Spencer of the club's financial controllers, Stoy Hayward and Company, said: "It is true that the current debt to the Inland Revenue is around £64,000 but we are meeting all of the tax demands as they come up. There is no question whatsoever of Chelsea being in default of current liabilities." However, the news that Chelsea had decided to leave their Mitcham training ground to rent a cheaper alternative at Molesey suggested that money was still extremely tight.

On the other hand, the club, and especially commercial manager Frank Milford, could not be criticised for failing to come up with ideas for raising cash. A limited edition 'Chelsea medallion' proved a real hit at £10, while the 75p 'Chelsea Snack-pack' – consisting of a roll, sandwich, sausage roll, fruit and biscuits – went down well with hungry fans travelling by rail to away games. Milford also arranged sponsorship deals for some home games, although to his frustration FA rules prevented any of the companies' names appearing on Chelsea's shirts. "We have our heads in the sand as regards sponsorship," he complained in the programme. "We are no more than playing at it by permitting only [shirt manufacturer's] logos on shirts...The time has come to allow – no, *welcome* is the word – sponsorship on a big scale as a means of bringing vitally needed cash into British football." In the absence of such commercial deals the onus fell on the fans to raise funds, through collections on trains to away matches and a 'cash for points' sponsorship scheme.

Fans who had signed up for that last scheme probably experienced mixed emotions as Chelsea's points haul slowed down in the build-up to Christmas with a defeat and three draws in December. Fewer points, after all, meant more to spend on the festivities. But the entertainment factor didn't slip. After a battling 3-3 draw against nearest challengers Wolves at the Bridge – a game in which the Blues scored two goals in the final minutes to maintain their unbeaten home record – Boxing Day threw up another appetising fixture, with Fulham making the short trip from Craven Cottage.

A massive crowd of over 55,000 squeezed into the Bridge for the game, many of them anxious to catch a glimpse of two football legends turning out for Fulham: Bobby Moore, England's 1966 World Cup-winning captain, and George Best. Graham Wilkins, one of the Chelsea defenders charged with keeping the quicksilver Irishman quiet, recalls the experience vividly. "On paper, I was up against their right winger, Brian Greenaway," he says. "But George used to like to change over wings so you couldn't take anything for granted. When you were up against him all you could do was watch the ball – because it wasn't just his feet that could trick you to go the wrong way, but his whole body. If you dived in he could make you look a right mug. And, off the mark, he was so quick. He was just an exceptional player. He would definitely be the best player I've ever played against – and, I guess, he feels the same way about me!"

Happily for Chelsea fans, Wilkins and co. kept a tight leash on Best while, at the other end, Kenny Swain and Mickey Droy, recalled to the side in place of the injured Steve Wicks, came up with the goals in a 2-0 home win. Indeed, the Fulham star was so frustrated at his lack of chances and his rugged treatment by the Chelsea defence that he ended up being booked for making gestures at the referee as the teams left the pitch.

Enjoyable though it was, the derby victory took a lot out of the Blues and two days later they put in a limp display at Luton, losing 4-0. The chasing pack were closing, but a 5-1 home thrashing of bottom-placed Hereford United on New Year's Day maintained Chelsea's four point lead at the top of the table. The club programme for this match made much of a good omen: for the previous seven seasons the club leading the Second Division at the turn of the year had gone on to win the title. Yet, for superstitious fans, the portents were not all good.

The day before Chelsea travelled to Southampton in the third round of the FA Cup the *Daily Mirror* ran a story which, for Blues fans who had some belief in the supernatural, was about as welcome as a smashed bathroom mirror. Below the bone-chilling headline,

'Curses! Chelsea get the evil eye treatment,' the paper reported: "Chelsea are doomed. They will be beaten by Southampton in the FA Cup tomorrow and will miss out on promotion. Who says so? Romark, the hypnotist, who correctly predicted last season's disappointments for Crystal Palace in the FA Cup and league. 'It will be doomsville for Chelsea,' he says. 'They will go downhill just like Palace did. I will stake my reputation on it. They will just collapse. Chelsea are too young to live with the pressure at the top.'" Romark, otherwise known as Ronald Markham, was no crank but a famous hypnotist who had appeared on his own BBC television show and, remarkably, had returned to the stage just eight weeks after suffering a massive stroke using his own mysterious 'hypno-think' energy-channelling technique.

While easy to dismiss as mumbo-jumbo, Romark's predictive powers proved to be spot on about the Blues' FA Cup chances – although, admittedly, the Saints needed a replay at a mud-clogged Stamford Bridge to fulfil his prophecy. More worryingly for McCreadie and his team, a run of seven league games with just one win in January and February threatened to turn the soothsayer's predictions of a dramatic collapse into a reality. "We saw the story in the papers but it didn't affect us," says Ray Lewington, refuting the suggestion that Romark's comments might have unsettled the players. "We weren't bothered about the curse, but we were concerned about the pitch which was rapidly deteriorating and didn't help our passing style in the second half of the season."

Meanwhile, the ongoing financial crises forced the club to introduce another hike in admission prices, entry to the terraces going up by 25 per cent to £1 for adults and 50p for children. The rise meant that, along with First Division Leicester and QPR, Chelsea were the most expensive club in the country to watch. "Entrance and ticket prices are out of line with the total costs of running the club," explained Martin Spencer in the programme for the disappointing 1-1 draw with Orient. "Supporters, both of the club and football in general, will have to accept that they must pay a proper price for their entertainment and it is that cold, hard fact alone which necessitates the admission price being raised."

The measure, though, was deeply unpopular. A week after the price rises came into effect, a crowd of just over 22,000 turned up for the home game against Plymouth – Chelsea's lowest league gate since August. However, group bookings for the match from Scandinavia, France, Holland and Germany indicated that interest in the Chelsea revival was still spread far and wide.

Addressing Chelsea supporters directly for the first time since August, McCreadie paid tribute to his team in the programme for the visit of relegation-threatened Argyle. "Considering the youth and shortage of experience of many first-team players, we're way ahead of schedule," he wrote. "I'd have been more than happy to see Chelsea a couple of points behind the leaders at this stage; instead, we've topped the Second Division for five months. Watching this side develop has been like planting a seed – which I consider we did last season – and watching it grow like a flower. I honestly believe you've seen nothing yet. We're only warming up!"

On a bumpy, rutted pitch, though, Chelsea looked tired and jaded and were lucky to escape with a 2-2 draw after Plymouth had a late goal controversially ruled out for offside. Following this poor result, even the normally ebullient McCreadie appeared to be having doubts about his side's ability to last the pace. "Being a manager is always hard, but it has been doubly difficult at this club," he said. "I would have liked to have been able to buy and sell players. Instead I had to push kids through when I was not certain they were ready."

The following week at Bolton, in front of the home side's largest crowd of the season, Chelsea looked set to be displaced at the top when they trailed the Trotters 2-0 at half-time. But, after the break, Finnieston latched onto Sam Allardyce's back pass to score his 18th goal of the season and Swain fired the Blues level a few minutes later. "At the finish, it still wasn't one of our best games of the season, but it was one of our best points," reflected McCreadie afterwards. "For the last five or six weeks we've been through a sticky patch. Having to play someone of Bolton's calibre, on their ground, was some test. They are such a good side, and I was most impressed with them."

Entering the final two months of the season, the promotion picture could hardly have been more exciting. Chelsea remained top, a point ahead of Wolves and two ahead of Bolton, but had played two more games than both their nearest rivals. Blackpool, Luton, Millwall and Charlton were also in the frame while Nottingham Forest, nine points behind the Blues but with four games in hand, could not be ruled out either. After yet another home draw, 2-2 against Blackpool, only served to fray nerves further among the Blues' followers three consecutive wins against Cardiff, Bristol Rovers and Blackburn provided some relief.

For a while, at least, thoughts at Stamford Bridge turned away from the vital promotion campaign and instead focused on former winger Peter Houseman, a key member of the 1970 FA Cup-winning side, who was killed in a car crash on the A40 near Oxford along with his wife, Sally, and two friends. The loss was especially keenly felt among his team-mates in that great Chelsea team. "He played in front of me for a very long time," says Ron Harris, the Blues' captain on the night of that famous triumph at Old Trafford. "He was a very under-estimated player. He didn't get the credit he deserved and he made my job a lot easier because he was a fit fellow and he used to do a lot of the work in front of me. I think we were sitting at home at the time when we heard the news. I believe it was on a Saturday after a game. I'd known Peter since he came to Chelsea as a kid. When I first started going out with my missus, Sally and her used to room together on the trips to the away games. So the four of us knew each other well. As you can imagine, the funeral was very depressing for us both."

Six young children, three from the Houseman family and three from their friends', were orphaned in the tragedy. In a fitting gesture, the club organised a fundraising match for the children at Stamford Bridge between the 1977 Blues and their 1970 counterparts, with former England star Alan Ball appearing in Houseman's old number 11 shirt. Nearly 17,000 fans turned up to the game, which the younger Chelsea team won 3-0.

Returning to competitive football, Chelsea began Easter badly with a 3-1 defeat at Fulham on Good Friday. Teddy Maybank, sold by the Blues to their neighbours a month earlier, played for the Cottagers, for whom George Best appeared on the scoresheet. The result allowed Wolves to claim top spot but Chelsea reclaimed first place the following day after a 2-0 win at the Bridge against Luton. Steve Finnieston grabbed his customary goal before John Sparrow, playing at left back instead of Graham Wilkins, wrapped up the points before half-time with a well-struck 20-yarder. Two days later, however, Chelsea crashed to a disastrous 4-0 defeat at Charlton – a game marred by serious crowd trouble – and slid behind Wolves again.

The loss made the following Saturday's game with promotion rivals Nottingham Forest even more of a crunch game. Having seen his side stutter throughout the second half of the season, and especially over Easter, McCreadie decided to make a number of changes to a team which had largely remained unchanged throughout the campaign. Ron Harris had already returned to the back four in place of eye injury victim David Hay, and the Chelsea boss felt the time was right to recall another of the old stalwarts from the 1970 side, Charlie Cooke. The longstanding Shed hero had only made two appearances all season, but McCreadie gambled that his experience, neat ball control and calm authority could play a vital role in the six-match run-in.

"It's a bit of a stunner," Cooke said at the time, clearly surprised to get the call to action. "I have had a lot of niggling injuries but I've kept pegging away. I don't feel any pressure and I am looking forward to playing in front of a crowd again. It is a tight situation for the club and I am prepared to do anything I can to help." Garry Stanley was the unlucky player to make way for Cookie.

Another change saw 19-year-old striker Tommy Langley, the leading scorer in Chelsea's championship-winning Football Combination side, pitched in for his first game of the season in place of Ken Swain. "A lot of people had been scoring goals and it had been very hard to get in the team," says Langley. "When you're trying to make your impression it's very difficult to sit back and watch it all happen. Then, Eddie decided to throw me in. I'm not quite sure why: maybe because the team was faltering a bit or because I was in exceptional form in the reserves. Either way, I knew it was a big chance for me."

Forest, who included such well-known names as Viv Anderson, Larry Lloyd, Martin O'Neill, Tony Woodcock and John Robertson in their line-up, were on a roll having taken 11 out of 12 points in their last six games – a run which had powered them to third place, two points behind Chelsea. A draw would not have been a disaster for the

Blues, but a defeat would have seen them drop to third behind Clough's men on goal difference.

In dry, blustery conditions, Forest had the better of the first half, passing the ball around attractively and occasionally creating decent openings. It was, then, no surprise when, just before half-time, O'Neill shot past Bonetti to put the visitors ahead. The game continued in much the same vein in the second half until, shortly past the hour mark, Ian Britton popped up with a priceless equaliser, his ninth goal of the season. Now Chelsea were pushing Forest back, but the Blues had to wait until the 86th minute for the winner, Finnieston smashing the ball home from close range after Wicks had knocked down Locke's cross.

While the Blues fans in the 36,499 crowd celebrated wildly on the terraces after the final whistle, Brian Clough stormed into the post-match press conference with an angry scowl across his face. Britton's equaliser, he claimed somewhat harshly, was "the only time he kicked the ball straight all day". But that sour barb was nothing compared to his diatribe about the inadequacies of the Stamford Bridge facilities. "How can they talk about the First Division when we are sitting in a pig-hole of a dressing room?" he railed, his cheeks turning more crimson by the second. "It's criminal. I suppose the directors are upstairs in plush surroundings. Can't they get some tiles on the rates? The dug-out is the worst in the Second Division. How the hell could I tell if Chelsea's winner was offside from that position?"

In fact, the *Match of the Day* cameras suggested the goal was legitimate. All the Chelsea fans cared about, though, was the two points which cemented the Blues' position in second place behind Wolves. They also had another reason to toast the club. Writing in reply to a letter in the Forest programme from a concerned fan, Brian Mears had attempted to dampen newspaper speculation that Chelsea were considering sharing Stamford Bridge with QPR. "We cannot prevent such speculation," pointed out the Chelsea chairman, "but neither can we prevent other clubs admiring our facilities and, perhaps, wanting to share them. Related to the club's best interests, everything has to be considered, and ground-sharing has been discussed from time to time. While it is not beyond the bounds of possibility, I would say the prospect is receding. Chelsea FC will never lose its identity. Chelsea will be Chelsea for always – and at Stamford Bridge."

And, he might have added, almost certainly back in the First Division the following season. Three points from the next three matches, the highlight of which was a stunning Ray Wilkins volley in a 4-0 demolition of Sheffield United at the Bridge, left Chelsea on the brink of securing promotion. A single point at leaders Wolves in the penultimate match of the season would confirm the Blues' return to the big time.

Yet there was still a chance for Romark's curse to strike – especially as Chelsea would be travelling to Molineux with the handicap of a government ban on their supporters which had been imposed following trouble at the Easter match against Charlton (see

Chapter Four, *Hello, Hello, We are the Chelsea Boys*). However, when the players arrived in the Black Country they discovered, to their delight, that thousands of Chelsea fans had evaded the ban and gained entry to the game. "We went out to get a feel of the pitch because you never know what it's going to be like at the end of the season," recalls Tommy Langley, "and as we stepped out there was a massive roar. We looked to the right-hand side and the bank was just full of Chelsea.

I knew then that we wouldn't lose the game. It was such a massive lift to see them all, the biggest lift we ever had. Everyone went back in to the changing room and people were saying, 'Did you see that?'"

The Blues knew that a win would give them a chance of the championship, and for most of the match they looked like claiming both points after Wilkins' superb defence-splitting pass found Langley, who drilled in a low left-foot shot from a tight angle. But 11 minutes from time Wolves striker John Richards equalised for Wolves, setting up what promised to be a tense finale. "I remember thinking, 'We could come under some pressure here,'" recalls Peter Bonetti. "But, possibly because Wolves only needed a point to be champions, it didn't turn out like that at all. They just passed it around at the back then, when they sent a long ball forward, they backed off and let us do the same. It was a real stand-off and quite a strange ending to the game."

All that mattered, though, was that the draw ensured that Chelsea had returned to the top flight – on the same day, incidentally, that Tottenham's relegation from the First Division was confirmed by a thumping 5-0 defeat at Manchester City. Unsurprisingly, the Blues' celebrations on the way back to London were unrestrained. "Coming back on the coach we were having a few beers when I decided to stick the buttered side of a sandwich on the top of Brain Mears' head," remembers Steve Finnieston. "He took it okay, fortunately. Then, when we got back to the Bridge, we went out to have a few more drinks in the pubs around the King's Road. The atmosphere everywhere was just brilliant."

But the party had only just started. The following week, when the Blues wrapped up a memorable season at home to mid-table Hull, a near-hysterical atmosphere enveloped Stamford Bridge. To thunderous chants of 'Chelsea are back!' and 'Chelsea up, Tottenham down, alleluia!' the squad began a pre-match lap of honour – which, annoyingly for the majority of supporters in the near 44,000 crowd, had to be aborted when hundreds of fans poured onto the pitch to join in. Chelsea's first two goals, both scored by Finnieston, led to more pitch invasions and when over 1,000 fans attempted to personally congratulate Ian Britton on his 82nd minute strike the match seemed likely to be abandoned. Eventually, the field was cleared and Eddie McCreadie, wearing his trademark dark glasses, strode to the centre circle with a microphone in his hand.

"You guys do us a favour," he pleaded. "If there are any more goals, stay where you are and let the game finish." Both sides seemed happy to play out the last few minutes without incident – with the exception of Steve Finnieston, who was desperate to claim his first Chelsea hat-trick. With two minutes left he charged into the box, only to be hacked down for a penalty which he prepared to take himself. "Butch Wilkins actually came up to me and said, 'Miss it!'" remembers Steve. "But I just thought, 'Yeah, right, like I'm going to deliberately miss it when it's for my hat-trick!'"

After drilling home the spot-kick to complete a glorious 4-0 Chelsea win, Finnieston's thoughts turned to the match ball. "A minute later the ref said, 'Get ready to run off, because I'm going to blow the final whistle.' But I wanted the ball. While all the other players were running off towards the tunnel, I managed to get it from Peter Bonetti's goal kick - but I was on the centre spot and got completely mobbed. I thought I was going to die from a lack of oxygen. It was really quite frightening. Everybody was pulling at my kit. I lost my boots, shorts and socks, but I managed to keep hold of my shirt, although it got ripped, and the ball."

The excitement was understandable. Considering the constraints McCreadie and his side had operated under, their achievement in gaining promotion at the second attempt was truly remarkable. What's more, the Blues had gone up playing an attractive brand of attacking football which had captivated neutrals as well as fans. But, as far as McCreadie was concerned, promotion was just the start – not an end in itself. "We are going into the First Division to liven it up – not looking to consolidate, but to cause a stir," he wrote in the Hull programme. "My ambition is for Chelsea to set the First Division alight inside two seasons."

For a few blissful weeks Blues fans everywhere revelled in daydreams of the Chelsea youngsters, led by the inspirational McCreadie, storming the ramparts at Anfield, Highbury and Old Trafford. Yes, the opposition in the First Division would be tougher but, as long as the Blues lived up to their rich potential, there was every expectation that they would make a strong mark at the higher level. Maybe, if everything went well, Chelsea might get back into Europe or, even better, challenge the likes of Liverpool, Everton and Manchester City for the title. But, on Friday 1st July 1977, contented musings along these lines were rudely interrupted by a shock announcement on the BBC's evening news bulletin: Eddie McCreadie had resigned as manager of Chelsea.

CHAPTER THREE
BACK UP... AND DOWN AGAIN
1977-79

For once, *The Sun's* headline writers could not be accused of any hype or exaggeration. 'McCreadie's Shocker' screamed the back page of the tabloid, while the sub-heading – 'Chelsea stunned as boss walks out' – neatly summed up the story that followed. The date above the headline read 2nd July 1977 but the bewildered Chelsea fans reading it might have wondered if it wasn't a belated April Fool's joke. It just didn't make sense: why on earth would McCreadie leave Chelsea just six weeks after guiding the Blues back to the First Division?

Some of the answers were contained in the report. McCreadie said that he had resigned "over a matter of principle". On closer examination, there appeared to be two sticking points in the negotiations that had been continuing between the club and the manager over the summer. "All I wanted was a contract and a car," complained the Scot. "Surely I deserved these two things after what I had done for the club."

Putting the club's case, chairman Brian Mears said Chelsea had offered McCreadie £18,000 a year – a figure still some way below the salaries commanded by the top First Division managers of the time, but double what he had been earning the previous season. "Talks broke down," explained Mears. "We got to the stage where the club couldn't go any further. It was a great shock when Eddie quit. We were ready to go for the new season. But there are limits."

Chelsea, Mears added, would not be advertising for a new manager. "I have no doubts that we will have a new manager soon, I hope by the time the players return for training in 12 days time. There is no chance of a reconciliation. Eddie has resigned and we have regretfully accepted. He did a great job and was one of the people mainly responsible for getting us back in the First Division."

In his book, *The Real Story*, published in 1982, Mears provided a few more details of the events which led to McCreadie's departure. The Chelsea manager, said Mears, had approached him on the club's post-season tour of North America and "just hit me between the eyes with his demands. Eddie said if he wasn't given what he wanted he would resign. It was a form of blackmail."

But, speaking to *The Sun* just a couple of days after the shock announcement, McCreadie stressed that the salary on offer was not a factor in his decision. "I had no dispute with the money," he said. "All I wanted were these two damn things – a three-year contract and a car. I was simply seeking security for my family after two years of uncertainty." That explained McCreadie's desire for a contract, but what about the car – the issue which is usually mentioned when his resignation is discussed in Chelsea circles?

"Till now I've had to travel to watch opposing teams in the club's old van," he pointed out, conjuring up comic images straight out of *Only Fools and Horses*. "A car is a necessary tool of a manager's trade. In any case it would belong to them, not me."

That, though, was not quite the end of the story as, three days after his resignation was announced, McCreadie attempted to get his job back. "I got the impression that Eddie was calling their bluff," says Peter Bonetti, one of McCreadie's old team-mates, "and that he certainly didn't want to leave. After he resigned, he rang me up and said, 'I want to come back. You're the senior pro, can you have a word with the lads and get them to back me?' I told him it was a bit tricky, because we all played for Chelsea and it wasn't really for us to tell the board what to do. But I spoke to the lads and we agreed that I should go to see Brian Mears to see if there was any way back for Eddie. But when I went to see him it was made clear that the board had made their decision. It was sad for Eddie but they'd made their minds up and it wasn't really our role to interfere."

McCreadie didn't just bank on 'player power' making a difference; he also phoned Mears to sound out a possible dramatic return to the Bridge. The Chelsea chairman told him, though, that it was "too late" and that the club had "already set the wheels in motion" with regard to appointing a new manager.

With McCreadie effectively out of the picture, media speculation moved on to his possible successor. Among those mentioned in dispatches were former Chelsea captain Terry Venables, then the up-and-coming manager of Crystal Palace; Manchester United coach Frank Blunstone, a member of the Blues' 1955 championship side, who had turned down the Chelsea job when offered it in 1975; and former Blues manager Tommy Docherty, who had just been dismissed as Manchester United boss after details of his affair with the wife of the club's physio had been revealed in the press.

Mears, though, had already decided on his man and on 7th July youth team coach Ken Shellito was unveiled as the new Chelsea manager. Shellito's salary was reported to be around £17,000 but, significantly, the package didn't contain the extras McCreadie had demanded. Certainly, there was no sign of a gleaming new car in the Stamford Bridge forecourt as Shellito, a right back for Chelsea in the 1960s whose career had been cut short by injury, attended his first press conference as the Blues' boss.

"It'll be hard to follow Eddie," he admitted. "I always worked very closely with him and realise it will be extremely difficult to do better than he did." Despite this tribute to his predecessor, Shellito suggested that he would be introducing some changes to the team's playing style. "We conceded a lot of silly goals last season," he pointed out, "and now I would like to see us more of a unit. If I could model the team on any other side it would have to be Liverpool whom I've admired for so long."

Interestingly, at a time when tactical nuances were rarely discussed in public, Shellito also announced a subtle change in Ray Wilkins' position. "Under Eddie we played a 4-3-1-2 formation with Wilkins operating just behind the strikers," he reminded reporters. "But Butch is one of the best passers of a ball in the country and at times I felt he was wasted tucked in so close behind the attackers." Against better quality opposition in the First Division Chelsea would need to get Wilkins on the ball as much as possible, so Shellito's decision to redefine his captain's role as that of the central midfield playmaker seemed a sensible one. For Ray Lewington, though, the new manager's plan was not so welcome. "That announcement was the writing on the wall for me," he says. "I knew he wouldn't play two deep midfielders and that Ray, because he was the better player, would be picked before me. From playing every game the previous season I only played half of them under Ken."

Significantly, Shellito made no tub-thumping McCreadie-style predictions of greatness for his new side. "All I want is for the team to go out and battle and get as high as they can," was the most he would say when asked to outline his targets for the season. That low-key response was fairly typical of Shellito, a modest and unassuming man who was well liked within the club. "Ken Shellito was a very different character to Eddie," confirms Peter Bonetti. "It was a bit like in the 1960s when Dave Sexton replaced Tommy Docherty. Ken was very tactically aware and had a lot of knowledge about the game, but he wasn't a shouter or ranter. He was much quieter than Eddie."

Ron Harris, though, wondered whether Shellito wasn't just too quiet. "Ken was a tremendous player, one of the best full backs Chelsea have ever had," says 'Chopper'. "But as a manager he was like he was as a player: he never kicked anybody, he never hurt anybody. I don't think he was the right type of fellow to be a manager – I don't think he was hard enough or ruthless enough to do the job. He wasn't the type of person who could come into the dressing room and have a moan at people when they deserved it.

Sometimes you've just got to steam into people, and I don't think Ken could do that."

The change in manager was not the only one at the Bridge: David Mears, Brian's brother, and Martin Spencer both joined the board of directors, while Ian Hutchinson took over as commercial manager. 'Hutch' was an unlikely choice for the role, as was his choice of picture for his programme column: medallioned and bare-chested, he looked as though he had just enjoyed a meeting with a couple of King's Road 'dolly birds' rather than a potential club sponsor.

Overall, the club's finances remained rocky but there were some hopeful signs. Crucially, Spencer had persuaded the creditors to agree to another 12 months suspension of claims for payment. Then, just before the season started the creditors rejected a once-and-for-all payout of 20p in the pound from Chelsea – hoping, instead, for an improvement in the club's financial position that would allow them to be paid in full in future. They, like the fans and players, had their fingers crossed that Chelsea could re-establish themselves as a serious force in the top flight: after all, success on the pitch was the best hope of a thriving club off it.

For the first game of the season at West Bromwich Albion, Shellito chose a side which showed just two changes from the team which had thrashed Hull: John Phillips replacing Peter Bonetti in goal and Garry Stanley returning in midfield at the expense of Charlie Cooke. The result, a comprehensive 3-0 defeat, did not augur well for the coming campaign. "I'm very disappointed," admitted Shellito afterwards. "We looked very green and inexperienced."

Four days later, sporting a new home kit which retained a white collar but featured a dozen Umbro logos inside a stripe along the sleeves, Chelsea chalked up their first points of the season with a 2-0 defeat of Birmingham City at the Bridge. Disappointingly, the match only attracted an attendance of just over 18,000 – a figure partly explained by the rain which turned the pitch into a swamp, but also by the club's decision to scrap concessions for children following the pitch invasions back in May. Not that there was any chance of those scenes being repeated: determined to prevent fans encroaching onto the playing area, the club had re-introduced fences at both ends of the ground.

The first third of the season was a difficult one for Chelsea. Serious injuries to Gary Locke, Steve Finnieston and Garry Stanley didn't help while David Hay's ongoing eye and knee problems, which would eventually cause him to retire the following season, reduced his appearances to a bare minimum. The main problem, though, was a simple one: a chronic lack of goals. In their first 13 games of the season, the Blues managed to find the net just seven times. True, one of those goals, a Bill Garner header against Manchester United, did help Chelsea achieve an unexpected victory at Old Trafford, but otherwise there was little to cheer for Blues fans during this period.

A first league defeat at Stamford Bridge for 16 months, against Coventry at the end of August, was especially painful although the fans in the Shed did their best to put on a brave face by defiantly chanting 'We never lose at home!' in the final minutes.

Briefly, for a few weeks at least, Shellito appeared to have found the solution to his goal-shy attack in the form of Trevor Aylott, a lanky young striker from Bermondsey. On two consecutive Saturdays at the Bridge, against Bristol City and newly-promoted Nottingham Forest, Aylott scored the only goal of the game, instantly achieving cult hero status with the Shed. The victory over Forest, riding high at the top of the table after having invested heavily in new players during the summer – including England goalkeeper Peter Shilton and Scottish international midfielder Archie Gemmill – was particularly impressive.

But Aylott's goals soon dried up – in fact, he failed to score again for Chelsea while making spasmodic appearances for the club over the next two years. Still, at least the defence was holding up well at the other end. Or, rather, it was until the Blues were humiliated 6-2 at Manchester City at the end of November.

Graham Wilkins, enjoying a run in the side at right back, had an especially forgettable afternoon. "I was up against Peter Barnes, the England winger, that day," he recalls. "He scored a hat-trick, I scored an own goal and got sent off. It was for two bookings. The first one I put him in the stands and the second one was for obstruction. It was quite difficult to get sent off in those days but I managed it that day. It sounds like I had an absolute nightmare, but that's not true. In the paper the next day he got 10 out of 10 and I got seven out of 10. So I had a good game, but everything he did came off."

The following week the Blues lost 1-0 at home to Everton, Ian Britton missing a late penalty which would have salvaged a point. The defeat left Chelsea in 18th position, just two places above the three clubs in the relegation zone, Newcastle, Leicester and West Ham. "We have to start scoring goals," Shellito admitted afterwards. "We had the chances but could not put them away." Asked by a reporter if the club had any funds to buy a striker, he replied, "I don't know if there is any money because I have never asked."

To nobody's surprise, least of all Shellito's, there wasn't any money to spend. Instead, he called up blond-haired winger Clive Walker for just his second ever start for the Blues' trip to mid-table Wolves. A 20-year-old youth product, Walker was the fastest player on Chelsea's books, having been clocked at 11.2 seconds for the 100 metres in a race at Stamford Bridge.

In addition to his pace, Walker could also cross the ball accurately and possessed a fierce shot – qualities which the Wolves defence just couldn't deal with. Chelsea won the match 3-1, Walker scoring twice, and the excellent result finally kick-started the Blues' season. Over the next two months the team climbed to lower mid-table, enjoying some extraordinary victories in the process.

On New Year's Eve, for example, the Blues completed the double over Birmingham, winning 5-4 at St Andrews. Chelsea's match-winner was the hard-running Tommy Langley, who took advantage of the improved service coming from the midfield and the wings to score a hat-trick. The feast of goals continued at the Bridge, where Ipswich were beaten 5-3 in January – but the game which really captured the attention of football fans around the country came in the third round of the FA Cup.

When the draw was made in December the Blues couldn't have been given tougher opponents, European and league champions Liverpool. The Reds were a formidable unit, boasting household names in stars such as Kenny Dalglish, Graeme Souness, Emlyn Hughes and goalkeeper Ray Clemence. Moreover, Liverpool had already beaten Chelsea 2-0 twice that season, at Anfield in the league and at the same venue in the second round of the League Cup.

Chelsea, though, had home advantage for the FA Cup tie. The backing of the fans would come in useful, doubly so because the Blues' preparations for the match had been thrown into turmoil by a series of niggling injuries. Skipper Ray Wilkins would definitely miss the game with a groin strain, while his brother Graham, Ron Harris and Mickey Droy, who had put in some sterling performances at the back after starting the season on the bench, were all doubtful. Then, on the morning of the match, Kenny Swain dropped out with flu.

In the event, Graham Wilkins and Harris were passed fit, while Ray Wilkins' absence was filled by Charlie Cooke, playing his last ever game for the club. Urged on by a noisy crowd of over 45,000, Chelsea tore into Liverpool from the start and on 16 minutes took the lead when Walker unleashed a magnificent swerving left-footer from outside the penalty area which flew past Clemence's near post. But the real drama came just after half-time when first Finnieston and then Langley put the Blues three goals up inside ten minutes of the restart. Liverpool pulled a goal back before Bill Garner unselfishly set up Walker for his second. A late goal by Dalglish – 'a real moaner' according to his limpet-like marker Ron Harris – proved academic as the Blues ran out 4-2 winners. In true Chelsea fashion, the team had produced their best performance of the season in the biggest game of the campaign. The key to a famous win, according to Tommy Langley, was the Blues' positive attitude: "We had respect for everybody, but feared nobody. We knew they came with great reputations but they didn't matter on the day."

Later that evening some of the players went for a meal out together at the Scotch Steak House in Hampton Court and celebrated their victory in unusual style. "The week before the cup tie John Sparrow announced that he'd always had an ambition to throw a custard pie in someone's face," remembers Ian Britton. "Anyway, the waiter, who was a big Chelsea fan, said he'd let John chuck a custard pie at him – but only if we beat Liverpool. So after we won the game, we all went off to the restaurant and watched John shove a custard pie in this guy's face. I think John enjoyed that as much as beating Liverpool."

For Chelsea's players the Sunday papers made satisfying reading the following morning. "Liverpool weren't just beaten – they were blitzed," suggested Ken Montgomery in the *Sunday Mirror*, while in the *Sunday Express* James Mossop hailed "the Chelsea

Youth show – an inexpensive, home-produced team that left the mighty Liverpool battered and bewildered." There was a laugh to be had, too, at reading Reds manager Bob Paisley's damning verdict on his team: "We were bloody pathetic. My players had sawdust in their heads today."

The Blues were rewarded for their brilliant win with a home draw against Second Division opponents, Burnley. After a waterlogged pitch caused the game to be postponed, Chelsea came from a goal down in the rearranged fixture at the Bridge to crush the Clarets 6-2 – six different players sharing the Blues' goals. The fans in the Shed could barely contain their glee as the scoreboard ticked over and with regular chants of "When Butch goes up to lift the FA Cup, we'll be there!" predicted greater success in the competition to come.

First, though, the Blues had to negotiate a tricky fifth round tie away to Orient. The Second Division club had famously knocked Chelsea out of the cup six years earlier, but only defender Phil Hoadley and midfielder Peter Bennett remained from that side. Otherwise, the Os' better-known players were ball-playing centre half Glenn Roeder and Peter Kitchen, a goal-poaching striker whose stocky build and Zapata moustache gave him something of the appearance of a Mexican *bandido*.

In a tightly-contested match at Brisbane Road, the Blues came away with a 0-0 draw. The closest they came to scoring was when Orient goalkeeper John Jackson brilliantly tipped over Ian Britton's 20-yard shot in the closing minutes. The headlines after the match, though, concentrated more on the overcrowding which led to the collapse of two walls at the ground shortly after kick-off (See Chapter Four, *'Hello, Hello, We are the Chelsea Boys'*).

Nine days later the teams met again at Stamford Bridge with a quarter-final tie away to either Wrexham or Middlesbrough the prize for the winners. An own goal by Orient defender Bill Roffey gave the Blues a half-time lead, but the home side were playing without the verve and sparkle of the previous rounds. Winning while not performing well was not a trick this young Chelsea side had mastered and, to the utter dismay of the Blues fans in the 36,379 crowd, two second half bullets fired by Kitchen ended their cup dreams for another year.

"That defeat just summed up the inexperience of the team," suggests Peter Bonetti, who was in goal that evening. "We'd beaten Liverpool who were European champions at the time, and possibly some of the players were thinking 'This is going to be easy' when we played Orient. But if you think like that you can guarantee it won't be easy, and it wasn't."

Remarkably, just five days after the devastating defeat by Orient, Chelsea beat Liverpool again at the Bridge to cement their status as one of the country's most unpredictable clubs. A Phil Neal penalty put the Reds ahead before a marvellous 20-yarder by Tommy Langley and two well-taken goals by Steve Finnieston, his last for the club before a summer move to Sheffield United, gave the Blues another unexpected victory. For a second time in two months, Bob Paisley left the Bridge in a huff. "That's seven goals we've given Chelsea," he complained. "We'll have to stop coming here."

The win gave the Blues a healthy eight-point cushion over West Ham, third from bottom of the First Division, and appeared to effectively end any lingering relegation worries. Suddenly, though, a gruesome run of nine games without a win in the spring, coinciding with a recurrence of Ray Wilkins' groin injury, changed the picture completely. Among these games a 3-1 defeat at Upton Park was particularly galling, as the Blues had been in front until Tommy Langley was forced to go in goal after John Phillips suffered a fractured jaw.

With just five games to go Chelsea were hovering above the trap door in 18th place. Newcastle and Leicester were already down, while the Blues would dispute the third relegation spot with West Ham, QPR and free-falling Wolves. A tense 1-1 draw at home to the Molineux club did little to ease nerves around the Bridge, but four days later the Blues were handed a 'get out of jail free' card in the form of a trip to Filbert Street. The Foxes were rock bottom, having won just four games all season, and goals by the returning Wilkins and Walker ensured they wouldn't make it five. "Without playing well we've picked up three points out of the last four and this could make all the difference to confidence," said Shellito afterwards. "There was so much tension. For the last couple of games we've been badly affected by the pressure. This club has been my life and I think I've been even more nervous than the players."

Three days later, though, the Blues were comprehensively hammered 6-0 at Everton and had to scurry back to the dressing room hoping results had gone for them elsewhere. The news was good: West Ham, despite being on a fine run of six wins in eight, had lost 2-0 at home to Liverpool and were relegated. "We are relieved to have survived," admitted Shellito. "But what team has gone four years without buying a player? Now we have got to buy." At the other end of table, the benefits of a free-spending transfer policy were plain to see: Nottingham Forest, promoted with Chelsea the previous season, were league champions.

If only, Blues fans must have thought, Chelsea could have gone on a spending spree like Forest's. There was, though, some good news on that front in the close season when Brian Mears, responding to a suggestion that Ray Wilkins might have to be sold, boldly announced: "In fact, far from selling Butch, we are now in the market for more high-calibre players. The bad times are behind us. We mean to prove that we are back in style."

However, the only player to join the club over the summer was Bob Iles, a goalkeeper signed from non-league Weymouth for £10,000 – Chelsea's first cash purchase for four years. Meanwhile, Charlie Cooke and John Dempsey headed for the Stamford Bridge exit door along with Finnieston, the two old Blues stalwarts crossing the Atlantic to end their careers in American football. Bill Garner was another player soon on the move, joining Cambridge United on a free transfer in the autumn.

If the fans were disappointed by the lack of new faces, they had another unwelcome surprise when they turned up for the opening game of the season at home to Everton: ticket prices had been increased yet again, with terrace admission rising to £1.50 and the top-priced seats in the East stand hitting the £5 mark. In the programme, the club's newly-appointed chief executive, Martin Spencer, explained that the price increases would help pay for patching up a decaying and unsafe stadium. The first phase of safety work, he pointed out, had already cost the club £230,000; even so, another £400,000 was required to bring the Bridge up to the standard required before the Greater London Council would issue a Safety Certificate.

Despite the unpopular increase in admission charges, Chelsea averaged over 30,000 for their first three home games of the season against Everton, Leeds and Manchester City. The fans' loyalty, though, was just about the only positive note to take from the matches, all of which ended in defeat. At least there was some comfort for the supporters in the Blues' away form, with the first four road trips producing a total of four points.

Amid much expectation, the Manchester City game had seen the home debut of Chelsea's first major purchase since 1974, Duncan McKenzie. Signed from Everton for £165,000, McKenzie was a crowd-pleasing ball-juggler who, unusually for the time, had enjoyed a spell abroad with Belgian giants Anderlecht. Equally extrovert off the pitch, McKenzie was famed for his whacky antics which included jumping over Mini cars and hurling a golf ball the length of the pitch.

The Shed loved him, but a thoroughly miserable 4-1 defeat by City suggested Chelsea's first priority was not a twinkle-toed forward, however gifted. With Mickey Droy, Gary Locke and David Hay all out with long-term injuries or illnesses, it was the defence rather than the attack which needed bolstering.

At the end of September, with Chelsea already deep in trouble in the relegation zone, there was some relief from the gloom enveloping the Bridge when New York Cosmos arrived in London for a high-profile friendly. The great Johan Cruyff, West German legend Franz Beckenbauer and Italian striker Giorgio Chinaglia all featured in the Americans' side, and helped attract an appreciative crowd of nearly 40,000 to the Bridge.

"Cruyff was nearing the end of his career but he was still excellent," says Graham Wilkins. "He did one 'Cruyff' turn on Ray Lewington and Ray fell for it hook, line and sinker and ended up on his arse!" After the match, which finished in a 1-1 draw, Ken Shellito attempted to persuade Cruyff to join the Blues, but the Dutch maestro turned down the offer.

Four days later Chelsea had a chance to put their own version of 'Total Football' into practice when they played Ron Atkinson's West Brom at the Bridge. What the Blues served up to just over 20,000 fans, though, was more like total rubbish as they sank to a 3-1 defeat, their fourth straight home league reverse of the season. "It was a disgusting and disgraceful performance," raged Shellito afterwards, in a rare outburst of emotion. "I told them there are too many prima donnas in the side and when you are bottom of the table there is no place for them. I don't care who we sacrifice. The club is not going down and I have told the players so."

Shellito would have been even more angry had he known how some of his younger players prepared for the next home game, against Bolton. "On the Friday night me and another Chelsea player went to the Morden Tavern, which we weren't supposed to have done, and we got pissed right up," says David Stride, a 19-year-old left back who had just broken into the side. "The intention was to go out and have a couple of relaxing pints but, you know what it's like, one leads to another. In the end I had about 12 pints and, I've got to admit, that was a regular occurrence – even on Friday nights. The fans wouldn't question us about being out at all - more like they'd be offering to buy us drinks!"

Bolton had already knocked Chelsea out of the League Cup at Burnden Park and, at half-time, were 3-0 up. It wasn't just the boozers, the whole Blues team looked hungover. The match appeared to be heading towards its inevitable conclusion in the second half when, with less than 20 minutes to go, Shellito finally responded to the increasingly impatient demands of the crowd and brought on his substitute, Clive Walker. "I'd heard the Shed chanting for me to go on," recalls Walker, "but I was beginning to think it wasn't going to happen."

What happened next has entered Chelsea folklore as, arguably, the most remarkable and unlikely 15 minutes in the club's history. First, Walker crossed for Langley to score what appeared to be nothing more than a consolation goal. Then, seven minutes later, Kenny Swain shot home from 10 yards. Now, the Blues had genuine hope of salvaging a point and urged on by constant chants of "Come on, Chelsea!" from all around the ground they launched a siege on the Bolton goal. Walker, tearing at the Trotters' defence down the left, was the chief threat and with three minutes left the winger ended a thrilling solo run with a low, angled shot past the Bolton keeper, Jim McDonagh. As the atmosphere in the stands and on the terraces moved up a notch from hysteria to delirium, there was still just enough time for the Blues to launch one last attack. Again, Walker had the ball. Again, he fired in a hard, low cross. And again, there was a player to smash the ball into the net at the Shed end. The fact that it was Bolton defender Sam Allardyce who had inadvertently rocketed the ball past McDonagh didn't matter – pandemonium broke out on and off the pitch as fans and players celebrated the goal which gave the Blues one of their most improbable victories ever. "It must have been a helluva finish to watch," said a delighted Walker afterwards. "It certainly was to play in, and for the rest of my career I don't imagine there'll be another match quite like that one."

Among the impressed spectators was the former Real Madrid and Red Star Belgrade coach Miljan Mandaric, who had been approached by Mears with a view to his becoming an 'advisor' to the club. Again, it was another imaginative idea which failed to come to anything – after witnessing the dramatic comeback against Bolton, Mandaric told Mears the spirit at the club was so good it had no need of his services. More to the point, perhaps, was the fact that Mandaric was lined up to become the coach of his country, Yugoslavia.

Despite the confidence boost provided by the Bolton victory, the Blues' results did not improve. The team's home form, especially, remained abysmal and as defeat followed defeat the crowd began to turn on some of the players. Graham Wilkins, perhaps because he was the brother of the captain but was not in the same class as 'Butch' as a player, became a prime target for the boo-boys on the terraces.

"The crowd couldn't stand me," he admits. "It got my then wife, Sandra, down more than me. It used to kill her. She got so distraught some days she wouldn't come to the game. It got quite nasty and unpleasant. After one home game I was driving Ray and my mum out of Stamford Bridge. We'd lost again and there was a group of supporters waiting for us outside the ground. We were surrounded by fans hurling abuse at us and I just couldn't move the car – the fans wouldn't move. My mum was getting a bit uptight and eventually I thought 'Sod it' and I just started moving the car forward. The fans edged away and while they were doing that I drove off. When I got home I could see there were dents in my car, where the fans had been pushing and shoving. So I wasn't very happy about that. Then, the next day, there was a knock at the door. It was the police. They told me that one of the fans had made a complaint because I'd driven over his foot and broken it. I thought I was going to be arrested but, after I explained what had happened, they dropped the charges."

The supporters' mood was hardly improved by a 1-0 defeat at home to Aston Villa in December which sent Chelsea sliding to the very bottom of the table. The loss was bad enough, but even more dispiriting was the Blues' feeble performance. "What surprised us was their lack of commitment," said Villa captain Dennis Mortimer afterwards. "They should be fighting for every ball but we had so much of it and so much space to use it that we were in danger of becoming lackadaisical."

Four days after the Villa game Shellito bowed to the inevitable and resigned. Well liked and respected for his coaching abilities, many of the players were sorry to see him leave the club. "He was a great lad," says Tommy Langley. "Everyone was very familiar with him – perhaps a little too familiar at the end. He was a great coach, but his hands were tied behind his back. He had to make do with what he had; I'm sure he would have liked to have got two or three experienced players in but it wasn't going to happen."

Reserve team coach Frank Upton was put in temporary charge and, believing the job was his for keeps, ordered the players to call him 'Boss'. He just had time to sell Kenny

Swain to Aston Villa before it was back to plain old 'Frank' when the new manager was announced the following day. The board's choice was a surprising one: Danny Blanchflower, the fabled captain of the 1961 Tottenham 'Double' team and the former manager of Northern Ireland, but a man with no practical experience of club management. "The first thing we want to know is what we need, then we must find out where to find it and finally how we can afford it," declared the Irishman in his first press conference. "I've even told the skipper that when the referee tosses the coin he's got to reach out an arm and grab it."

The laughter of the press pack ringing in his ears, the gag-cracking Blanchflower joined his new players on the plane for the journey to Middlesbrough, where the Blues were scheduled to play the next day. Among the players named in his first line-up was Peter Osgood, the Shed legend's second debut for the club coming a month after he had re-signed for the Blues from American outfit Philadelphia Furies. Osgood, who had returned to England in September nursing an ankle injury, had virtually pleaded with his old club to sign him. "I would go on my hands and knees to play for Chelsea again," he told reporters. "I want to get back to Stamford Bridge." Initially, Shellito had reacted coolly to these overtures but, with the Blues' season going from bad to worse, had eventually decided that the second coming of the 'King of Stamford Bridge' might provide the club with the lift it so desperately needed.

Bizarrely, however, Osgood would not be playing in his customary striker's role at Middlesbrough but at centre half. Not that he was complaining. "I'm delighted to be back where I started, and where I shall end my playing days," Ossie told fans. "I feel I've got plenty to offer and am ready to play anywhere to prove it – sweeper, centre half or up front. I just want to help Chelsea wherever I can."

Up at Ayresome Park, Osgood scored from a corner to put the Blues a goal up, but everything went downhill from that point: 3-1 behind at half-time, Chelsea lost 7-2. It was a shocking defeat, but Blanchflower still managed to find a positive angle in his post-match debriefing. "I'd been marking their right winger, Terry Cochrane, who'd scored two and made five," recalls David Stride. "Danny came in all smiles afterwards and said to me, 'Well done, you've marked an outstanding international winger out of the game!' Marked him out of the game? He'd slaughtered me! But that was Danny for you. He was the nicest man in the world, but he wasn't a manager."

That view was shared by most of the Chelsea players. "Danny had been out of football too long, to be truthful," says Ron Harris. "He was very out of touch and his ideas were non-existent." To be fair, Blanchflower did have a game plan of sorts, namely to get the Blues playing the 'pass and move' football which had been his hallmark in his Tottenham heyday. "Danny came in with weird ideas of turning Chelsea into Bill Nicholson's Double-winning side of 1960/61– one touch football and all that," remarked Duncan McKenzie later. "I thought to myself, 'Hang on, Danny, you'll need some pretty good players to do that.'"

But if the Blues struggled with Blanchflower's tactics, that was nothing to the confusion generated by his training sessions. "Danny had been a great player but, boy, did he have mad ideas!" says Tommy Langley. "One day, during a practice match, he threw a second ball on the pitch and said, 'If you can play with two balls, imagine what you could do with one on Saturday!'" Amid blank looks all round, the players would try to score at one end while, simultaneously, making sure the opposition didn't net at the other end. "We just didn't know what the fuck was going on," says David Stride candidly. "He used to say, 'When I blow the whistle, pass the ball' but we had two balls on the pitch. We were getting absolutely mullered that season and we had enough problems playing with one."

Surprisingly for a man who hailed from Ireland, one of the wettest countries on the planet, Blanchflower had a deep-rooted hatred of rain. So much so, in fact, that training would be abandoned if the clouds opened above Molesey. "If it was raining, instead of training, he'd keep us in a room," recalls John Bumstead, an energetic and tough-tackling young midfielder who made his Chelsea debut that season. "Danny used to tell great stories. He'd talk for about an hour and a half, then we'd go home."

"Danny was woeful, bless his soul," adds Graham Wilkins. "He didn't have a clue about coaching or training, so all we used to do was play games against each other. He didn't coach us or do anything about set pieces or who was picking up who at the opposition's set pieces. Nothing. So in games, it was all off the cuff, nothing planned. We just had to try to sort things out between ourselves on the pitch.

"One incident summed him up, really. We were training at Stamford Bridge on the Friday morning before the game and there were a few supporters just above the tunnel. As we came out onto the pitch we threw the balls out of the ball bag and dropped the bag on the ground. Just at that moment a couple of fans shouted 'C'mon Danny, keep it going!' He turned round to wave to them, walked a step backwards and tripped up in the ball net!"

Briefly, though, it appeared that Blanchflower's unconventional methods might pay dividends. Following a 5-1 thrashing at Ipswich and a 3-0 FA Cup third round defeat at Manchester United, the Blues' fortunes revived with a 3-2 win at an icy Maine Road. In their next game Chelsea beat fellow strugglers Birmingham 2-1, Ray Wilkins scoring both goals, in a match which saw the debut of Eamonn Bannon, a skilful, ball-playing midfielder signed from Hearts for £200,000. The victory left the Blues still second bottom but within four points of QPR and safety.

There was to be no dramatic escape from the relegation zone, however. The next 13 games produced no wins and just two draws, against champions-elect Liverpool and Derby. The creditable goalless draw against the Reds attracted the biggest crowd of the season to the Bridge, over 40,000, and was notable for the debut of Petar Borota, an acrobatic and flamboyant goalkeeper signed from Partizan Belgrade on the recommendation of Miljan Mandaric. "Borota is an engaging mixture of eye-catching reflexes, mind-boggling courage and weird positioning, who is clearly destined to become a cult figure at the Bridge," predicted Jeff Powell in the *Daily Mail*. His new team-mates were equally impressed, if a little nonplussed by some of the Yugoslav's unorthodox antics. "He was the first goalkeeper I've seen to go up for a corner," says Ron Harris. "He instigated that tactic when we played Liverpool at home. But I found him alright to play with. He was a very good shot stopper, and a good keeper generally." Typically, Blanchflower had his own unique take on his exciting new signing, saying, "If he makes an ass of himself he will do it in style."

Borota, though, could do little to halt Chelsea's slide back into the Second Division. Now without Steve Wicks, sold to Derby for £275,000, and Duncan McKenzie, who moved back north to Blackburn, the Blues increasingly relied on young, unproven players. "It didn't add to the continuity of the team," says Tommy Langley. "Because we were always reading about players possibly being sold, it got to the stage where we didn't know who would be there on a week-by-week basis." Rather than selling players, Chelsea needed to buy. "We had a nucleus of five or six good young players," adds Garry Stanley, "but we needed to replace our senior players who were nearing the end of their careers. If we could have brought in three or four good, experienced pros like Nottingham Forest had done it would have been a different story. But the club didn't have the money."

A 6-0 thrashing at Forest in the rain signalled that the end was nigh, before a 5-2 defeat at Arsenal on Easter Monday confirmed Chelsea's demise to the satisfaction of the mathematicians. There was still a month of the season to run and Blanchflower used the remaining games to give further experience to a number of youth products including elegant midfielder Mike Fillery, versatile defender Gary Chivers and centre back Micky Nutton.

"Danny was eccentric, but he was very good for the youngsters," says Gary Chivers, one of the few players to offer a positive assessment of Blanchflower's management style. "He offered us a load of encouragement which was very helpful. He turned round to me one day in training and said, 'Football's an easy game, complicated by idiots' and he was completely right. He wanted the easy game, see what you see and pass the ball. He encouraged the passing game. I was a ball-playing centre half and, at 18, he wanted me to play football rather than booting it – which a lot of teams in our position would have done."

Five days after being relegated a largely youthful Blues team gave their fans – by now invariably described as 'long suffering' – something to cheer with a 2-1 home win over Middlesbrough, the last of just three Chelsea wins at the Bridge that season. "It was a great day because it was the first game we'd won in something like 15," says Chivers, who made his debut in the match. There was no doubt, though, who was the happiest man on the pitch. Scoring his one and only Chelsea goal with a sweetly-struck 20 yarder, Graham Wilkins provided the best possible response to his critics in the stands. "I was absolutely flabbergasted when it went in," he admits. "I didn't have a clue what to do, so I just stood there – then I got completely mobbed!" David Stride, though, was less thrilled after being knocked out following a collision with Boro's Staurt Boam. "I got a severe elbow to the head," he recalls. "I was out cold and the game was held up for 10 minutes. When I came round I was on the stretcher and Graham Wilkins came over and said, 'You're taking the piss, Stridey!' Then when I got to hospital I was told I had a fractured skull. But that was typical Graham, always taking the piss."

Three weeks later, Chelsea's last home game of the season against FA Cup winners Arsenal was a poignant affair. Not only was it a farewell to the First Division, it was also Peter Bonetti's 600th and final league game for the club. Fittingly, the match programme paid fulsome tribute to one of the all-time Chelsea greats: "Words cannot adequately express what he has meant to Chelsea in all his years: masterly goalkeeper, sportsman supreme, model clubman and a shining example to all who have been privileged to play in front of him for so long in the Chelsea team."

After the game, which finished in a 1-1 draw that confirmed Chelsea would finish the season in bottom place, Bonetti had no time for a farewell party. Instead, he was dashing up the motorway to begin a new life north of the border. "It was an emotional evening for me and it was real break in more ways than one," he says. "Apart from my oldest daughter, who was studying at drama college, my family had already moved up to Scotland where we had bought a guest house. My daughter was waiting for me after the game, and we drove up to Scotland all through the night. So I didn't just leave Chelsea that night, I left the country too."

Bonetti's departure marked the end of an era for the Blues. The Seventies, a decade synonymous with Chelsea cup glory, were almost over and, on the face of it, the club could not look forward to the new decade with much optimism. Yes, the Blues had some promising youngsters but, on the other hand, the older players in the squad were largely past their best. Yes, their manager was one of the most famous names in football but many people, including some of his own players, had serious doubts about his ability to perform his role competently. Yes, again, the Blues had one of the biggest stadiums in the country, but it was a crumbling wreck – and, in any case, would the fans who had stuck by the team during the worst ever top-flight season in the club's history continue to tolerate second-rate, and second-tier, football on a regular basis? As the curtain came down on a season to forget there were, as so often at the Bridge, more questions than answers.

CHAPTER FOUR

'HELLO, HELLO, WE ARE THE CHELSEA BOYS'

I n the second half of the Seventies there was little or no stability at Chelsea: the team pinballed wildly between the First and Second Divisions, players came and went with bewildering frequency and the comfy chair in the manager's office had a built-in ejector-seat. The only constant factor remained the fans, who gave loyal backing to the club during some very difficult years.

Owing to its bowl-like design, the old Stamford Bridge was never the most intimidating of venues for visiting teams. The noise produced by the famous Shed at the Fulham Road End could be deafening when you stood in the middle of the pulsating throng but, by the time the chants and songs had floated across the huge open space behind the goal and drifted onto the pitch much of their impact was lost. Nonetheless, the Bridge crowd played its part, especially during the 1976/77 promotion season when the Blues remained undefeated at home in the league – a feat the club had only managed once before in its history.

Away from home, Chelsea possessed a huge army of travelling fans – many of them boisterous, excitement-seeking, adrenalin-pumped teenagers. Even when the club was in the Second Division, up to 10,000 fans would travel the country supporting the Blues, providing the club with one of the largest away followings in the Football League. Many of these fans had become hooked on the Blues during the glory years of the early 1970s and by no means all of them hailed from London or the Home Counties. Yorkshire, in particular, was something of a Chelsea stronghold, the Blues having been embraced by the local anti-Leeds faction during their epic 1970 FA Cup final clashes with the Elland Road club. Chelsea away games would also see flags and banners proclaiming the support of fans from numerous other areas of the country, including the midlands, Wales and the south-west.

Inevitably, there were elements within this huge support who were up for a scrap – this, after all, was a period when it was difficult to open a newspaper without reading that one match or another had been 'marred' by football hooliganism, so widespread was the phenomenon. However, possibly because Chelsea were a bigger club than most, episodes of violence involving Blues supporters tended to attract additional media attention and coverage. Soon, it seemed, that no mention of 'Chelsea fans' in the press was permissible without the preceding adjective 'notorious' or its close cousin 'infamous'.

Which isn't to say that the supporters' appalling reputation was completely unjustified. Far from it. Between 1975 and 1977, in particular, Chelsea fans were involved in so many incidents of violence, vandalism and general mayhem that, along with those from Manchester United, they were subject to sanctions not only by the club, but also by the Labour government of the day.

One of the first headline-grabbing incidents during this period occurred at Luton in September 1975. Having invaded the pitch and attacked the Hatters' goalkeeper during the Blues' 3-0 defeat, Chelsea fans then smashed the windows of dozens of shops on their way back to the train station. Even though more than 100 supporters were arrested, the day's anarchy was far from over. On the return journey to London, to a background chant of "Chelsea sing, Chelsea fight, Chelsea set their trains alight!" the Blues fans turned one of their British Rail 'specials' into a blazing inferno.

One of the fans on board the train was Chris Ryan, then aged 16 and living in Greenford. "All I could see was smoke coming past, as if we were on a steam train," he recalls. "The train stopped outside Cricklewood, everybody got off by the side of the track and it was really quite chaotic. At the time it was quite common for fans to smash up the 'specials' but setting fire to the train was a new one. The trains were terrible, they didn't quite have broken windows before they set off, but they were really old. Setting fire to them was probably the best thing you could do to them. In a way, these incidents were quite enjoyable – and everyone wanted to hear about them in school on Monday."

British Rail, however, was appalled by the damage. It promptly stopped running football specials for all clubs for the rest of the season and refused to sell cheap tickets until after 3pm on Saturdays. If fans wanted to travel, British Rail announced, the club itself would have to charter special trains and be responsible for any damage caused.

The Police Superintendents' Association's knee-jerk response to the disorder was to suggest that matches should be classified in the same way as films with under-16s banned from 'X-rated' games unless accompanied by an adult. Chelsea, along with other clubs, were not impressed with the bizarre proposal. "Who would decide which matches were selected?" asked Chelsea chairman Brian Mears pointedly. England manager Don Revie, meanwhile, publicly advocated 'the return of the birch' saying, "We have tried everything else, we might as well try this dramatic deterrent."

Startling though they were, the events at Luton were just a warm-up for the following season when Chelsea's promotion push saw even more fans sign up for 'Eddie McCreadie's blue and white army' – a chant that was heard throughout 1976/77 from Plymouth to Carlisle. Early on in the campaign the Blues played Millwall away – the first league meeting between the clubs for 46 years – in a match which, in terms of its potential for trouble, wasn't so much 'Category X' as 'Category XXX'. If anything, Millwall's fans were even more notorious than Chelsea's, thanks in part to a *Panorama* investigation into football hooliganism which had introduced the TV-watching public to blood-chilling characters such as 'Harry the Dog' and his psychopathic mates in 'F Troop' and 'The Treatment'.

"We got down there early," remembers Cliff Auger, who was 16 at the time and living in Southall. "I was with a few Chelsea – we were sort of mob-handed which you had to be for your own protection – and we were very wary, looking over our shoulders. Our plan was to 'take' the Millwall end by getting in there very early and at about 1.30 pm we entered the Cold Blow End. We held it for about two minutes before Millwall came from everywhere – you could walk round the ground in those days – and we jumped over the low terrace wall and scattered across the pitch in various directions. I ended up going out of the ground at the other end and back into the street. I was sitting on a wall about 200 yards from the ground with some other Chelsea fans, wondering what to do next, when a horse and cart came up the street. There were a bunch of fellows sitting on the back of it, so I thought, 'That's a funny way of going to the game!' It pulled up next to us, a load of Millwall fans clambered off and steamed right into us. We were chased all over the place. I got away, but I'd had enough by then and didn't go back into the ground to see the game. I got back to Ealing Broadway and found out the score in a TV shop there."

Patrick Kenny, from Reading, was also in the group of Chelsea fans which attempted to get one over their Millwall rivals by occupying their territory. "We all met up at Chelsea, went down there on the tube and, about an hour and a half before kick-off, chased them out of their end. But, by ten to two Millwall were coming back in big numbers and by two o'clock we were back out on the street again. We got a hell of a kicking. I was trying to get out of the ground and some bloke had me by the hair, trying to pull me back in. People were punching and kicking me but I managed to get out.

"After that we regrouped, with the idea of getting in at the other end where the Chelsea fans should have been. We went down there and we ran into a group of Millwall fans.

There were about 200 of us and only 50 of them so we started to charge them – but they didn't run. As we were running towards them they suddenly brought out meat hooks, baseball bats and other weapons and they battered us again. I've been everywhere with Chelsea and I always felt wherever we turned up we'd have a go, but that day we got done."

The Chelsea firm may have taken a hiding at Millwall, but it didn't deter them from embarking on similar escapades at other grounds. At every away match the home end would be invaded by many of the travelling Blues, who would often wait until the match started before revealing their true colours. Soon, even the Chelsea players knew that not all their supporters would be found in the away end. "When we were playing away we'd kick off and that was the signal for the blue and white scarves to start waving in the home end," recalls Ian Britton. "After a while the fans would be escorted down the other end. But you can't take it away from the fans at the time, they were tremendous."

For the club, though, the antics of some of their away fans were a complete embarrassment. An item in the Chelsea programme in November 1976, a week after 26 fans had been arrested during disturbances at Nottingham Forest, was fairly typical of the time. "The one serious blot on our day last Saturday was the outbreak of hooliganism at Nottingham – violence on the terraces, stabbings, arrests before, during and after the match," it read. "It is lamentable that at a time when so many people are pulling so hard for Chelsea – players, management, backroom and groundstaff, fundraisers and the vast majority of supporters – a tiny, mindless minority continue spasmodically to besmirch our name with their hooligan behaviour." Chelsea manager Eddie McCreadie, meanwhile, always made a point of distinguishing between the "thousands of good supporters" and the "tag-along hooligan element" in his infrequent programme notes.

For a number of years, the club seemed at a loss at how to tackle the issue of hooliganism. Stamford Bridge, like all other grounds at the time, didn't have CCTV cameras so the trouble-makers could not easily be identified. In any case, most of the problems came away from home, in town centres and at stadiums where the local police forces were undermanned, ill-equipped and unused to dealing with large numbers of travelling fans. The upshot was that supporters who traded punches with opposing fans, threw objects on the pitch or even smashed windows in shopping centres would, in all likelihood, escape arrest – a state of affairs which, inevitably, only encouraged them to cause more mayhem the following week.

Three months after the Forest match, however, the club did act, threatening to stop arranging rail travel to away matches after a train returning from Cardiff was smashed up by "alleged Chelsea supporters". Fans who had been on the train, though, vehemently denied that they were responsible for the damage. "The train I came back on was held up outside Cardiff and again at Newport," wrote one fan in the following week's home programme. "Part of it stopped over a bridge, and we were subjected to stone and bottle throwing, from under the bridge, by Cardiff supporters, and they broke a few windows to add to those already smashed when we got on the train to go home. In short, I am amazed at this allegation of damage 'by alleged Chelsea supporters'." Nor was this an isolated incident of Blues fans coming under attack – three buses containing Chelsea fans were bricked at Liverpool in 1978, for example, while grounds such as Filbert Street, Goodison Park and Loftus Road were notorious for coin throwing.

It wasn't long, though, before the hooligans in Chelsea's following were cementing their reputation as among the most uncontrollable in the country. On Easter Monday 1977 Chelsea fans lit fires on the terraces at Charlton during their side's crushing 4-0 defeat. After the match, the disgruntled mob targeted the Addicks' supporters club, setting it alight and breaking all its windows.

"There were Chelsea fans everywhere, we had three sides of the ground," recalls Chris Ryan. "The fires were all along the big side terrace they used to have at the Valley. They weren't big fires because there wasn't much to burn – just programmes and newspapers. It was just something to do, really. The team was playing crap, we were getting stuffed and maybe there was some frustration because we were so close to promotion.

"A friend of mine, Johnny, got arrested after the game. He was Scottish, and had just started living down in London, but he started coming to football with us and got a bit carried away. Again, it was just wanton vandalism – he overturned a hotdog stand. He got a big fine for the time – about £200, I think – and his name and address appeared in the papers. He had the *News of the World* parked outside where he lived, hoping to get a picture of him and an interview. He worked for the civil service and just about managed to hang onto his job, but when he was at home his flat-mates had to vet his calls in case it was the press."

More than 100 Chelsea fans were reported to have been involved in the disturbances, which attracted grisly headlines in the papers. For some commentators, especially those on the right of the political spectrum, the events at The Valley were not merely a blot on the football landscape but symptomatic of a breakdown in law and order under a directionless and indecisive Labour government. Mob violence on the picket line at Grunwick in north London, vicious street clashes between the right-wing National Front and the Anti-Nazi League, riots at punk rock concerts and football hooligans rampaging around the country every weekend: the government, argued its critics, was doing nothing while Britain went to the dogs.

Under fire from the opposition and the media, the government reacted to the events at The Valley by making an example of Chelsea. Speaking in the House of Commons, the Minister of Sport and Recreation, Dennis Howell, first of all criticised the courts for the small fines they had imposed on fans charged with offences at Charlton. "The use of detention centres seems to have more merit than inadequate fines," he said, adding that the government was considering raising fines for hooliganism to £1,000. Howell then announced that future Chelsea away matches – like those of Manchester United, another big club with a large hooligan following - would be all-ticket with no terrace tickets made available to the club. "This sort of behaviour has got to be stopped," he told rows of nodding heads in the Commons. "If it means fans shall be denied access to the terraces then that is what we shall do. It is not the first time.Chelsea supporters have been involved in something like this."

Howell's measures came into effect for Chelsea's last away match of the season at Wolves, a game the Blues needed to win or draw to guarantee promotion back to the First Division. 'Eddie McCreadie's blue and white army' had travelled all over the country in support of their team but now, it appeared, most of the foot soldiers would not be present at the final, dramatic chapter of a tumultuous season. The only Chelsea fans who would definitely be at Molineux were those lucky season-ticket holders who had snapped up the small allocation of stand tickets provided by Wolves.

For the remaining thousands of loyal Blues, there were no encouraging words from the club. "If you haven't got a ticket, do not travel next Saturday under any circumstances," cautioned the Chelsea programme, emphasising the point by printing the warning in capital letters. What the club didn't know, however, was that many fans already had tickets for the match or were making arrangements to get them in the days leading up to the vital clash.

The chief organiser of Chelsea's unofficial ticket allocation was the acknowledged leader of the Blues' travelling support, Danny Harkins, more commonly known as 'Eccles'.

"He sorted out tickets for lots of the Chelsea fans who went up there," says Cliff Auger. "We were coming back on a special train from Burnley two weeks before the Wolves game and Danny was collecting deposits for Wolves. He took a pound off everybody for the tickets and altogether he charged £2; the face value was £1 so he made a right killing! But it was the only way to get tickets, because he was either sending people up there to buy them or he had contacts in Wolverhampton."

Thanks to the success of Eccles' and other similar operations, many Chelsea fans were able to travel to Wolves with a ticket in their pocket. Others didn't have tickets but still planned to go. Soon, it was common knowledge that, rather than the expected couple of hundred fans, four or five thousand would be travelling up from London. To the fans' delight – and, no doubt, the annoyance of the government – British Rail announced that it would be providing a direct, 'relief' train from Euston to the Midlands. "We are running the train because we know Chelsea supporters have tickets for the game and will be travelling to Wolverhampton," stated a BR spokesman.

For the media, the fact that thousands of Chelsea fans were flouting a government ban with the apparent backing of British Rail was a big news story. "Joan Thirkettle from ITN was on the concourse at Euston, interviewing loads of fans," recalls Dave Johnstone, editor of the popular Chelsea fanzine *cfcuk*. "She asked me 'So, are you going up there without a ticket?' and I said, 'No, I bought it last week at Chelsea' – I'd got it from Eccles – and I took it out for the camera. I don't know if the clip was ever shown on TV, though."

In the Black Country, especially, the media helped spread rumours that the invading force from the capital were set on pillage and destruction. Understandably, the local inhabitants were more than a little apprehensive on the day of the match. "Our train pulled up outside Wolverhampton station before they let us off and, in the houses by the tracks, people were hanging out of their windows with looks of disbelief on their faces," continues Dave. "You could almost hear them saying, 'They're here!' Some of them looked terrified because it had been all over the papers that Chelsea were going to smash up the town." The fears of the residents were hardly eased as the Chelsea fans stormed out of the station, scarves waving, chanting their new tongue-in-cheek battle-cry, 'We're worse than Man United!'

When they arrived at Molineux, the fans with tickets had no problems entering the ground – while the ticketless ones were helped out by a surprising source. "When we got to the ground a policeman came over to us with a wad of about 50 tickets and handed them out free," remembers Patrick Kenny. "I suppose the police thought they'd rather have us in the ground than outside. So I got a free ticket to get into the game." All the same, the police strategy was only partially successful as fighting inside and outside the ground resulted in 111 arrests, most with London addresses.

For the vast majority of Chelsea fans, though, the day was a joyful one as the Blues gained the point they needed to go up. Both sets of supporters invaded the pitch at the final whistle, many of them hacking at the Molineux turf to claim a treasured souvenir. "I took a bit of the pitch, put it in my pocket and kept it for about three seasons," remembers Chris Ryan.

The following Saturday the Bridge was in party mood for the visit of Hull – a match which was interrupted by a number of celebratory pitch invasions. "I was sitting in the West stand benches," recalls Patrick Kenny. "When everyone ran on the pitch before kick-off I was one of them. The ball just happened to come out to me on the edge of the penalty area. I shot, Peter Bonetti dived and the ball went in. That got a cheer from the Shed. At the end of the game everyone was crouched by the touchline, waiting to rush on, and people were trying to grab the corner flags to keep as souvenirs. It was just completely chaotic." After the final whistle an estimated 10,000 fans poured over the barriers onto the pitch, most of them heading towards the East stand where the players eventually appeared to revel in the crowd's adulation.

"The atmosphere in the Shed for that match was just fantastic," says Robert Howard, a Chelsea fan from Hillingdon. "But it was great throughout that whole season. Virtually every fan had a scarf and we used to hold them up while singing 'You'll Never Walk Alone'. Nobody seemed to mind that, really, it was a Liverpool song. There were loads of flags, as well, mostly Union Jacks with 'Chelsea' scrawled over them so, all in all, the Shed was awash with colour – not just blue and white, but also red, white and green from the old early-Seventies away kit. The crush on the terraces for the big matches was extraordinary. For some of the games, like Hull, when it was really packed, you couldn't stand face on to watch the match – there were so many bodies you got turned sideways and you had to twist your neck to see what was happening on the pitch by peering over your shoulder. By the end of the game you had a cricked neck and all the bobbing up and down left you feeling exhausted but, if we'd won, you just didn't care..."

The anarchic scenes at the Hull match were fired by over-exuberance rather than any malicious intent but, nonetheless, the authorities were unimpressed. A number of fans were arrested, one for kicking a policeman who prevented him from entering the players' tunnel, and Horseferry Road Magistrates' Courts subsequently handed out fines ranging from £3 to £50. There was a knock-on penalty for all young Blues fans, too, as Chelsea chairman Brian Mears announced that, for the following season, there would be no concessionary price for children. If they wanted to watch the Blues from the terraces they would have to stump up £1, just like the adults.

In general, though, there was much less trouble at Stamford Bridge during this period than there was at Chelsea away games. Except when the likes of Millwall or West Ham were the visitors and their firms would attempt to take the home end, the Shed was a safe place to stand and it was here that the most vocal followers congregated.

Terrace style during the late mid-to-late Seventies reflected London's rich variety of cults and tribes: skinheads, ageing hippies and big-haired and wide-collared disco fans. More alarmingly, the baleful influence of the Bay City Rollers could still be seen in occasional dashes of tartan and the widespread preference for scarves to be worn tied to the wrist rather than round the neck. The various groups mingled more or less happily together, united by their common passion for Chelsea and, initially at least, by a shared loathing for the latest cult to emerge from the London underground scene: punk rockers.

Alan Delaprelle, better known as 'Punky Al', was one of the few Chelsea fans in the Shed to embrace the controversial new look. "I had the spiky hair, the bondage trousers and all the other punk gear," he says. "Some of the other lads I went with were into punk, but I was the only one who wore the stuff. The reception from the other Chelsea fans was hostile to start with. It wasn't physical, but people had a go at you. Then, within about a year, everybody accepted it. Remember, a lot of the punk band members were Chelsea fans. Charlie Harper from the UK Subs used to go to games from time to time, and I sometimes saw Paul Cook and Steve Jones from the Pistols drinking in the Swan pub before matches."

Not that there was much time for mingling with these punk icons down the boozer.

For many fans pre-match drinking was a hurried affair – a consequence of the need to get into the Bridge at least an hour before kick-off to be sure of grabbing a favourite spot on the terraces. Once inside the stadium there was nothing to do except read the match programme or join in the terrace singing which, as the clock ticked down to three o'clock, would get louder by the minute.

Chants and songs ranged from some of the old Chelsea classics – 'You are my Chelsea', 'Super Chelsea', 'One team in London', 'We're proud of you, Chelsea' and so on – to witty insults aimed at the visiting fans, who were corralled into a corner of the North stand terrace by the East stand. Northern fans, in particular, would often be ridiculed by a reworking of the folk song, *In your Liverpool Homes*:

In your Liverpool* slums
In your Liverpool slums
You look in a dustbin for something to eat
You find a dead rat and you think it's a treat
In your Liverpool slums
(* Unless the Reds were the visitors, the away team's name would be substituted for 'Liverpool')

In those days, the visiting team always came out of the tunnel first, to be greeted by a cacophony of boos, whistles, jeers and 'wanker' gestures from the Shed, which would then launch into a deafening chant of 'Who the fuckin' hell are you?' regardless of whether the team in question were no-hopers Hereford United or reigning European champions Liverpool. A swift pause for breath would be followed by a rousing rendition of 'Bring on the champions!' – a chant which seemed to be all the more popular for having no real basis in fact. The Blues' eventual appearance would then be greeted by the biggest cheer of the day, bar those generated by Chelsea goals.

Once they were out on the pitch, the players were hailed individually with their own personal song or chant. Ray Wilkins, like Peter Osgood before him, was worshipped as 'The King of Stamford Bridge'; leading goalscorer Steve Finnieston was greeted with a staccato chant of 'Su-per Jock'; Kenny Swain was 'here, there and every fuckin' where'; while Ian Britton and 'Flasher' Walker were, according to the fans anyway, always to be found 'on the wing'. Then there were the players of whom, as their songs said, there was only one: Tommy Langley, Garry Stanley, Eamonn Bannon and the rest. Few players, if any, would be missed out.

Once the game kicked off, a palpable sense of excitement would ripple through the Shed whenever Chelsea attacked. Corners and free-kicks in dangerous positions would be met with urgent and repeated cries of 'Come on, Chel-sea!' while, conversely, sloppy play by the Blues at the back might produce the critical chant 'Wake up Chel-sea, wake up!' sung to the tune of *Auld Lang Syne*.

A SERIOUS CASE OF THE BLUES

A Chelsea goal would, of course, be the cue for mass pandemonium, as Robert Howard recalls. "The first time I went in the middle of the Shed was against Bolton in 1976. Garry Stanley hit a 20-yard rocket past their keeper and in the next instance I was sent flying about the same distance down the terrace steps. Then everyone surged back to roughly their original positions. It was a bit like being caught up in a powerful human wave – you just had to go with the flow and hope you didn't fall over. I somehow managed to stay on my feet, but I lost one of my trainers in the melee. I thought I'd never see it again and have to go home minus one shoe. Then I looked around and saw somebody holding up my trainer in celebration – he was holding it aloft as though it was the FA Cup. I managed to grab it off him just before the Shed launched into 'Knees Up Muvver Brown' and 'Let's Go Fuckin' Mental' and we were all sent spiralling down the steps again."

If the opposition scored first, on the other hand, the Shed would usually respond with a defiant chant of 'Chel-sea, Chel-sea, Chel-sea!' to the tune of 'Amazing Grace'. Then, the celebrating away fans would be subjected to a barrage of abuse and threats:

'You're gonna get your fuckin' heads kicked in,' was straight to the point, while 'It's a long way to Fulham Broadway', sung to the tune of 'It's a long way to Tipperary', possessed a slightly more subtle menace. Finally, the Shed would issue a call to action to the Chelsea fans standing at the away end: 'North stand, North stand, do your job, North stand, do your job!'

The sprawling North stand was a crumbling, dilapidated terrace with weeds growing between some of the steps. Unlike the Shed end, there was no cover to shelter under when it rained – hence the gleeful cry from the Shed during torrential downpours of 'You're getting wet, you're getting wet, we're not, we're not!' Yet, for some Chelsea fans the fact that this was the designated 'away' end made it an attractive spot to watch the Blues. Incredibly, even as late as 1976, there was no segregation on the North stand – even for a big London derby. "I was in the North stand for the FA Cup game against Palace in 1976," recalls Patrick Kenny. "The Palace fans came into the ground singing 'Eagles, Eagles' but Chelsea fans were waiting for them at the top of the steps and piled straight into them."

"I was in the Shed end for the game but you could clearly see the Palace and Chelsea fans all mingled together on the North stand," adds Cliff Auger. "Then, all of a sudden, a gap appeared and a Chelsea fan launched himself across it with a kung fu kick and tried to knock someone's head off with his foot. There wasn't a lot of fighting, it was pretty much that one incident – but it was so dramatic I think a lot of people remember it."

Incidents like that persuaded the club to introduce segregation at the North stand, but the terrace remained the place to go for hardcore scrappers who fancied 'steaming in' on the opposition. A direct assault over the fence was sometimes attempted but, more often, the Chelsea fans would wait for half-time. "The police would put the away fans in their section and lock the gate," explains Patrick Kenny. "We used to stand in the other section under the floodlights by the tea bar, which was the only one on the terrace. At half-time the away fans had to walk past the Chelsea fans to get to the tea bar, so they'd get a slap as they went to buy a cup of tea."

Away fans who bought a ticket in the stands were not much safer, either. "One game I distinctly remember was at home to Manchester United in 1978," says John Kiely from Essex. "We were 2-1 up when, in the last minute, United were awarded a penalty. Some of their fans in the West stand, who had kept quiet until then, jumped up with excitement and within seconds people were piling in on them."

The aggressive chanting and full-on violence only helped to confirm Stamford Bridge's reputation as one of the most hostile and partisan venues in English football. Even, it seemed, the behaviour of the well-wadded fans in the posh seats left a lot to be desired. "Frankly, we wish we were without those spectators whose behaviour is dragging Chelsea's name down," sighed Blues captain Ray Wilkins in 1978. "Some of them are on the terraces, but there are also many obscenities coming from the stands – from the expensive seats, too."

By the late Seventies the Bridge, in the popular imagination at least, had become the Beirut of London football: once a glamour spot frequented by actors and pop stars, now a pock-marked battle-zone populated by crazed thugs and foul-mouthed yobbos. Understandably, perhaps, some parents were reluctant to let their offspring set foot in this intimidating and frightening arena. "My dad used to go to work on the train from Orpington and, unfortunately, my request to go to a game in the Shed coincided with 10-foot high graffiti appearing in the station that said 'Shed Chelsea Boot Boys Kill,'" recalls John Ingledew, a photographer for the Chelsea programme and club magazine. "So he had a certain reluctance to let me venture up on the train to Charing Cross and, in fact, I wasn't allowed to go to Chelsea until I was 15.

"My first game was against Burnley in the FA Cup in 1978. It was everything that I'd expected. The queues outside the ground were enormous even an hour and a half before kick off. Then we heard a tannoy announcement – 'The game is off due to a waterlogged pitch...' There was a big groan, then everybody charged back into Fulham Broadway station and I've never heard a noise like it. We were under the old glass roof by the ticket office and everyone was chanting, 'If you're all going to West Ham clap your hands.' So I got on the tube with two or three thousand other fans. But by the time we'd reached Victoria most people had got off, and when we got to West Ham it seemed it was just me and my mate in our blue and white scarves. And, of course, West Ham were playing QPR – so we decided it might be a good idea to wear our scarves under our crombies."

Chelsea easily disposed of Burnley in the rearranged match and, in the next round, travelled to Orient. A huge army of Chelsea fans crossed London to Brisbane Road, and comfortably outnumbered the home fans in the 25,123 crowd. "I was about 10 from the front behind the goal Chelsea were attacking," remembers Scott Buckingham from Sidcup. "The first time we attacked their goal, people leant forward to see and the wall at the front of the terrace collapsed. Another wall collapsed at the side of the ground. It was simply the pressure of people. In those days clubs used to let in as many people as wanted to go in and that was the problem that day – in years to come that's what happened at Hillsborough." As a number of Chelsea fans were carried away on stretchers the rest, shocked and angered by the incident, sang 'Oh, what a shitty ground' to the tune of the ancient Mary Hopkin hit *Those Were the Days*.

Bizarrely, however, Orient chairman Brian Winston refused to accept that his club's sub-standard stadium was at fault. Instead, he pointed the finger of blame at the visiting supporters. "We've had threatening phone calls all week from Chelsea fans saying that if they lost they would push our walls down and smash up the ground," he told reporters afterwards. "Obviously we didn't believe them but we did restrict the attendance. Before the match they were pushing and pushing until the walls went. There was nothing sudden or spontaneous about it. They had been working at the crash barriers on the terracing with steel rods. They will bring acetylene cutters with them next. The walls weren't faulty. The groundstaff had checked them beforehand. It was the Chelsea crowd that caused the trouble."

However, John Kiely, who also attended the match, is adamant that the Chelsea fans were not responsible. "I got in the ground early and didn't see anyone chipping away at the walls," he says. "The walls had most probably been built before the war and weren't used to supporting the weight of that many people. It was just lucky nobody was killed or seriously injured."

During that season, 1977/78, the club launched the Chelsea Official Supporters Club. One of its main aims was to control the distribution of tickets for away matches. After the Wolves fiasco, Dennis Howell had wisely decided to relax the ban on Chelsea fans attending away games, but the all-ticket policy was maintained. In turn, Chelsea restricted the sale of stand and terrace tickets for away games to season-ticket holders and club members.

"The policy worked quite well from the club's point of view because there was less trouble that season," says Robert Howard. "But for the fans it was a hassle because you had to get your ticket in advance rather than just turn up on the day. On one occasion, I bunked off school to go to the Bridge to buy a ticket for West Ham away and watch the reserve game that was on that afternoon. After I bought the ticket I was hanging around the forecourt with three other lads when we were approached by a steward. He asked us if we wanted to be ballboys for the reserve game so, of course, we said 'yes'.

"It was a slightly surreal experience. We got changed into club tracksuits in the referee's dressing room, then we waited in the tunnel with a few of the Chelsea players who were having a laugh together. About 20 minutes before kick-off Chelsea's opponents, Ipswich, turned up. They were all in club suits, and looked very serious. Then I saw why. Bobby Robson, the Ipswich manager, was with them. He was already firing them up: 'Get changed quickly, start concentrating, let's have a good attitude...' He couldn't have been more animated if it had been a cup final rather than a meaningless reserve fixture. Then they disappeared into the dressing room.

"During the match I was so excited I kept running up and down my touchline, along by the East stand, almost as though I was a player. At one point I nearly tripped up the linesman and he ticked me off. I hardly got a touch of the ball, though, because whenever it went into the stand one of the couple of hundred fans there would throw it back. Meanwhile, one of the other ball boys had propped himself up against a goal post and spent most of the game chatting to Ipswich's goalkeeper, Laurie Sivall. I can't imagine Robson was very impressed by that. I was only interested in the Chelsea players, though, and after I'd picked up my 25p match fee I had quite a long chat with Clive Walker, who had been playing, and Ray Wilkins, who had come along to watch his brother Steve. All in all, it was much more fun, and in some ways more educational, than going to school!"

Depressingly for club and fans alike, by the end of the Seventies Chelsea's attendances for first team matches were beginning to resemble reserve game crowds. The side's poor form and the fear of violence convinced many fans that there were better things to do with their time on Saturday afternoons than to go along to the Bridge.

One fan who stopped attending matches during this period was the writer and comedian David Baddiel. "I was a regular, standing in the Shed, from about 1975 to 1978 or 1979," he told the official Chelsea magazine, "but then I actually stopped coming because Chelsea became very shit and also the atmosphere got very hard. Some friends of mine were attacked and one had his nose broken. I remember being in the Shed for one game at the end of the Seventies. We were losing and half of the crowd was shouting to the other half, 'Where were you at Molineux?' – a reference to a fight that had broken out at Wolves the previous week – and then a fight broke out *within* the Shed. It just got really dangerous and so I stopped coming for a bit."

Baddiel was far from alone in boycotting the Bridge. In April 1979 the midweek visit of Derby County attracted a pitiful attendance of just 10,682, one of the lowest post-war Chelsea crowds at that point. For the hardy few it was a depressing experience, watching a once-great club struggling with a poor and under-funded team in a near-deserted stadium. What none of those fans realised, however, was that in the unremittingly bleak years that followed crowds of that size would become pretty much the norm at the Bridge, as the Blues spiralled deeper and deeper into decline and decay.

CHAPTER FIVE
A WORLD CUP WINNER ARRIVES
1979-81

S eason 1978/79 had seen Chelsea set numerous club records. Unfortunately, they were all of a type none of the players wished to be associated with: lowest points total, most league defeats, fewest wins and so on. Indeed, only draws in the Blues' last two games against Arsenal and Manchester United had prevented them from equalling the post-war low of 18 points held jointly by Leeds and QPR. There was no getting around it: the campaign had been a season from hell with few, if any, redeeming features.

If the recent past was depressing, so too was the outlook for the immediate future. Chelsea returned to the Second Division in 1979 in even worse shape than when they had plummeted out of the top flight in 1975. Back then, Eddie McCreadie, while untested as a manager, was a genuinely charismatic leader who had the support and respect of his squad. The same could not be said of the bumbling Danny Blanchflower, although his constant stream of one-liners was guaranteed to keep a smile on his players' faces. Four years earlier, McCreadie, while weighting his rebuilding plans heavily on the side of youth, had also been able to call on vastly experienced pros such as Peter Bonetti, John Dempsey, Ian Hutchinson, Charlie Cooke and Ron Harris. Now only a visibly declining Peter Osgood and Harris, his fearsome tackles getting later and later as time moved on, remained of the side which had captivated the fans in an altogether happier period.

A SERIOUS CASE OF THE BLUES

Whether the squad, despite the presence of talented and committed individuals such as Gary Locke, Ian Britton and Mickey Droy, could mount a sustained promotion bid was very much in doubt. Even more concerning, were the continued financial problems at the club which, by now, tended to dominate any discussion about Chelsea's prospects.

There was, though, some better news on this front. By April 1979 a total of £1,190,000, or 35 per cent of the original debt, had been repaid to creditors or settled by negotiation. Most of the debt repayment had been made from profits earned in the club's first season back in Division One, 1977/78, when attendances at the Bridge averaged a healthy 28,734. A much smaller sum had been paid to the club's two main creditors, Barclays Bank and W.C. French (Construction) Limited, the following season because of the cash needed for ground improvements. Much work, though, still needed to be done to bring the stadium in line with the statutory requirements of the Safety of Sports Grounds Acts but, lacking the necessary funds to complete the job, the club settled for the simple expedient of fencing off sections of unsafe terracing. The result was that the Bridge's capacity for the 1979/80 season was restricted by the GLC to just 36,000. It seemed unlikely, though, that many fans would have to be turned away – rather, the worry for chief executive Martin Spencer was that a decent number would turn up in the first place.

Meanwhile, in a move which would have lasting repercussions in the future, the Mears family transferred the remaining debts and ownership of the ground to SB Property, a company created on the advice of Spencer specifically for that purpose. At the time, with Chelsea directors holding the vast majority of shares in SB Property, there seemed no cause for concern at this separation between club and ground, although the distinction would soon become of vital importance.

A few days before the season began Blues fans heard the news they had been dreading all summer: Ray Wilkins had been sold to Manchester United, where his old Chelsea manager Dave Sexton was now in charge. The transfer had been on the cards for some time: back in April, Blanchflower had announced, somewhat optimistically, "If I can get someone to buy two of our defenders for a million pounds, I won't sell Butch Wilkins." Unsurprisingly, considering Chelsea's woeful defensive record, there were no bidders. The only consolation as Wilkins departed for Old Trafford was the fee, a club record £875,000. Meanwhile, two other key members of the 1977 promotion team also left the Bridge around the same time: Garry Stanley joining Everton for £300,000 and Ray Lewington crossing the Atlantic to play for Vancouver Whitecaps.

Spencer's assurances that the transfers had not been forced by financial pressures were unconvincing, especially as Chelsea failed to re-invest any of the incoming money in new players. There was, though, a significant arrival behind the scenes in the shape of Geoff Hurst, who was appointed as first team coach. The 1966 World Cup hat-trick hero had been managing non-league Telford United and, initially at least, had been reluctant to leave. A telephone chat with Sexton, however, persuaded him that his future lay at Stamford Bridge.

Danny Blanchflower was completely in favour of Hurst's appointment – in fact, it had been his idea in the first place – partly, or so the players suspected, because it gave him more time to concentrate on his chief passion: golf. "Danny absolutely loved golf," says Gary Chivers. "He used to start the training session then go into his office. He had this green BMW – that would disappear and we knew he'd gone. He'd left the training ground and gone off to play golf. He'd leave it all to Geoff." With Hurst in charge training became more professional, and sessions were no longer abandoned at the first sign of rain.

Taking time out from working on his handicap, Blanchflower appeared cautiously optimistic about the Blues' promotion chances. "When Chelsea were last relegated it took them two seasons to win back their place," he pointed out. "This time I'd like to do it at the first attempt – but it's not going to be easy." Among the favourites in a competitive field were the other two relegated clubs, Birmingham and QPR; West Ham, whose strong side included such famous names as Trevor Brooking, Billy Bonds, Alvin Martin and Frank Lampard; and Leicester City, for whom a young striker by the name of Gary Lineker was beginning to make a name for himself.

Chelsea got off to a reasonable start with a 0-0 draw at home to another highly-fancied team, Sunderland, and a 1-0 win at West Ham. After an early goal at Upton Park by rookie striker Gary Johnson – who was shortly to go down with a bout of German measles – the Blues were indebted to a superb goalkeeping performance by Petar Borota, suggesting that Peter Bonetti might not be missed as much as the fans feared. "If we keep getting one point at home and two away we'll get promotion the Irish way," quipped Blanchflower. The first week of September was a disaster, though: the Blues lost 2-1 at Newcastle after having the lead at half-time, went out of the League Cup at home to Third Division Plymouth, and then lost at home again to Birmingham.

Three days after the defeat by the Brummies, Blanchflower's ill-starred tenure at the Bridge came to an end. "I always said I would go when the time was right," he declared, after having handed in his resignation. "The club now needs to appoint a younger manager more in touch with the modern game – especially off the pitch. I tried to help the younger players, to be friendly and to respond to their demands. But I must have looked and sounded like an old man to them."

Geoff Hurst was immediately installed as caretaker-manager, taking charge for the first time for the following Saturday's decidedly unglamorous trip to Shrewsbury.

Future Chelsea chief executive Trevor Birch lined up for the Shrews against a young Blues team and helped the home side notch up an easy 3-0 win. "Disappointed as I am with the result, I am more disappointed with the players' attitude," admitted Geoff Hurst in the post-match press briefing. "This is the area we must work on. I've already had quite a moan about it. It's been happening a long time. Chelsea go a goal down and heads drop straight away."

Over the next few weeks Hurst's 'moaning' clearly had an effect, as the Blues racked up five straight wins – a run which coincided with the return of flying winger Clive Walker from an extended summer season in the USA with Fort Lauderdale Strikers. Hurst was now clearly a strong contender for the Chelsea job on a full-time basis, but his was far from being the only name in the frame: Terry Venables, Fulham's Bobby Campbell and Norwich's John Bond were all mentioned in the media as possible candidates. The board, though, were unwilling to rush an appointment. Shellito and Blanchflower had both proven to be poor choices; this time they had to make the right decision.

"I'll be judged by my results and I'll be going if things do not go my way," Hurst had said on becoming caretaker-manager. But results had gone his way, and now he was becoming impatient. "If you don't make up your mind soon, I'll quit," he informed the club via the newspapers. With the fans urging the board to "Sign him up!", Hurst was eventually formally interviewed by Brian Mears and club director Sir Richard Attenborough. The meeting took place at a Chinese restaurant in Richmond and, after the trio had polished off a crispy aromatic duck, Hurst was offered a three-year contract. The salary, negotiated a few days later with Martin Spencer, was £28,000 a year.

Despite the team's improved form, not all the players were thrilled by Hurst's appointment. Peter Osgood left the club almost immediately, following a training ground row with the new boss. "Quite frankly, Geoff was an absolute disgrace," he said. "He became manager and announced a squad of 16 players with me as number 16. He asked if anybody had any questions, and I said: 'Yeah, why am I number 16, Geoff?' When he told me that I wasn't fit, I replied: 'You've been coach here for three months. How long does it take to get a player fit, then? You've sat on your backside, stabbed Danny – a great man – in the back, and I can't work for you. I'll pick my cards up.'" Osgood did exactly that, and never played for Chelsea – or any other club – again.

David Stride also moved on, joining Eddie McCreadie's new side Memphis Rogues, after a clash with Hurst. "I started the season under Danny then I got injured," he recalls. "I got back in the squad and the following week we were playing Bristol Rovers. Graham Wilkins dropped out with flu, and Geoff pulled me into his office and said, 'It doesn't matter how well you play, he'll be back in next week.' We beat Rovers, I had a blinding game and sure enough the next week I was out. I spoke to Ronnie Harris about it and he said, 'The best thing you can do is to get out of it, mate.' So that was it."

Trevor Aylott and Eamonn Bannon were also sold but Hurst's efforts to bring in new players – including England captain Kevin Keegan, who had tentative talks with the Blues while he was with Hamburg before opting to join Southampton – came to nothing, primarily because he was unable to persuade Martin Spencer to open the club's tightly-fastened purse strings. Hurst, though, was able to bolster his staff with two important signings: assistant manager Bobby Gould, another former West Ham player, and youth development officer Gwyn Williams.

In an innovative move, Hurst also brought in Olympic athlete and keen Chelsea fan Seb Coe to train the team once a week. "He was fantastic, a smashing fellow," says Clive Walker. "He gave new meaning to the term 'being fit'. We would do ten runs of 60 yards each and he would do double that amount with ease. On one occasion we were up against each other in a 60-yard race and we were both dipping for the line, it was that close. He also showed us some new stretches, but mainly he simply impressed us by being a super-fit guy – he was on a level which we'd never achieved. It really helped us having him around, he was top drawer."

Two straight defeats – against relegation-bound Fulham at home and away to Sunderland – saw the Blues drop to mid-table, but another five-match winning run lifted Chelsea to the top of a tightly-packed division. The first of these games was an extraordinary 7-3 victory at Orient, which the away fans celebrated by chanting 'Who needs Kevin Keegan?'. Lee Frost, a 21-year-old striker who promised much before fading away, scored a hat-trick, while Clive Walker, showing no signs of tiredness after his sojourn Stateside, grabbed two goals. "From being 3-0 up at half-time, the second half was like a basketball game with both sides going up the other end and scoring," remembers Colin Pates, who made his debut for the Blues after Mickey Droy was injured in the warm-up.

With the strikers banging in the goals up front, Fillery and Bumstead offering a mixture of creativity and industry in midfield, and Chivers and Droy providing good protection to the brilliant but unpredictable Borota in goal, Chelsea looked to have as good a chance of going up as any of the other half dozen teams in the race. Tommy Docherty, manager of fellow promotion hopefuls QPR, certainly held that view. "They're as good as any team we've played," he enthused, after an entertaining 2-2 draw at Loftus Road. However, John Toshack, boss of mid-table Swansea, was altogether less taken with the Blues' style. "Chelsea are the least impressive of the top six," he observed shortly before Christmas, despite having seen his side comprehensively beaten 3-0 at the Bridge.

There was also some press criticism of Chelsea's playing style, which in some quarters was felt to be over-reliant on long balls hit from the back to the strikers. Tommy Langley, however, argues that the Blues were not as one-dimensional as their critics suggested. "Geoff was a striker and target man and he would encourage us to hit the front player, whether that be with a long ball or short ball, and feed off him," he says. "From my perspective, the long ball game wouldn't have suited me because I couldn't head the bloody thing. If it went in behind the defence it wasn't a problem, though."

Certainly, the fans weren't complaining when the Blues thrashed Newcastle 4-0 in January, in front of a near full-house crowd of 32,281 and the *Match of the Day* cameras.

Two days later, though, on a bitterly cold Monday evening, Chelsea crashed out of the FA Cup 1-0 at home to Fourth Division Wigan. A similar lack of consistency plagued the Blues in the following weeks, much to Hurst's irritation.

"A few good results and they began to think they were great players and could stroll through games – now they know," he told the press after a surprising 4-2 home defeat by bogey side Shrewsbury in February.

In the same month there was some relief from the league slog when Chelsea played an International XI featuring Bobby Moore, Jimmy Greaves, Ian Botham and Portuguese legend Eusebio in a testimonial at the Bridge for John Dempsey. "Eusebio was about 84 by then," quips Gary Chivers. "He only lasted about 10 minutes, bless him. He had bandages all round his legs – I think he was sponsored by Band Aid." Jimmy Greaves scored the only goal of the game, which was watched by a crowd of just under 8,000.

In an effort to maintain the faltering promotion bid, Hurst squeezed over £300,000 out of Spencer to buy three players: Colin Lee, a tall, powerful striker from Tottenham; former England midfielder Colin Viljoen from Manchester City; and left back Dennis Rofe from Leicester City. Lee's aerial power would have given the Blues' attack a different dimension, but a hamstring injury picked up in training severely limited his appearances. The other two purchases, meanwhile, made only a marginal impact.

In a division lacking any outstanding sides, Chelsea's campaign suffered from the same maddening inconsistency which bedevilled their rivals. A 5-1 away defeat against a Birmingham side featuring Alan Curbishley, Frank Worthington and Archie Gemmill suggested the wheels were about to come off, but the Blues then put together a three-match winning run which lifted them back to the top of the table, ahead of Birmingham, Leicester and Sunderland.

The final seven games would decide the success or otherwise of Chelsea's season. At this crucial stage, the Blues hit a sticky patch, picking up just two draws in four games. It didn't help that skipper Mickey Droy, a colossus at the back, was struck down with chicken pox, but Hurst's cautious attitude also contributed to some nervous displays. "I felt we weren't playing the right tactics, that we were defending more," says Gary Chivers. "I think Geoff just wanted people behind the ball, instead of going at teams. We had a half decent team, so it was disappointing." A neatly headed goal by Chivers, though, gave the Blues the points in a scrappy 1-0 win over Notts County at the Bridge, leaving everything riding on the final two matches.

The first of these games was at Swansea, a mid-table side who had won successive promotions in the two previous seasons. Urged on by a good proportion of the 18,000 fans inside the Vetch Field, the Blues went ahead after just four minutes, Tommy Langley shooting high into the net from a difficult angle. It was the perfect start, but Chelsea failed to drive home their advantage on a bumpy pitch and, 15 minutes later, Jeremy Charles equalised for Swansea. In a game of few chances, Chelsea had to wait until five minutes from the end for their best opportunity, but Fillery headed Chivers' excellent cross narrowly wide from a good position inside the six-yard box.

"Everyone goes on about the header at Swansea, but it wasn't as easy as people made out," said Fillery later. "Geoff Hurst didn't help, though. The following week he went on *Grandstand* or *On the Ball*, I'm not sure which one, and said in front of millions of viewers: 'Mick knows he should have scored that header.' So I'm sitting there watching it just before we played our last game of the season at home to Oldham and I think, 'Cheers, Geoff, thanks very much.'"

Still, there was no disputing that it was a vital miss. After the draw at Swansea, Chelsea dropped out of the top three for the first time in two months. Leicester, two points clear of the Blues and with superior goal difference, could not now realistically be caught. Birmingham, in second place, were a point ahead and also had better goal difference. Sunderland, in third, were level on points with Chelsea but had a game in hand, at home to FA Cup finalists West Ham, which was scheduled to be played nine days after the final round of league matches. Chelsea's promotion hopes were still alive, but even the most optimistic fan had to admit that the Blues' chances of going up were now slim.

All Chelsea could do was beat Oldham and hope for the best. The Blues fulfilled the first part of the equation comfortably, winning 3-0 with goals by Fillery and Walker (2). At the final whistle fans stormed onto the pitch, chanting 'We are going up!' but the news from elsewhere was not good. Leicester, as expected, had beaten Orient and were confirmed as champions; Birmingham's exciting 3-3 draw with Notts County guaranteed them promotion as well; Sunderland, though, had only drawn at Cardiff, meaning the Blues now occupied third place – but a draw at home in their last match would be enough for the Rokerites to claim the final promotion slot.

Some of the celebrating fans seemed to have overlooked this small matter. The players certainly hadn't, though. "I think we realised it was all over," says Colin Lee. "I think we felt it was a foregone conclusion. It was out of our hands." To no one's surprise West Ham, having beaten Arsenal in the FA Cup Final two days earlier, went down limply 2-0 at Roker Park. "We were out in Spain on a club tour when we heard the news and we weren't at all surprised," says Gary Chivers. "West Ham were never going to get a result in a million years. As if they were going to try in the last game against Sunderland." And so a campaign which had promised so much finished ultimately in disappointment.

At the end of the season Ron Harris, a Chelsea icon for almost 20 years, left the club to become player/coach at Brentford. "I was offered a coaching job at Chelsea," he says, "and if it had been any other management team except Geoff Hurst and Bobby Gould I would have stayed. But I didn't get on with them so I took the Brentford offer. I thought they were a couple of 'Harry Nash' geezers. I think Gouldy was the type of bloke who would stab anybody in the back to get on, but that's just my opinion. Geoff came to the club on the back of the three goals in the World Cup final but his management track record was abysmal. I'd played a bit and seen a few managers but those two weren't my kettle of fish."

Harris was far from alone in having severe reservations about the Hurst–Gould management duo. Despite being club captain, Mickey Droy was less than enamoured with the pair. "Geoff just didn't endear himself to people, especially when he brought Bobby Gould with him," he says. "I didn't personally get on with Bobby either. I thought his ideas on the game were crap to be honest. He liked to be up front when we went running – as a player he'd always run around like a headless chicken – but on the coaching side he wasn't very good at all. The style of play was boring long ball stuff; it wasn't my cup of tea at all."

Graham Wilkins, meanwhile, was equally unimpressed by Hurst and Gould, dubbed 'the smilers' by some of the players for their beaming countenances. "Geoff was so arrogant," he says. "He thought what he'd done we should be doing as well. He intimidated us because of what he'd done. He used to strut around the training ground. I didn't like him at all. As for Bobby Gould, he was a nightmare. Another one who thought he was a lot better than he was. The two together were horrible."

Other players, though, took a totally different view – of Hurst, at least, if not Gould. Colin Lee, a centre forward in the Hurst mould – tall, strong and good at bringing team-mates into play while holding off defenders – was a big fan of the former England star. "I got on really well with Geoff and learned a lot from him," he says. "Geoff used to join in training sessions every so often and, even at that age, he was a class above. He was fantastic: he held the ball up brilliantly, he never gave the ball away, he had a great shot on him. He was a class act. I knew he was good because of what he'd achieved but I didn't realise what a great player he was until I saw him in those sessions. When Gouldy joined in at the same time, it was chalk and cheese because Geoff was class and Bobby was more of an all-out trier."

"Geoff was great to us, he was OK," adds Gary Chivers. "The style of play wasn't direct for me, because I kept on playing my own stuff. He encouraged me to go forward, I was coming out with the ball and it was enjoyable football." Like most of the players, though, Chivers was less keen on Hurst's sidekick. "Gouldy was a strange guy," he continues. "He wanted to be your pal, but he wasn't your pal. On the other hand, he's done well wherever he's been, so you can't knock him. But I don't think he was a good coach. In his training sessions he wanted to lump it, really, and when he was manager of Wimbledon he got them to lump it all the time. But when you're coming to a team like Chelsea who have been brought up to play the passing game for years and years, it was difficult to have him there."

Interestingly, Chivers also suggests that Gould had his eye on the top job. "You never felt they were together. There wasn't tension between them, but you always felt there was an underlying sense that Bobby really wanted to be the manager. Whenever we had a team meeting, Bobby would pull you out for criticism or whatever and you could always detect that Bobby probably wanted to have the job."

Whatever differences there were between Hurst and Gould, the pair showed a united front on Chelsea's pre-season tour of Scotland in July 1980 when they fined most of the team for going into a pub the day before a match with Hearts (see Chapter Thirteen, *Chelsea on Tour*). The incident was the final straw for Tommy Langley, leading scorer in two out of the three previous seasons and a tireless chaser of lost causes, who promptly asked for a move. "At the time my head was completely screwed up," he says. "My mother had died not long before. I'd got married in May of that year – I had other things going on. The incident with Geoff and Bobby just pushed me over the edge. I heard West Ham were in for me and that was unsettling. I wasn't playing well, I was unhappy and I made the biggest mistake of my life. I'd been a Chelsea season-ticket holder since I was five, but for some reason decided I didn't want to play for them anymore." Langley joined QPR for £425,000 shortly after the start of the season. "As soon as I walked out, I knew I'd made the wrong decision but it was too late," he adds. "When I played for Chelsea I loved playing football, but once I left it just became a job."

In his programme notes for the opening day visit of Wrexham, Hurst drew a veil over the pub bust-up describing the Scottish trip as "very rewarding and enjoyable". He also mentioned that the club had moved to a new training ground in Harlington near Heathrow Airport, having rented a ground at Ember Court from the Metropolitan Police during the previous season. That made it four different training grounds in four years, a record of change and disruption which mirrored the overall instability at the club.

There was significant changes, too, to the team's kit. Having taken over from Umbro as the club's official kit suppliers, le coq sportif came up with a radical new design. Controversially, the familiar all-blue jersey was now adorned with thin white pinstripes, while the tired floppy white collar was replaced with a more fashionable v-neck. As if that wasn't enough for traditionalists to swallow, for the first time a hint of red appeared on the kit – along with the trimmings on the collar and sleeves, the lion's staff on the club crest also turned crimson. In yet another ground-breaking innovation, the crest itself was moved from its customary place on the left of the shirt to the centre. The pinstripe design also featured on the away kit, although the lines on the traditional yellow jersey were blue rather than white.

There were far fewer alterations to the Blues' playing staff. The only player Chelsea had signed over the summer was Chris Hutchings, a forceful left back and part-time bricklayer who arrived from non-league Harrow Borough. He didn't make the team for the game against Wrexham, although there was a place for the posh-sounding Peter Rhoades-Brown, a pacy left winger who had made a handful of appearances the previous season. Rhoades-Brown scored his first goal for the Blues in a disappointing 2-2 draw, a result which was followed by another five league games that the Blues failed to win and a League Cup exit away to Cardiff.

A 1-0 defeat at home to West Ham, however, was the undisputed low point of a poor start – especially for Graham Wilkins, whose own goal in the dying minutes gifted the points to the Hammers. "Trevor Brooking hit a ball from the right wing, it came through a crowd of players and hit me on the knee and went in," he recalls. "It was a terrible feeling at the time but you just have to put it behind you." Unfortunately for Graham, it turned out to be a moment which continued to haunt him, even after he'd retired from pro football. "Fifteen or so years later the Chelsea Old Boys played a testimonial at a place called Binfield," he continues. "We were all sitting down having a beer after the game and I got a tap on the shoulder. This geezer looked at me and said, 'You owe me money!' I said, 'What are you talking about? I've never seen you before in my life.' He said, 'You know that own goal you scored against West Ham at Stamford Bridge? I had a bet on for Chelsea to draw 0-0. I want my money!' Then, Mickey Droy stood up and said, 'Why don't you go away, just fuck off?' And, of course, he took one look at Mickey and shuffled off."

The week after the West Ham game a Colin Lee goal gave Chelsea a 1-0 win at Cambridge, a result which set the Blues off on an 11-match unbeaten run that lifted them into the promotion positions. The highlight of this period was a magnificent 6-0 demolition of Newcastle at Stamford Bridge, which Hurst described as "the best performance since I've been here". Phil Driver, a turbo-charged winger signed from Wimbledon for £20,000, had a scintillating match while Colin Lee grabbed the headlines with a hat-trick. The goal of the game, though, was scored by Gary Chivers – a superb team effort which came second in *Match of the Day*'s 'Goal of the Season' competition. "It started with a corner to them on the right-hand side which I headed out at the near post," recalls Gary. "I was always encouraged to get forward at the time so I started running out. Someone played a one-two, it was all first-time football, and then it went out to Colin Lee, who held it up. He laid it off to Mickey Fillery and I just kept on running – it was from box to box really – and Mick played Clive Walker in down the line. Clive took the full back on, crossed it and I had the easy task of knocking it in from six yards. I think I'd run about 90 yards to get there, but it was just a fantastic team goal."

Two weeks later Hurst picked up the divisional Manager of the Month award before a dull 1-0 win over Oldham. Colin Lee again scored the vital goal, with a header from Walker's cross, but the game was memorable for some eccentric goalkeeping, if that's what it could be termed, by Petar Borota. "Once Borota gave a good impression of a speedy winger," reported John Moynihan in the *Sunday Telegraph*, "dummying the bemused (Paul) Atkinson and back-heeling the ball deftly out of play." Such manoeuvres would earn huge applause from the fans who, by now, had developed a huge affection for the whacky Yugoslav.

Four days later, Derby ended the Blues' unbeaten run but good wins at Wrexham and at home to fellow promotion hopefuls Sheffield Wednesday cemented Chelsea's place in the top three alongside West Ham and Notts County. The signs looked good: Lee and Walker were scoring at a prolific rate; Fillery, Bumstead and Rhoades-Brown were combining well in midfield; while the defence, marshalled by Droy and Chivers, was one of the tightest in the division. Then, quite suddenly, everything went very terribly wrong.

The first signs that Chelsea's season was going off the rails came in a dismal 0-0 draw at the Bridge against Swansea. The game was so poor, and so utterly devoid of entertaining action, that the promised extended highlights on *The Big Match* were reduced to around 30 seconds of underwhelming footage. The Blues then failed to score in their next four league games, which included another dreary home 0-0 draw with Bristol City. "There is a nervous twitch about Chelsea these days as they stumble through one of those bad patches that afflict most promotion candidates," Lance Masters suggested in his match report for the *Sunday Telegraph*. "Anxiety showed as Chelsea tried to accomplish their purpose, at a pace which would have done credit to the 'Keystone Kops'. There was hustle and bustle, but nobody with a cool head, or the vision to dissect the City defence."

The following week the Blues did, at least, manage a goal but still crashed out of the FA Cup, 3-1 at Kevin Keegan's Southampton. The league drought continued, however, and the Blues gradually slipped down the table. "We all find the present loss of form terribly frustrating but a wholesale change of players or tactics is not the answer," Hurst wrote in the programme for the visit of Shrewsbury at the end of January, a match the Blues won 3-0 to keep themselves in the promotion hunt. There was some player turnover, however: Lee Frost and Gary Johnson departed for Brentford, while journeyman striker Alan Mayes arrived from Swindon for £200,000.

The signing of Mayes didn't exactly excite the fans, especially as the club had been in discussion with two somewhat bigger names: Dutch legend Johan Cruyff and his former international team-mate Robbie Resenbrink, a member of Holland's team which reached the World Cup final in 1978. The transfer talks, which were carried out by Martin Spencer rather than Hurst, followed a friendly at Stamford Bridge between Chelsea and the pair's club, DS 79 Dordrecht, but ultimately nothing came of them. Hurst, though, was furious to have been excluded from the discussions. "I have not been involved in any negotiations so far," he told the press. "I'm angry about it. I'm supposed to be the manager."

Not that there was much sign of Hurst's managerial skills rubbing off on the team: as the goal famine continued, Chelsea's promotion hopes ebbed away. To the dismay of the fans, jokes began appearing in the media about the Blues' appalling run: they were, literally, a laughing stock. In the *Daily Mirror*, for example, Frank McGhee, quipped: "To

Chelsea FC: the architect's report on their new stand reveals a terrible flaw – it was built facing the pitch." Hurst appeared to have no answers, falling back instead on football truisms in his programme notes: "Just as a team can get into the habit of winning, so too can it get into the habit of losing and not scoring, so if you go a goal down, the confidence visibly drains away."

Meanwhile, the players had their own ideas why the team was struggling so badly. "Before Christmas we were full of goals and we were playing well," says Gary Chivers. "Then the communication between the manager and the players seemed to deteriorate. I didn't think Geoff and Gouldy had the players' interests at heart, to be honest, and the players' faith in them dropped. We went on silly trips to the Isle of Wight and things like that to get us going again but it didn't work. We used to play practice games and we couldn't score in training either. We weren't getting turned over by teams but as soon as they got a goal we knew that was it because we weren't going to score. It got that bad."

The strained relationship between management and players eventually came to the boil in a dressing room row at Newcastle in late March. "We were 1-0 down at half-time," recalls Colin Lee. "It was a heated situation and revolved around an implication by Bobby Gould that we were frightened and not really playing. That's what he suggested to a few individuals and he included me in that, and that really riled me. He tried to put me in the same category as some players about whom he was probably right, but I wasn't having that. We had a right old barney because I thought he was totally out of order – I've never shirked a challenge in my life and, once I crossed that line, I would do anything to win a football match."

Having lost at St James' Park, the Blues then failed to find the net in their next four games – taking their latest scoreless run to seven games. Three days after the last of these matches, a 2-0 home defeat by Luton, Brian Mears called Hurst into his office and told him that he was being sacked. The dreadful run of results was not the only factor in Mears' decision; he also felt that Hurst was reluctant to accept advice and that he and Bobby Gould were too critical of the players. Hurst still had 15 months of his contract to run but the club were reluctant to pay him off, citing alleged 'negligence' on his part. Hurst took legal action and the case was eventually settled in his favour in an out of court settlement.

Bobby Gould was put in temporary charge of the team for the final two games. The first, a 3-0 defeat at Swansea, suggested that there would be no easy solution to Chelsea's steep and dramatic decline. In the week after the game Colin Lee requested a meeting with Chelsea chairman Brian Mears. "I just couldn't see where Chelsea were going," he says. "During the meeting Brian Mears said he had a big name lined up to become manager, and there was talk in the press of Brian Clough coming to Chelsea. He said to me, 'Just be patient, I'll get the right manager in,' but I told him, 'Look, I'm not in support of what you've done to Geoff Hurst and I'd like to know how you see Chelsea going forward, because that's what I want to see. If I don't see that, I would find it very difficult to stay at a club that has no ambition.'"

Before the final game of the season, at home to Notts County, the fans were asking similar questions as Lee. The difference was that some of them, at least, thought they had answers. Around the ground, on the street and in pubs and cafes, fans distributed leaflets with a simple message: 'Shed no tears! It's the end for Mears!' (see Chapter Seven, *The Gloomy Years*)

Before, during and after the game fans chanted "Mears out!" and, after Rachid Harkouk scored County's second goal, the match looked likely to be abandoned when around 1,000 protesting supporters invaded the pitch. Some of the fans grouped together under an anti-Mears banner in the centre circle, while others rushed over to the East stand to make their feelings known in front of the directors' box. "They completely engulfed the pitch and just ran riot," recalls Gary Chivers.

"That was one of the lowest situations in my time there," says Colin Lee. "But the fans were more or less echoing what I'd said to Brian Mears: they wanted to know where their club was going and they wanted the success I was looking for. We didn't want to be has-beens. We knew of the teams before us – their success and their style. We wanted to achieve something similar and, most of all, we wanted to know where the club was going."

Chelsea lost to County 2-0, taking their scoreless streak to nine consecutive games. An even more damning statistic was the one which showed that the Blues had failed to score in an incredible 19 of their last 22 league matches. They had, at least, managed to win the three games where they had found the net but a meagre total of 12 points in the second half of the season had resulted in Chelsea slipping out of the promotion places and to within just four points of the relegation zone. Little wonder, then, that the fans had been so angry at the last home game.

At first, Mears dismissed the pitch protest, saying, "I don't feel under any pressure. Why should I?" Then, at the end of May, he appointed the former Wrexham and Middlesbrough manager John Neal as Chelsea's new boss. With a new manager installed and a new season approaching Mears looked set to extend his 12-year chairmanship of the club. But, on 2nd June 1981, came a bolt from the blue: the club issued a statement saying that Brian Mears had resigned as chairman and a director of Chelsea FC for 'personal reasons'. The fans had got their way: as the leaflet had predicted it really was the end for Mears.

CHAPTER SIX
FLIRTING WITH OBLIVION
1981-83

Brian Mears may have brushed them off, but the protests at the Notts County match made his position as Chelsea chairman virtually untenable. His fellow directors certainly held that view. Following a secret meeting, the club's vice-chairman Viscount Chelsea, son of the enormously wealthy Earl of Cadogan, informed Mears of the group's unanimous verdict. "We all think you should stand down as chairman," he was told, "and we don't think you should stay on the board either." This was a shattering moment for Mears, a director of Chelsea since 1958 and chairman since 1969. True, he did retain a role at the club as vice-president but this was very minor compensation for what Mears perceived, perhaps understandably, as the treachery of his former allies. In the round of musical chairs that followed Mears' resignation, Viscount Chelsea, a club director since 1964, became the new chairman while Mears' brother, David, took over as vice-chairman.

For John Neal, appointed as Chelsea manager just a couple of days before the boardroom bloodletting, the sudden and dramatic sidelining of Mears was a concern. "I thought, 'What the hell's going on here?'" he said later. "I'd been in the job two days and now I could be out on my ear. It was chaotic." Ultimately, though, Mears' departure proved to be only a temporary distraction from Neal's main focus: improving the Blues' fortunes on the pitch. "You walk in here every day and you look out there and you get a tingling down your back," he said shortly after his arrival at the Bridge. "It's a tremendous set-up. Tremendous supporters. It's all there to be done. It's just a case of getting the team right."

The former manager of Wrexham and Middlesbrough, Neal was well respected in the game but didn't have a high profile among fans and the media – or, indeed, some of the players. "John Neal wasn't the big name that had been described to me by Brian Mears," says Colin Lee. "He was a man of few words, but when he said something it always meant something. He was a quiet man who got on with his job."

Neal's first task, and that of his assistant Ian McNeill, was to restore confidence and self-belief to a side that was still wondering when it might score again. With no money to invest in new players – despite the cost-cutting efforts of Martin Spencer, the club's balance sheets still made grim reading – Neal had to work with what he had. To put it mildly, he wasn't overly impressed with the squad of players he had inherited, which was unchanged from the season before minus John Sparrow who joined Millwall. "They thought they were good players but they weren't," he said later. "They were ordinary players and it was very, very difficult."

Still, at least the team managed to finally lay to rest their non-scoring bogey on the opening day of the season against Bolton at the Bridge, Colin Lee driving home Clive Walker's cross for the Blues' first goal for 876 minutes. Three minutes later Mickey Droy added a second with a powerful header from Colin Viljoen's centre to wrap up a 2-0 win in front of a delighted crowd of 16,606. "Chelsea thoroughly deserved their win against a strangely uncertain Bolton side," suggested John Wasbrough in the *Fulham Chronicle*, "but the victory margin should have been greater and John Neal, Chelsea's new manager, will doubtless be thinking hard about the numerous scoring chances his side wasted."

The following week the Blues doubled their points tally to six, the Football League having introduced three points for a win at the start of the season, with a hard-fought 2-1 victory at Cardiff. Alan Mayes, who had hardly set the Bridge alight since his arrival from Swindon, scored both goals in a fine team performance which "oozed class" according to the *Sunday Mirror*. "It's a marvellous start for us," said Neal afterwards. "It will lift the depression at Stamford Bridge."

A week later Chelsea's best crowd for nine months, 20,036, turned up for the visit of a Watford side managed by Graham Taylor and featuring future England star John Barnes as well as ex-Blue Steve Sherwood. Chelsea slumped to a 3-1 defeat and followed that disappointment with another deflating reverse, 1-0 at Shrewsbury. "Chelsea showed few signs that their unrealised promotion ambition is still justified," concluded the *Sunday Mirror* after the match at Gay Meadow. Among the fans, meanwhile, the early season optimism had melted away as quickly as it had appeared.

The erratic start set the tone for the whole season: a couple of good results would be followed by a pair of poor, even occasionally shocking, ones. Frustrated by this inconsistency, Neal identified a couple of areas which needed to be improved. "We must learn to become a bit more ruthless in our finishing, to be a bit more 'nasty' if you like," he reflected after one defeat. Perhaps, though, a bigger concern for the new manager than wayward finishing was a sloppy attitude which he identified among some of the players.

If only, Neal mused aloud in his programme notes, he had more players like tigerish midfielder John Bumstead. "His attitude and application were faultless," the manager pointed out after a 2-2 draw with Charlton in late September. "'The John Bumstead approach to the game', if you like, is what I would like from everybody out there but I'm not getting it at the moment. I think I'm right in saying that his performances have gone largely unnoticed for a lot of the time, but I consider him to be a wonderful professional and I'm quite carried away by the lad."

Despite the implied criticism of Bumstead's team-mates, the side as a whole was capable of raising its game on occasions. In October the Blues knocked First Division Southampton out of the League Cup, following up a 1-1 draw at The Dell in the first leg with a 2-1 victory in the return back at the Bridge. Goalscorers Clive Walker and Mick Fillery naturally grabbed the headlines, but the defensive net cast around England captain Kevin Keegan was just as vital to the Blues' triumph.

"I man-marked Keegan in the two games," recalls Gary Chivers. "He was buzzing around all over the place but I was very fit so I could handle that. He had a squeaky-clean image with the public but he kept swearing at me the whole game, because I was marking him so tightly. I wasn't dirty but I wouldn't let him out of my sight, and it got to him. I got the full blast from him. I wasn't bothered – I'd never liked him that much because of his silly permed hair!"

Not for the first time that season, a fine win was followed three days later by a humiliating defeat – 6-0 at Rotherham. Petar Borota, his crowd-pleasing eccentricity turning into head-in-hands incompetence, had an awful game and only played once more for Chelsea afterwards. "Petar Borota was a great shot stopper but I can honestly say that five of the goals were down to him," says Chivers. "He had a complete and utter nightmare. The writing was on the wall for many of us with John Neal after that, and I think in some respects he wanted us to fail so he could make the case for bringing in new players."

Borota's replacement, 17-year-old Steve Francis, had made his debut in the League Cup at Southampton and returned to the side for the third round tie at Fourth Division Wigan. He didn't have the best of nights, either, as the Blues crashed out of the competition, losing 4-2. Other new faces to feature in the team, meanwhile, included occasional midfielder Kevin Hales and left back Chris Hutchings, who established himself in the side at the expense of Graham Wilkins.

With the Blues mired in mid-table, excitement centred on the FA Cup. In the third round Chelsea were handed an easy-looking draw at home to another Fourth Division side, Hull City, but could only manage a 0-0 draw in a rearranged fixture played on a bitterly cold Monday night. Three days later the teams met again at Boothferry Park in front of Hull's biggest crowd for almost two seasons, 13,238. Only a couple of hundred of these fans were from Chelsea, the reduced numbers resulting from another ban on the club's away supporters – introduced after a riot at Derby two months earlier (see Chapter Seven, *The Gloomy Years*) – and transport problems caused by a national train strike. The match, played on a boggy pitch which made passing football difficult, appeared to be heading for extra-time until Alan Mayes struck a sweet left-footer past Hull keeper John Davies with just over 10 minutes to play. Shortly afterwards, a header by Bumstead confirmed Chelsea's passage to the next round.

The Blues' good win, though, was marred by an unpleasant incident after the match. "We'd already left the ground and as we were coming back on the motorway there was an almighty crash," recalls Colin Lee. "A bottle had been thrown at the coach and Steve Francis, who was sitting by the window which was smashed, caught the bulk of it all. Thankfully, he wasn't injured badly but it was quite scary." Francis, who had made some fine saves in the match, required treatment for cuts to his face while Kevin Hales was also cut on the hand.

Less than 48 hours later the Blues played their third FA Cup match in five days, drawing 0-0 at home to Wrexham in the fourth round. Mayes, Walker and Lee all spurned good chances, which they had cause to rue further on Monday lunchtime when the fifth round draw gave the winners of the Chelsea-Wrexham tie a plum home fixture against reigning European champions Liverpool. Purely from a financial viewpoint, this was not a game Chelsea could afford to miss out on, adding extra pressure to the following evening's visit to the Racecourse Ground.

Again Wrexham, struggling near the bottom of the Second Division, proved a tough nut to crack and only Alan Mayes' late equaliser kept Chelsea's cup hopes alive. The saga picked up again at the start of February when the Blues returned to north Wales for the second replay and came away with a 2-1 victory, thanks to goals in each half by Mickey Droy and Alan Mayes. "There could be no doubt that Chelsea deserved to go through," was Colin Wood's verdict in the *Daily Mail* on the final act of the long-running drama.

The game against Liverpool was the biggest at the Bridge for years, and attracted a full house of 41,422 (the GLC having permitted an increase in the stadium capacity following recent ground improvements). Apart from the lucky fans inside the Bridge, hundreds more found vantage points in flats and balconies overlooking the ground at the Shed end, while some even clambered onto roofs to get a bird's eye view of the action. The turbo-charged atmosphere soon turned into something uglier, Chelsea and Liverpool fans clashing on the North stand terraces.

Without his favourite player, the injured John Bumstead, Neal pushed Colin Pates into midfield with Kevin Hales, bringing in the mop-topped Mickey Nutton to partner Droy at the back. Chelsea's plan was a simple one: to harass Liverpool at every turn, while looking for the pace of Walker and Rhoades-Brown on the flanks to launch devastating counter-attacks. "We always thought if you ran at them they struggled," reveals Mickey Droy. "Their back four, which included Alan Hansen and Mark Lawrenson, were good players but not quick. So we wanted to get Clive Walker and Peter Rhoades-Brown running at them." As plans go, this one couldn't have worked any better.

In only the eighth minute Colin Lee dispossessed Terry McDermott, one quarter of Liverpool's all-international midfield, and put Rhoades-Brown in the clear. The winger outpaced the Reds' defence before calmly slotting the ball past Liverpool goalkeeper Bruce Grobbelaar with a well-placed left-foot shot into the far corner.

It was the perfect start for the Blues who could now concentrate on denying Liverpool time and space to develop their renowned passing game, while knowing that each passing minute edged them closer to a famous victory.

Deep into the second half Chelsea were still grimly hanging on when Walker made a rare foray forwards. His cross was palmed out by Grobbelaar, bounced off Phil Neal's knee and fell invitingly into the path of Colin Lee, who joyfully slotted the ball into the net. "Even now I can remember scoring my goal," he says. "It was a bit of a defensive mix-up and I just had to put it in with my left foot. Once we got that second goal there was no way we were going to let them back into it. By that stage we'd frustrated them because we'd worked so hard as a team to nullify them."

The 2-0 win, hailed ecstatically by the Chelsea fans inside and outside the ground, came as a genuine surprise to John Neal. "To be honest, I didn't quite expect the lads to respond in the manner they did," he said afterwards. "I think it was a marvellous experience for everyone present to witness the way in which we won the match."

Bob Paisley, back at a ground which held nothing but unhappy memories for him, was understandably less thrilled by his team's performance. "They caught us day-dreaming," he told reporters. "When we move and play we look the best team in the world. When we stand and play we look like some Russian chess player."

Chelsea's reward for a memorable victory was another mouth-watering home tie, against arch rivals and FA Cup holders Tottenham. The Spurs side, managed by Keith Burkinshaw, was one of the most exciting in the country, containing household names such as Glenn Hoddle, Ray Clemence, Steve Perryman, Garth Crooks and Ossie Ardiles, the Argentinean World Cup star. Attractive though they were to watch, Tottenham were not as ruthlessly efficient as Liverpool and their defence was prone to schoolboy errors. Having beaten the Reds, the Blues' confidence was sky high and they fancied their chances of reaching a first FA Cup semi-final since 1970.

However, Chelsea's hopes of pulling off another upset where dealt a blow when striker Colin Lee was sent off in a league match against Cardiff and was given a suspension which ruled him out of the Spurs game. Mickey Droy then picked up an injury in a 2-1 defeat at Norwich which sidelined him for the next six weeks. Without the pair, the two tallest and most physically imposing players in the club, Chelsea would be lacking aerial power at both ends of the pitch.

Again, another huge crowd, over 42,000, poured into the Bridge, filling even the smallest of spaces on the terraces. The programme cover made interesting reading: against a black background, the club appealed in capital letters for the fans to behave themselves: "If you are here, masquerading as a football supporters, but your sole purpose is to cause trouble, then you are *not* welcome," it read. The decision to print the warning on the cover, rather than the normal action shot, was taken following the violent scenes before the Liverpool tie. In an attempt to prevent a repeat Spurs fans were allocated the whole of the North stand, while a staged handshake between two rival supporters on the pitch shortly before kick-off was also designed to defuse the potentially explosive atmosphere.

Despite being below strength, the Blues had the better of the first half against Tottenham and deservedly took the lead when Mike Fillery drilled in a 25-yard free kick. After the break, however, Spurs quickly turned the match around with three goals in 18 minutes by Steve Archibald, Hoddle and Mick Hazard. Alan Mayes, ploughing a lone furrow up front in the absence of Lee, pulled it back to 3-2 but Spurs hung on to book a semi-final place against Second Division Leicester City.

"That was one of the best games I ever played in," said Fillery, whose goal briefly had Chelsea fans dreaming of a trip to Wembley. "We played really well and were unlucky to lose." Colin Lee, meanwhile, is convinced that the result would have been very different if he and Mickey Droy had been on the pitch rather than watching from the stands. "I really think we would have beaten them if the pair of us had played," he argues. "Our size at free kicks and corners would have worried Tottenham, just for a start. We had a feeling in the camp that we could have won the cup, we really sensed that we could have gone all the way. The trouble was we didn't have so many internationals to bring in when we had a couple of players out!"

After the cup defeat the rest of Chelsea's season rather fizzled out. A final placing of 12th, a massive 31 points behind champions Luton, equalled the club's lowest ever league position set the year before. Worryingly, crowds at the Bridge dropped to a post-war low with the midweek home games against Cambridge and Orient only just clearing the 6,000 mark. These two pitiful attendances pulled the season's average down to 13,133, the lowest in the club's history at that point. After two disappointing seasons, the fans were beginning to vote with their feet.

Off the pitch, there was more change in the boardroom. At the start of April Ken Bates, a former chairman of Oldham and director of Wigan, became the club's new owner and, shortly afterwards, chairman. As well as his previous involvement in football, Bates had a long and sometimes controversial track record as a businessman which included stints as a builder in Burnley, a developer in the Caribbean and a financier in Ireland. Most recently, he had returned from supposed retirement in Monaco to buy a dairy farm in Beaconsfield in 1981. It was in Monaco that Bates renewed an old acquaintance with Brian Mears, a frequent visitor to the south of France. The subject of Chelsea and, specifically, the club's financial problems featured prominently in the pair's discussions.

Back in England, Bates put in an offer Chelsea. With the club losing £12,000 a week, Bates was able to buy Chelsea for just one pound in a deal that, as far as the fans and the media were concerned, came completely out of the blue. He was, though, unable to reach an agreement with David Mears to buy SB Property, the company which owned Stamford Bridge. Instead, on 19th August 1982, Bates signed a seven-year lease with the company, which gave Chelsea an option to buy back the ground at any time until August 1988 (see Chapter Fifteen, *The Battle for the Bridge*).

"I know that Chelsea is one of the most exciting clubs in London, a sleeping giant, a stately home run down," Bates told fans, while outlining his plans for the club. Much of his immediate focus was taken up with overhauling the club's finances – with the eventual target of paying off the £1.75 million debts – and changing the existing business practices at the Bridge. To say these did not meet with the new owner's approval would be something of an understatement. "When I took over the club in 1982 the so-called commercial department had a staff of seven but so dismal was their operation that the money they generated did not even cover their wages," Bates recalled later. "The club shop lost money, the promotions department lost money and even the lottery lost money! It was a farce."

One of Bates' first policy decisions was to announce increased admission prices for the 1982/83 season. "With an anticipated current loss of nearly £300,000 and cash needed to strengthen the playing squad and spruce up the Bridge, which looks shabby, there is no alternative," he informed supporters. "However, one thing I promise is, your money will be spent very carefully. The slogan at the new Chelsea is 'every penny wasted is a penny less for the team.'"

The supporters may have groaned at the price hike, which meant admission to the Shed now cost £2.50, but the players had reason to be thankful to the new owner, as Clive Walker reveals: "When Ken Bates turned up, we hadn't been paid for six weeks. Then this Messiah pitches up who pays you and guarantees your wages for the rest of the season. You couldn't help but like him."

With funds extremely limited, John Neal and Ian McNeill wheeled and dealed over the summer in an attempt to improve the playing squad. Petar Borota, Graham Wilkins, Ian Britton, Colin Viljoen and Dennis Rofe were among those to leave the club, while their departures were balanced by the arrival of a trio of new signings, solid midfielder Tony McAndrew and two strikers, the veteran Bryan 'Pop' Robson and David Speedie. As was the case with many signings in recent years, these were not big box-office names who would have the fans clamouring at the gates of the Bridge – although McAndrew and Robson had decent enough reputations. Of the three, Speedie, a short, fiery Scottish-born striker whose impressive leap made him a threat to even the tallest of defenders, was the least known having previously knocked around the lower leagues with Barnsley and Darlington. Another playing pushing for inclusion was Paul Canoville, a young black winger signed from non-league Hillingdon Borough.

Of the new faces, 'Pop' Robson was the first to endear himself to the Chelsea fans by scoring the winner on the opening day at Cambridge. The victory, however, did not provide the launchpad for an early season promotion bid. Despite the new additions, and the arrival of former Liverpool left back Joey Jones from Wrexham in October, the team was as inconsistent as ever. Indeed, it wasn't until December that the Blues managed to string together consecutive victories in the league, with 2-1 wins over Bolton at the Bridge and QPR on the newly-installed plastic pitch at Loftus Road.

Perhaps unsurprisingly, given their haphazard form, Chelsea only managed to survive one round in each of the cups before losing in the Milk Cup to Notts County and Derby County in the FA Cup. At the latter match Chelsea fans threw seats on the pitch after Kevin Wilson's last minute winner, an incident which produced yet more grisly headlines.

Not that, according to new boy Joey Jones, all the players would have been that downcast by the defeat. "I didn't realise how bad it was at the Bridge, until I had played a few games there," he said later. "There were a few players who couldn't care whether they won or lost."

Still, with the team safely treading water in mid-table, the occasional defeat hardly seemed like the end of the world. Indeed, a 6-0 thrashing of Cambridge at the Bridge in mid-January, in front of a desperately poor crowd of under 8,000, suggested that the second half of the season might see a dramatic improvement in the Blues' fortunes. It didn't happen. Instead, Chelsea embarked on a horrendous run of just two wins in their next 16 league games which saw the Blues tumble down the table towards the relegation zone.

These were some of the darkest weeks in the history of the club. As defeat followed defeat, a sense of all-pervading gloom enveloped the Bridge. With the exception of the visit of local rivals QPR at Easter, a game which attracted a crowd of nearly 21,000 to see the Hoops triumph 2-0, attendances hovered around the 7,000–8,000 mark – a new low watermark for Chelsea. The loyalists in the Shed did their best to encourage the players but, inevitably in such a large and open stadium, their chants drifted away on the wind. The fans who were dotted around the rows of empty seats in the East and West stands, meanwhile, could clearly hear the shouts of the players on the pitch. The flat atmosphere was hardly helped, either, by the almost complete lack of away fans. Often only a couple of coachloads would make the journey south, a result partly of a deep recession in the economy which had left millions unemployed but also of the dread conjured up by the very words 'Stamford Bridge' among non-Chelsea supporters. For many away fans the Bridge at this time was a virtual no-go area: visiting coaches were regularly attacked on their way to the ground (see Chapter Seven, *The Gloomy Years*) and opposition fans could expect to be picked off if they were foolish enough to stray from their tightly-escorted group. Little wonder, then, that the usual 100 or so away supporters would huddle together nervously in their gated section of the North stand, a bit like a herd of anxious wildebeest in a lion-infested plain.

In an effort to improve results during this depressing period but with no available funds to bring in new players, John Neal juggled his squad around. Long-serving right back Gary Locke left for Crystal Palace on a free transfer, Tottenham striker Mark Falco appeared briefly on loan, while numerous other players were picked for a game or two and were then left out again. Gary Chivers was one of the players who could no longer be sure of his place, and sometimes found himself playing reserve team football. While unhappy about his demotion, Chivers was able to enjoy the odd light-hearted moment in the less tense atmosphere of the 'stiffs'. "I used to do zany things just to ease my nerves before games," he says, "and so I climbed into the laundry basket before a reserve game just for a joke. Tom McInerary, the reserve team manager, walked back in to the dressing room and started his team meeting sitting on the laundry basket. I was looking out through the holes of the basket and I could see all the other players laughing, but nobody said where I was. Then, Tom said, 'Where's that Gary Chivers?' and someone said, 'I think he's out on the pitch doing his warm-up', so Tom said, 'Well, tell him to come in!' Somebody went out, came back and said, 'I can't see him.' So Tom went out to have a look himself. At this point I quickly jumped out of the laundry basket, ran into the toilet and then came out of the toilet making out I'd been in there the whole time."

Life in the first team, though, was decidedly less fun. "It was dreadful," says Chivers. "The team was very much split between John Neal's men and the rest. You always knew the ones he wanted and the ones he didn't really want, and he made it plainly obvious. It's very hard playing for someone who doesn't really like you or want you to play. He never liked Clive (Walker), he never liked myself, he never liked Mickey Fillery, probably because we would speak up about the team. My attitude is if there's something wrong you need to address it, you need to be vocal. But he didn't like the vocal ones. He liked the ones who just nodded."

As the season wore on, the poor team spirit in the side became apparent even to members of the opposition. In April, during a 2-0 defeat at home to Newcastle, former England captain Kevin Keegan, who had arrived on Tyneside from Southampton the previous year, detected that all was not well inside the Chelsea camp. "Keegan turned to me on the pitch and said, 'You've got big problems here,'" recalls John Bumstead. "I wasn't going to argue with him. By that time, there were a lot of petty divisions within the players. We weren't all together and we'd lost the ability to play our basic game. The divisions weren't so much between individuals but between different parts of the team. The defence, midfield and attack would all be blaming each other when things went wrong."

Meanwhile, in the programme for the same match a page-long letter from Edinburgh University student Mark Everard summed up the supporters' frustrations. "Sooner or later it must be realised that in our present first team we have only four or five players capable of holding their own in the First Division," he wrote. "Our team is no more than a very average Second Divison side, as proven by our current league position. The games against Palace (0-0) and Barnsley (0-3) I have seen since my Easter break began, have been little short of disgraceful. That the few thousand who made the short trip to Palace should be treated to a lack of commitment from certain members of the side was disgusting."

The fact that the club should decide to print such a critical letter was highly significant, and suggested that the views expressed by the fan were shared by important figures at Stamford Bridge. However, if the intention was to buck the players up, it didn't work: the week after the defeat by Newcastle, Chelsea lost 3-0 at fellow strugglers Burnley and slipped into one of the three relegation places. With just four games left, the Blues were facing the very real prospect of relegation to the Third Division for the first time in the club's history.

Out of form and with a dressing room divided into factions, Chelsea looked odds on to go down. The Blues, though, did have two thin straws to clutch at: first, three of their remaining four games were at home, and second, no fewer than ten clubs were caught up in the relegation dogfight and Chelsea still had to play three of these rivals. In other words, the club's fate was still very much in the hands of the players and, if they could get their act together, there was still no reason why they couldn't save the Blues from the indignity of the drop into football's third tier.

Of the four games, the first one against lowly Rotherham at the Bridge looked the easiest. Watched by just 8,674 fans, Clive Walker gave the Blues the lead before Kevin Arnott equalised for the Yorkshiremen. After the match, which finished 1-1, hundreds of supporters demonstrated inside the ground, demanding the resignation of John Neal and the reinstatement of old favourite Eddie McCreadie. Three days later David Speedie jumped above his marker to power a first-half header into the Sheffield Wednesday net, but the Blues had to settle for a point once more when Gary Bannister levelled the scores after the break. Again there were vocal anti-Neal demonstrations after the final whistle, which only ended when the police moved in.

Two points from two home games was a disappointing return, but they did lift the Blues one place clear of the relegation trapdoor. In their penultimate fixture, though, Chelsea faced a tricky away game at Bolton, who were also struggling desperately against the drop. Although, with one game still to come, nothing could be decided on the day the result of the match would go a long way to settling the fate of the two teams.

Facing the biggest game of his Chelsea career at that point, John Neal agonised over his team selection. He knew that David Speedie, who had formed a decent 'little and large' partnership with Colin Lee up front, would be suspended for the game and had to be replaced. Another doubt concerned Clive Walker: would it be too much of a gamble, he wondered, to play the occasionally brilliant but sometimes anonymous winger in such a vital match?

Eventually, Neal decided to consult Blues captain Mickey Droy before deciding on his team. "When you're looking at an away game like that, the only way we were going to win it was with a breakaway," says Droy. "So we needed somebody quick up front. Clive Walker wasn't the bravest player in the world – although he got braver as he got older – but he could nick you a goal. The trouble was John didn't fancy him; he thought Clive was a bit of a fairy, a player who would jump out of tackles. But I said to John there are players like that – but you've got to concentrate on what they can do, not what they can't do." Neal was persuaded by Droy's logic and decided to stick with Walker. Convinced, too, by the skipper's argument that pace on the counter-attack could prove decisive, Neal opted for Paul Canoville to fill Speedie's number 10 shirt.

On a rain-soaked pitch, the match developed into a predictably tense affair, with few chances for either team. Then, deep into the second half, Clive Walker collected the ball just outside the Bolton penalty area and struck a spectacular left-footer into the far corner past Trotters keeper Jim McDonagh. The 3,000 travelling fans, who were by now thoroughly drenched, celebrated like never before – every one of these hardcore supporters knew how important Walker's goal could prove to be. After that, the Blues hung on in the remaining minutes for a crucial win which eased their own relegation worries while increasing those of Bolton.

"The Chelsea fans were fantastic, cheering throughout the game," recalls Gary Chivers. "At the end of the game I ran over to them with Mike Fillery and Clive. We took our shirts off and threw them into the crowd as a show of thanks. When we got back to the dressing room John Neal asked us where our shirts where. We said we'd chucked them to the fans and thought no more of it – until we found the cost of a shirt had been deducted from our wages!"

In truth, the celebration was a trifle premature. Despite starting the last game of the season in 15th place Chelsea were still not safe, and required another win over visitors Middlesbrough, another side who were looking anxiously over their shoulders to guarantee their Second Division status. In the event a 0-0 draw suited both sides, as results from other matches determined that Bolton, Burnley and Rotherham would go down. The final whistle was the signal for a pitch invasion by jubilant Chelsea fans in the 19,340 crowd, relieved that the nightmare scenario of relegation to the Third Division had been averted.

The celebratory mood did not, however, extend to the dug-out or the directors' box. "It has been a very disappointing season," John Neal admitted afterwards. "It has been a season in which we have had to fight for our lives, but the experience will make the players better people and professionals." Ken Bates' programme notes for the final match, meanwhile, must have sent a cold shiver down the backs of many of the players. "It is obvious to everyone that the present playing staff is too small and lacks the strength in depth required to overcome the problems of injuries and suspensions," he wrote, "whilst quite frankly there are also some who are simply not good enough."

Bates ended his notes by making a firm commitment to the club's long-suffering fans: "One thing I promise – never again will Chelsea find itself in the position which we were in before today's match." That one sentence must have given the fans hope over the summer, as did Bates' hint that the club would be looking to buy new players over the coming weeks.

The 1982/83 campaign had been little short of a disaster. At the end of a season to erase from the memory banks Chelsea had escaped the humiliation of league fixtures with the likes of Newport, Exeter and Lincoln by just two points. In a five-year period of consistent underachievement, false dawns and outright failure – offset only by the promotion near miss of 1980 and the exciting FA Cup run two years later – the brush with relegation to the Third Division was the absolute nadir, the blackest of the black days.

But the Blues had survived and, looking at their position in the most optimistic light, were still only one good campaign away from an overdue return to the top flight. And there were some positives for the fans to cling to: Bates had promised new players, there was press speculation about a new manager arriving at the Bridge and, despite the poor attendances in recent seasons, the occasional big cup game had shown that the crowds would come flocking back to the Bridge if the team was at least moderately successful.

On his arrival at the Bridge in 1982, Ken Bates had compared Chelsea to a run-down stately home. The comparison was still a valid one a year later. The big question, though, was this: could the once sumptuous mansion be restored to its former glory with just a lick of paint or would the whole crumbling wreck needed to be gutted?

CHAPTER SEVEN
THE GLOOMY YEARS

Where were you when you were shit?' It's a chant which rings out from the away section at Stamford Bridge at virtually every Chelsea home game these days. Usually delivered with pointed index fingers in the direction of the Matthew Harding stand, the jibe is designed to suggest that all Blues fans are middle-class Johnny-come-latelys who only started supporting the club when Ruud Gullit, Gianfranco Zola or even Jose Mourinho arrived on the west London scene. The intended effect is to stun the home fans into embarrassed silence – yet this never happens. Instead, the Harding invariably replies with a rousing chorus of a song which was first heard at the Bridge in the spring of 1986: 'When Pates went up, to lift the Members Cup, we were there!'

The implication is that the mid-Eighties were some sort of low watermark in Chelsea's fortunes. However, apart from the club's triumph in the much-mocked Full Members Cup, season 1985/86 also saw the Blues put in a serious bid for the First Division championship (See Chapter Twelve, *A Title Challenge*) The truly 'shit' years were a little earlier when, as we've seen, Chelsea struggled even to stay in the old Second Division and regularly performed in front of crowds of less than 10,000. Indeed, so miserable where these seasons, especially the ones between 1979 and 1983, that the period is quite often referred to among Blues fans who were there simply as 'The Gloomy Years'.

"The early Eighties were very grim," says Tim Harrison, who now reports on Chelsea matches for the west London *Informer* group of newspapers but at the time attended home games with a group of friends from Kingston. "You came along with a sense of foreboding and very often went away at the wrong end of a drubbing. It was rough, too. On one occasion I was standing in the Shed and half a house brick just missed my head by about an inch and hit some poor bugger in front of me. I've no idea who threw it or why, it just came out of the blue from the back of the Shed. After that I tried standing as far back as possible but, with the distance involved, it was like watching ants performing.

"There was another awful occasion around that time when I was handed a knife in the Shed. I was standing with a group of people and there was a girl standing next to me. She was a real hard nut, with a skinhead haircut and drainpipe trousers. From a distance, I could see some policemen who seemed to be pointing at me from their raised platform at the back of the Shed, but obviously they were pointing at this girl. Then, one of these little lines of coppers in their yellow jackets came snaking towards me and this girl started looking very panicky. She said, 'Hold this!' and held this bone-handled hunting knife out at me. Like an idiot, I just instinctively put my hand out and took it. As the police closed in I quickly chucked it away. They must have had a tip-off that she was carrying a weapon or something because they nabbed her and didn't pursue me. But that was a scary moment and one that could have changed my life, I suppose, if I'd got a conviction."

This bleakest of eras began with Chelsea's relegation from the top flight in 1979, an event the fans pretended to celebrate with the witty chant, 'Division One kiss my arse, Division Two we're back at last!' Such gallows humour would be called on again as the club descended into its very own Dark Ages, but during the 1979/80 season the fans could enjoy some of the benefits of life in the lower tier: winning, rather than losing, most weeks; the chance to visit new, quaint grounds like those at Shrewsbury, Cambridge and Wrexham; and, most excitingly, the opportunity to renew acquaintances with old rivals West Ham.

"West Ham, like Millwall, was always a nasty place to go," recalls Scott Buckingham. "Even Chelsea's proper geezers used to bottle out of going there. It was a case of not going in the official Chelsea bit because there was always likely to be trouble in that area. At West Ham I used to go in the 'Chicken Run', which wasn't where their big mob was. I used to go with a mate of mine who was a West Ham fan and, of course, you couldn't wear your colours or celebrate a Chelsea goal.

"I went to the game in August 1979 when Gary Johnson scored the only goal and Petar Borota had the game of his life. On the walk back to the station there were West Ham fans hanging about all over the place – there was a real threatening atmosphere. I walked back in silence with a Chelsea-supporting friend. We got on the tube, got on the train at Charing Cross and only then did we go mental. That was the first point we felt safe enough to cheer."

Patrick Kenny was also at the match, attending the game with an identifiable group of Chelsea supporters. "We all came off the tube at Upton Park tube and West Ham attacked us outside the nearby market," he remembers. "We got to the ground and felt there was a bad atmosphere in our end – a group of lads weren't singing or joining in – and we realised they were West Ham. Then more West Ham tried to climb over the walls to get at us from the 'Chicken Run'."

Ironically, at the end of the 1979/80 season a handful of Chelsea supporters went up to Sunderland to *support* West Ham, when the Blues' last remaining hope of promotion lay with the Hammers pulling off an unlikely victory at Roker Park. Many fans, though, didn't fancy a return visit to Sunderland after an unnerving incident at Chelsea's match there earlier in season. For once, the travelling Blues fans were clearly not to blame for the violence which erupted following Chelsea's 2-1 defeat. "On the way home after the game we went to the local train station at Roker Park," recalls Scott Buckingham. "Sunderland fans were waiting in side streets trying to have a go and when the train moved off bricks went through every window. A few people got cut by flying glass and everyone crowded into the guard's van because that was the only part of the train that had wire mesh up over the windows. Even the London Old Bill, who used to travel on the trains with us, were in there. We had to change at Newcastle where we saw all the Chelsea team – but I don't think they'd received the same treatment from the Sunderland fans."

This incident failed to make the national press – perhaps because Chelsea supporters were the victims, rather than the instigators of the violence – but a similar episode at Swansea six months later during the promotion run-in was mentioned by Vince Wright in *The Times*: "The ugly crowd scenes before and after the match were depressingly familiar," he wrote, "but even I had not bargained for a brick being hurled through the window of my compartment on the train travelling back to London. Amazingly no one was hurt but I had experienced at first hand the unacceptable face of football."

In the same season, Chelsea played at Shrewsbury for the first time in the club's history. Typically, at these smaller clubs there would be little trouble, mainly because the home fans didn't have a big enough firm to put up against Chelsea's massive travelling support. "We were being frogmarched back to the station by the police when everybody at the front started running and veering off to the right," remembers Scott Buckingham. "I thought, 'there's not going to be a ruck here, surely?' There wasn't. But there was a big paint factory that was open and everybody steamed into it and started throwing paint at each other. At Shrewsbury train station the police were nicking everybody who had paint on them – although they were the ones who had paint thrown on them, not the ones who were nicking it."

Such light-hearted incidents became commonplace during 'The Gloomy Years'. The fans' philosophy seemed to be that if there was little in the way of entertainment on the pitch, they would have to create their own fun off it. In the Shed, for example, there was always much excitement when the digital clock on the club's electronic scoreboard ticked over from 68 minutes to 69, setting off the chant 'Sixty-nine, sixty-nine, sixty-nine!' Meanwhile, the occasional appearance by a group of cheerleaders at half-time, or even a sole female programme seller walking in front of the Shed, would inevitably provoke a chorus of 'Get your tits out for the lads!' Benny Hill, you felt, would have enjoyed himself hugely at the Bridge.

At Southampton in January 1981, Chelsea supporters even gave the impression they had had enough of the game altogether and 'confiscated' the ball during the Blues' 3-1 FA Cup defeat. "Minutes passed as the players waited for the ball to be returned to the goal," reported Robert Oxby in the *Daily Telegraph*. "The appeal from the Chelsea players was ignored and not until Bobby Gould, Chelsea's assistant manager, strode behind the goal was the ball returned." Southampton's Kevin Keegan scored a goal from a corner after this incident, leading Oxby to suggest that "Chelsea's notorious supporters, as ill-mannered as ever, must bear some of the responsibility for their team's exit from the FA Cup."

In the same year Blues fans livened up a dismal match at Cambridge by performing some unsolicited ground renovation work on the Abbey stadium. "The game was terrible, we were getting stuffed, there was no one to fight, and then someone realised that this bit of rusty terracing was really loose," recalls Scott Buckingham. "Everyone was heaving at it until it came out of the ground. The rest of the terracing was in the same poor condition and the Chelsea fans spent the whole of the second half pulling them up and passing them down to the front. The Cambridge stewards were just shaking their heads and putting these old iron bars on the side of the pitch."

Despite these pranks, it would be wrong to assume that Chelsea fans had a wholly fatalistic attitude to the team's decline. Quite the contrary. Many supporters remembered the glory days of the late Sixties and early Seventies when Chelsea were feared because of their prowess on the pitch, rather than the antics of some of their fans off it. Younger fans, too, recalled the days of 'Eddie McCreadie's blue and white army' just a few years earlier, when for a while at least the Blues looked set to become a power in the land once more. To see Chelsea consistently lose at third-rate grounds against no-mark teams was heartbreaking for these fans but what, apart from offering their continued and unstinting support to the team, could they do?

Towards the end of the 1980/81 season when, as we've seen, the Blues went on a long scoreless run, a group of fans decided to act. Led by a supporter called Ray Lloyd, who worked for a printing firm, they produced a leaflet calling for Brian Mears to resign as chairman. The famous 'Shed no tears, it's the end for Mears!' leaflet was distributed to fans at the last game of the season at home to Notts County and were snapped up by supporters eager to see the back of the *ancien regime* at the Bridge.

Throughout the game, chants of 'Mears out!' echoed around the ground. Then, in the second half, with Chelsea trailing 2-0, the first group of fans invaded the pitch. "It was the Shed and the West stand benches who came on," recalls Punky Al. "It happened two or three times towards the end. I don't know if they were planning to disrupt the game, but if they were it certainly wasn't on the leaflet."

"Notts County got promoted to the First Division that day, so there was an element of envy," says Chris Ryan. "There was a lot of frustration that a little team like Notts County were getting promoted and a big club like Chelsea was going nowhere.

"But there was a point to it: to get rid of Mears, because we were skint, directionless and couldn't score any goals. Altogether, about 1,000 fans ran on the pitch and held up the game three times." The most dramatic scenes, though, came at the end of the game when fans broke the crossbar at the Shed end and only left the pitch after a charge by police on horseback. Even so, anti-Mears protests continued inside the ground for at least half an hour after the final whistle.

The feeling that Mears' time was well and truly up at this point is echoed by Scott Buckingham. "There was a lot of anti-Mears sentiment generally because by then it was clear we were not going forward in any way, shape or form," he argues. "He was the antithesis of Ken Bates: he was never interviewed, he never told the fans anything. Bates would say a load of stuff which would be entertaining and often controversial, but Mears was very aloof. So if you're not getting the answers you want you do get frustrated. The stadium was falling apart, the team was falling apart, the crowds were down and you'd think 'Someone's got to get hold of this and do something!'"

During this long period of ongoing under-achievement, the fans' ire tended to be directed squarely at the boardroom rather than the managers' dug-out. "I don't recall a lot of chanting against any manager," says Scott. "There was certainly not a lot of support for Geoff Hurst, for example, but the mentality of most Chelsea fans is that if someone's the manager or wearing a blue shirt you get behind them. You can slag them off in the pub before and after the match but during the 90 minutes you support them. The way the crowd might get at the manager is by singing the name of, say, Clive Walker, when he was on the bench. That's sort of anti-manager, but it's a bit more subtle than calling for his head. At the end of games when you're frustrated maybe there was something like that, but I don't recall chanting for a manager to go."

In any case, many fans simply accepted what was served up in front of them with a fatalistic shrug of the shoulders. "I went to all the games in 'The Gloomy Years' and I quite enjoyed them, even though we were crap," says Paul Baker, who attended matches with a group of friends from Hayes. "You just accepted the football was awful but it was still Chelsea, so you kept going. The atmosphere at Stamford Bridge was still OK, although maybe it depended where you were. We moved from the middle of the Shed to the side of the Shed by the West stand and there was always a big crowd of us there. It wasn't a big chanting area but we weren't big singers anyway. A lot of the songs were the same as the ones today, but there were a few that you don't hear now like 'Always look on the bright side of life' and 'All we are saying is give us a goal' to the tune of John Lennon's 'Give peace a chance'."

"It was a dour period," adds Robert Howard. "The colour seemed to go out of the game, not only on the pitch but on the terraces as well. All the scarves and flags which you saw on the Shed in the late Seventies gradually disappeared. The bloke on his stall outside Stamford Bridge shouting 'Wear your colours!' must have done terrible business because the only people you saw wearing scarves were old geezers or kids, and there weren't too many of either – it was all lads with, at best, a small Chelsea badge pinned on their bomber jacket."

For the hardcore fans who attended regularly the sparse crowds at the Bridge during this period, especially for midweek games, provided a few benefits: the chance of a seat on the tube to Fulham Broadway, no queuing outside the ground and, once inside the Shed, a choice of spots to watch the game from. "You could stand where you liked," recalls Tim Harrison. "You'd have rows of empty terracing, although the middle of the Shed would still be full an hour before kick-off. And, often at the away end, there would just be one coachload of fans, nonchalantly leaning against the terrace rails, who had trekked down from Carlisle or Wrexham or somewhere.

"Mind you, the coaches always used to get bricked so was it any wonder they didn't turn up in vast numbers? I once saw a Leeds United coach outside the Rose pub [now the Legless Ladder] on the King's Road being attacked. It was very early, two hours or more before the game, and this coach had obviously got a bit lost and was trying to do a U-turn. Suddenly, a huge mob of about 50 or 60 Chelsea fans surrounded it and smashed in all the windows. I could hear all the screams from inside the coach, it was petrifying. The coach was completely wrecked. It was that sort of era, that was the norm. But you couldn't deny there was a certain grim thrill about the fighting, there was a fascination often because the football on the pitch was so mediocre."

Possibly because it was viewed as an internal club matter, the pitch invasions against Notts County did not lead to any punishment by the Football Association. The club, though, responded by making the West stand enclosure open only to members of the Official Supporters Club. The transfer cost from the terracing remained 50p and the area proved popular with fans as it provided a much better view of the game than behind the goal in the Shed.

The following season again saw Blues fans hit the headlines when they were involved in a riot at Derby County in November 1981. Bricks and bottles were thrown on the pitch, three policemen and a steward were injured and around £2,500 worth of damage was caused to the Baseball Ground. Among the dozens of Chelsea fans to be collared by the police was Dave Johnstone, although his role in the day's events was minor to say the least.

"All I did was to give the 'wanker' sign to some Derby fans who were having a go at us," he says. "A couple of coppers came along and they must have thought, 'He's an easy nick, we'll have him.' I was marched along the touchline to the cell underneath the ground. The cell had 'Harry the Dog, Millwall' scratched on the ceiling. He was a big name, because he'd been featured on a *Panoroma* programme about hooliganism. I wanted to add my name, but I was too small to reach the ceiling.

"We had to go back to the court the following Thursday and it was like a Chelsea home game, choc-a-bloc with fans. I was charged with threatening behaviour and a breach of the peace. We were dealt with in groups of eight and we all agreed to plead 'not guilty'. So the first fan was asked how he pleaded and he said 'not guilty,' as we'd planned. The magistrate glared at him and said, 'Right, you're signing on at a police station at half past three every Saturday and eight o'clock every Wednesday until this case goes to Crown Court'. Of course, that meant he'd miss all Chelsea's next lot of matches. So everyone just changed their minds and pleaded 'guilty'. The prosecuting officer read out the charges against me and said, 'The defendant was seen gesticulating by the arresting officer and shouting abuse to suggest masturbation'. At this point somebody in the back of the court shouted out, 'Yeah, wankers!' and everybody pissed themselves laughing except the magistrate. He looked furious and he just shouted out 'Hundred pound fine!' So I got the fine and was bound over for a year. It was a hell of a lot money and I had to pay it off at £15 a week for the next two months. That had an effect on me: after that, I was very sensible and stayed out of trouble."

As in 1977, having titillated readers with graphic accounts of the violence at Derby, the media urged the Football Association and the government to act. By now, the Conservatives, led by Margaret Thatcher, were in power. Part of the Tories' successful 1979 election campaign had been based on a strong commitment to 'law and order' but the early years of the Thatcher government had seen at least as much mayhem and disorder on Britain's streets as the last years of the previous Labour administration. The summer of 1981, in particular, had been a disaster for the Conservatives as inner city after inner city had exploded in flames as young, disaffected rioters looted shops and engaged in street battles with the police. Similar scenes involving football hooligans just a few months later were guaranteed to provoke a strong reaction from the authorities.

Under pressure from a government determined to clamp down on what Neil Macfarlane, Minister of Sport, described as "the sickening behaviour of these vicious thugs", the Football Association announced that all Chelsea's away games until the end of the 1981/82 season would be all-ticket. After meeting at the Baseball Ground, where it inspected the damage to the ground, the FA's disciplinary committee issued a statement saying: "No tickets will be sold on the day and Chelsea will pay compensation of £1,000 to each club involved. It is hoped that Chelsea, the other clubs involved and the police will take every step to keep Chelsea fans away from these games."

Chelsea vice-chairman David Mears said the hearing was "fair and sympathetic" and took the opportunity to warn fans that any further trouble by hooligans "could put us out of business". Club chairman Viscount Chelsea delivered a similar message in the next home programme for the 2-1 win over Sheffield Wednesday. Chelsea, he said, could go out of existence if "the lunatic fringe are allowed to continue their destructive ways."

Neil Macfarlane was also happy with the FA's ruling, saying, "I strongly support the FA's stand, and if what is now proposed does not have the desired effect, then I will support even stronger action in the future. It is about time these mindless louts realised that they are putting at risk the future of one of our most famous football clubs."

Initially, the ban appeared to be having the desired effect. The first game under the new all-ticket provisions, at Bolton in January 1982, was attended by just 7,278 fans. The previous season nearly 12,000 fans had attended the corresponding fixture – the shortfall largely being made up of Chelsea fans who had taken to heart police warnings that they would not be let in if they travelled to Burnden Park.

Some fans, though, were still determined to see the Blues in action, especially as the next away game was an FA Cup replay at Hull. Once again, just as during the 1977 ban, resourceful supporters thought up ways of getting tickets for the big game. This time the leading figure was a Chelsea fan called, bizarrely enough, Plasticine. "His real name was Gary but he'd got the nickname because he had a rubbery face like Plasticine," explains Punky Al. "For the FA Cup game he took the day off work, went up to Hull and bought a badge in the club shop. Then he went to the ticket office and said he was running a coach for the Bristol branch of the Hull Supporters Club and wanted 50 tickets for the Chelsea game. They gave them to him without asking any questions – whether they were gullible or just thought they'd get a low attendance if they didn't sell any tickets to Chelsea fans, I don't know. Anyway, Plasticine came back to London and met six or seven of us at Euston that evening to hand them out. That wasn't the end of our problems, though, because a train strike was starting on the day of the match. So we had to run a coach up to Hull and I'd say there were only 200 Chelsea there. When we scored there was a sort of ghostly roar, but you couldn't see anyone making it if you were anywhere else in the ground."

After Chelsea's 2-0 win at Hull the club announced that it would challenge the away ban ruling on the grounds that it couldn't be held responsible for the conduct of its supporters. In the meantime, the ban stood for the two FA Cup games at Wrexham, when again Plasticine volunteered to get dozens of tickets for fellow fans from the Welsh club's box office.

So far, the four away games at Bolton, Hull and Wrexham had not provided the local police forces with any major problems. The small number of Chelsea fans who had turned up had behaved well on each occasion. The next league game, at the beginning of February against Watford, promised to be somewhat different. In the absence of matches against Arsenal and Tottenham, fixtures with the Hornets were among Chelsea's biggest of the season. Although not quite a local derby, the visit of the Blues usually attracted Watford's largest home crowd of the season and many of the fans at the game, of course, would normally be following Chelsea.

If the ban could work at this game, it was fair to assume it would successfully remain in place until the end of the season. It didn't work. More than 3,000 Chelsea fans – fewer than would usually go to Vicarage Road but a substantial number nonetheless – turned up without tickets at Watford and the police decided to let them all in. The ban had been smashed, just as it had been in 1977 at Wolves. The message on the fans' T-shirts – 'You'll never ban a Chelsea fan!' – had proved to be prophetic.

In any case, the ban was never likely to work simply because of the sheer numbers of supporters who followed Chelsea away throughout the early Eighties. "We had quite a poor team but going away from home we took lots of fans," says Paul Baker. "For London games we could fill any end and up north we'd have a good few thousand – probably not as many as people made out, but I still reckon we were one of the top four teams in the country for away support."

Simple expediency had dictated the police policy at Watford: in their opinion, it was better to have the Chelsea fans inside the ground rather than walking through the streets of the town, frustrated and annoyed. All the same, on that occasion there was no denying that the police had acted in the interest of Chelsea fans. Generally, however, the boys in blue, shortly to be dubbed 'Maggie Thatcher's boot boys' for their role in the miners' strike, were less obliging. "The attitude of the police was outrageous sometimes," says Ron Hockings, who organised train travel to away games for members of the original Chelsea Supporters Club for many years. "The only time I got hit was at Wolves in 1983. These Wolves fans just went on the rampage, hitting and pushing everybody in their way. I got punched, and so did the three women I was with. I was so angry I wanted to run after them. But my friend Eileen went over to a copper to complain and he said, 'Well, you shouldn't bloody well be here.' That was disgraceful."

Many ordinary Chelsea fans felt that, apart from not intervening on occasions when they should have, the police also contributed to the intimidating atmosphere at away games.

"The police set the tone, with dogs barking as soon as you arrived somewhere," says Ron Hockings. "Then herding us towards the ground. It didn't help."

"You'd arrive at the train station and the police would try to mob you up and march you off somewhere," adds Punky Al. "Sometimes they'd take you straight to the ground or into a pub. The trick, if you wanted to avoid being treated like sheep, was always to pal up with someone who was on the train but not going to the football, like a family with kids. So you'd walk out of the station chatting to them to make the police think you were nothing to do with the football. Then you'd meet up round the corner with the others who'd got away with it and go off to find your own pub."

On one famous occasion over-zealous policing almost landed a Chelsea player, Joey Jones, in severe trouble. In January 1983 Chelsea played at Derby in the fourth round of the FA Cup. The Blues lost 2-1 but the game is better remembered for a mini-riot by Chelsea fans late in the second half which the police alleged was provoked by the Welsh defender. "Kevin Hales got injured right in front of the County fans," Jones recalled later. "I went over to see how he was and called over our physio, Norman Medhurst. As Norman approached, the Derby fans started throwing coins at me. One hit me over the eye and cut it. The blood was pouring down my face. Out of the corner of my eye, I saw Norman picking up the coins and pocketing them. He was a great physio, but boy was he tight.

"Anyway, Chelsea fans started chanting my name. So I turned round to them and raised my fists to the crowd. But when they saw the blood over my shirt, they ripped the seats from the stands. After the game, I was arrested for inciting a riot. I was up in court at Derby, but just before the date, they dropped the charges."

Fans who attended the game, however, insist that Jones' role in the events was limited to the point of non-existent. "Chelsea fans were ripping up wooden seats up and chucking them on the pitch," says Chris Ryan. "Ken Bates came on to try and get them to stop but all the seats started flying at him and he had to retreat. Joey Jones had nothing to do with it."

Around £10,000 worth of damage was caused at the Baseball Ground, just a week after Leeds fans had wrecked 600 seats at the same ground. Twenty-five Chelsea fans were arrested during the disturbance which led Vince Wright in *The Times* to question whether football should continue to be played at all: "Seeing people conduct themselves in such a manner, despite the heavy police presence, makes one wonder whether the game is worth preserving."

However, violent incidents like the one at Derby were not the norm. The majority of Chelsea games during the period passed off peacefully, thanks in part to the attitude of responsible fans like Ron Hockings who attempted to stamp out disruptive behaviour before it could spread. "On my trains I only had trouble twice," says Ron. "Once we found some Chelsea slogans sprayed in a carriage toilet. I knew it wasn't one of our Supporters Club fans because we spotted a bloke with paint on his shoes. I got him nicked at Euston and it went to court as well.

"Another time we were going to Birmingham, and I told everyone, 'Listen, they're a load of bastards up there. If you want to be safe turn left when you come out of the station, not right, because that's where the Birmingham fans will be waiting for us.'

These idiots went right and got beaten up – one of them lost his eye. On the way back I said to them, 'You asked for it – I bloody told you not to go that way!'

"On another occasion we were being marched to the Sunderland ground by the police and one of the supporters in our club threw a beer bottle through a pub window so I barred him for the rest of the season. I chucked out another fan because I saw him run on the pitch with a gang of people at Cambridge. Later, I saw him in a café up at Aston Villa and he was going 'C'mon, let's get at the Villa' – so I barred him again. Generally, though, ours was a really nice group: very social and very supportive. I was criticised by some people for allowing 'hooligans' on my trains. But, apart from those few exceptions, when they were on my trains they behaved themselves."

Despite the threat of violence from opposing fans, the provocative attitude of the police and the occasional FA ban, Chelsea fans were always there to support their team. Even the most meaningless game involving the Blues would see a turn-out of supporters, as Scott Buckingham recalls: "In December 1979 we played a testimonial down at Weymouth on a Tuesday night. The game had been arranged at very short notice after one of their players was hurt in car crash. Anyway, at the Saturday home game we decided we'd go. There were no proper trains down there so we had to get a little cattle truck. About 20 of us turned up from London and when the team came out we went on the pitch to get our photographs taken with the players. Gary Johnson just looked at us and said, 'What the fuck are you lot doing here? You must be mad!'"

Such dedication did not go unappreciated by the players, especially those who played for the club during the early Eighties when the Blues were struggling both on and off the pitch. "What I've got to say is that through all this bad period the Chelsea fans were magnificent," says Colin Lee. "It's easy to support Chelsea now, but I still see people who were following the club during that period and they are fantastic supporters. They are, easily, the best supporters in the world in my opinion."

The loyalty of the fans, as described by Lee, deserved better than the results and performances of the team throughout 'The Gloomy Years'. Chelsea's near-relegation to the Third Division in 1983, in particular, tested that loyalty to the limit – but, happily for the fans and everyone else associated with the club, much better days were just around the corner.

CHAPTER EIGHT
REVIVAL AT LAST
1983-84

Shortly after the 0-0 draw with Middlesbrough confirmed the Blues' place in the Second Division, Ken Bates arranged a lunch meeting with John Neal. Having read stories in the newspapers linking the likes of former Blues boss Tommy Docherty and ex-Manchester City manager John Bond with his job, Neal could have been forgiven for fearing the worst when the Chelsea chairman picked up his bread knife. He needn't have worried. Bates had already decided to retain the hard-working, straight-talking Geordie, but he did want to see other changes at the Bridge.

"I told John that as a fan I didn't want to watch dreary defensive games, even if we won 1-0," revealed the Chelsea chairman later, "and that I wanted to build an exciting new Chelsea where everybody plays with skill and enthusiasm, and provided such entertainment that they got a standing ovation from the fans even if they lost. I felt that I was speaking from the heart of every committed Chelsea supporter. I finished by saying that the money was there to enable him to make a fresh start."

Neal and Ian McNeill, a noted talent-spotter, wasted little time in spending the limited funds made available to them, raiding Scotland and the lower English leagues for young, hungry players who they felt possessed the talent, desire and belief to succeed at a higher level.

The first player to sign was Eddie Niedzwiecki, Wrexham's highly-rated goalkeeper, who was snapped up for a bargain £45,000. The son of Polish survivors of a German concentration camp, Niedzwiecki was a steady, technically sound keeper with a strong kick. Since the retirement of Peter Bonetti four years earlier Chelsea had struggled to find a reliable keeper – both Borota and Francis, while occasionally brilliant, were prone to making costly errors – but the unflappable Welshman promised to bring some much-needed consistency to the Blues' back line.

The defence was further strengthened with the acquisition of Morton's Joe McLaughlin, a tough centre-half and former plumber who had been interesting Arsenal and Celtic. Neal pencilled him in to start the season alongside new skipper Colin Pates, McLaughlin's aerial ability complementing Pates' intelligent reading of the game and accurate distribution from the back. Chelsea negotiated a fee of £80,000 for the Scot with a further £20,000 to be paid to Morton once McLaughlin had played 30 first-team matches.

Another player to arrive from Scotland was Pat Nevin. Virtually unknown south of the border, the diminutive winger possessed remarkable dribbling skills and ball control, facets of his game which he had honed as a child under the watchful eye of his father. Clyde, Nevin's club, initially demanded £185,000 for their prize asset but eventually had to settle for around half that figure when the fee was decided by a transfer tribunal. The knockdown fee was a bonus, but Neal was simply delighted to capture a player he would later describe in the following glowing terms: "What a gem he was. He was a genius."

Unlike Niedzwiekci, Nevin and McLaughlin, the next player to arrive at the Bridge had not been on John Neal's original hit list. Ken Bates had an agreement with Wigan, where he had been a director, that the Blues could have their pick of the Latics' team in lieu of money owed to the Chelsea chairman. Attending a match between Wigan and Bournemouth Neal was impressed by the Cherries' hard-running midfielder, Nigel Spackman. David Webb, the former Blues legend who was then managing Bournemouth, swiftly put a £125,000 price tag on Spackman but Bates, knowing that the south coast side were desperate for cash, was able to reduce the fee to a much more reasonable £35,000.

The final piece in the jigsaw was Reading's Kerry Dixon, who had topped the Third Division goalscoring charts the previous season despite playing for a side which ended up being relegated. Strong in the air, quick and a powerful finisher, Dixon had been attracting the attention of a number of clubs including Graham Taylor's Watford, Coventry and Norwich. Reading, keen to sell to the highest bidder, held out for a fee of £150,000 plus another £25,000 if Dixon won two England caps which Ken Bates initially rejected as being too high. But, after a sleepless night, the Chelsea chairman phoned Roger Smee, his counterpart at Reading, to tell him: "You win. Get the boy down here."

Along with the new faces, three old ones turned up for pre-season training in Aberystwyth: John Hollins, Peter Bonetti and Alan Hudson, team-mates in the great

Chelsea side of the early 1970s. Hollins arrived from Arsenal as player/coach, a role for which a fourth member of that legendary side, Ron Harris, had also been approached. Bonetti, back from self-imposed exile in Scotland, was signed as goalkeeper coach, a position he would keep throughout the Eighties. Hudson, out of contract following a spell in America with Seattle Sounders, was nearing the end of his career and, as it turned out, would not make a single first-team appearance during his short second spell at the club.

While half a team of new players arrived, a number of established names left the club. Gary Chivers moved on to Swansea, Mick Fillery signed for QPR, while Alan Mayes, 'Pop' Robson, Mick Nutton, Bob Iles, Phil Driver and Kevin Hales also departed the Stamford Bridge scene. They were soon followed by Chris Hutchings and Peter Rhoades-Brown who joined Brighton and Oxford United respectively in the early months of the new season.

The training sessions in Aberystwyth, which involved a lot of cross-country runs across beaches littered with sand dunes, proved to be a tough induction for the newcomers. Not that the more experienced players found it any easier. "That summer in Aberystwyth was absolute hell," recalls Colin Pates, who took over as team captain at the start of the season. "Running up and down those sand dunes all day was murder. I threw up on a regular basis." On the training pitch, meanwhile, Pat Nevin delighted in showing off his repertoire of bamboozling ball skills to his new team-mates. "There was a classic with Mickey Droy in my first few days there," says Pat. "The ball came to me and I did a double feint, went to go one way and went the other. Mickey shouted, 'I'm too fuckin' old for this game' in a real London accent and I felt a wee bit embarrassed because he was a great pro who'd done a lot and I had a lot of respect for him."

All the hard work looked to have paid off on the opening day of the 1983/84 season when a radically revamped Chelsea side, featuring Hollins at right back and all of the five major new signings except Nevin, trounced Derby 5-0. Nigel Spackman, who opened the scoring after a couple of minutes with a long-range shot, and Kerry Dixon, who found the net twice, both marked their debuts with goals while McLaughlin and Niedzwiecki also impressed. Fittingly, the new team showcased a new kit, le coq sportif turning their trademark vertical pinstripes on the classic blue shirt into horizontal white and red ones – a theme which was developed further with blue and red bands around the white socks. Further changes saw the V-neck collar replaced by a round-neck and the club badge return to its traditional place on the left breast.

Chelsea's good start was maintained over the following weeks, although there was a slight blip in September when the Blues lost 2-1 at early pacesetters Sheffield Wednesday and then drew 0-0 at home to Middlesbrough. A stray elbow from Paul Ward, a former Chelsea youth player, broke Clive Walker's jaw in the Boro' game and ruled him out of contention for a couple of months. Pat Nevin took Walker's place and helped the Blues achieve a 3-2 win at Huddersfield the following week, with the prolific Dixon again grabbing two of the team's goals. A buzz was starting to develop around the new-look Blues and Huddersfield chairman Keith Longbottom only added to the hype by gushing, "Chelsea are the best team we have seen here in umpteen years."

The following week the Blues took centre stage when an upcoming England European Championship qualifier in Hungary led to all First Division matches being postponed. Chelsea's local derby against Fulham, however, went ahead and attracted a sell-out crowd of nearly 25,000 to Craven Cottage. Bobby Robson and his England team were among the spectators who enjoyed a thrilling 5-3 Chelsea win, which included Pat Nevin's first goal for the club as well as, inevitably, a Dixon brace. The Chelsea centre forward, now dubbed 'Kerrygoal' by the press (presumably much to the delight of the marketing people at 'Kerrygold' butter), was in demand for interviews after the game but, typically, preferred to praise his team-mates rather than revel in his latest achievements. "We've got a system here now which helps me tremendously with two wingers playing down the flanks, plenty of support from midfield and even defenders coming through to score," he told reporters. "Colin Lee and I seem to complement each other, too. He does a lot of work, he's good in the air and people can't afford to leave him alone. His experience helps me greatly."

Despite this tribute from Dixon, Lee's place was under threat from his old striking partner David Speedie who had been scoring goals for fun in the reserves and was desperate to return to first team action. When Speedie hit five goals in a reserve team fixture against Charlton at Stamford Bridge in mid-October, Neal could no longer resist his claims for inclusion. The combative striker repaid the faith in him by scoring twice against Charlton as the Blues maintained their excellent form with a 3-2 home win, Kerry Dixon notching the other Chelsea goal.

After that first game together the Dixon–Speedie partnership went from strength to strength. Three days after a defeat by West Brom in the League Cup third round, a superb 4-0 home victory over fellow promotion hopefuls Newcastle, whose line-up included Kevin Keegan, Peter Beardsley and Chris Waddle, provided the high point of the first half of the season. Two well-taken Speedie goals underlined his fine form, but the whole team had performed superbly. "We expected one of our hardest games of the season," said Neal afterwards, "but in fact it turned out to be one of the easiest because of the tremendous form shown by every one of our players."

The manager had every right to feel proud of his team. In front of the assured Niedzwiecki the defence was looking solid, largely due to the formidable partnership Colin Pates and Joe McLaughlin had formed in the centre. In midfield, John Bumstead and Nigel Spackman invariably wore down the opposition with their non-stop running and tackling, while the creativity of Pat Nevin, who provided one of the moments of the season against Newcastle with a mazy dribble from one end of the pitch to the other, presented Second Division defenders with a set of problems they were unused to encountering. Finally, the striking duo of Dixon and Speedie provided the Blues with a cutting edge which incorporated a whole raft of different qualities: speed, power, aggression and lethal finishing ability on the air and on the ground. All in all, Chelsea were playing with a verve, swagger and style which hadn't been seen at Stamford Bridge for a long time.

For the Blues supporters in the 30,628 crowd against the Geordies, the club's highest league attendance for three and a half years, the five-star display was something they could only have dreamt about a few short months ago. Whereas in previous seasons the fans had often left the Bridge feeling frustrated and depressed after yet another lacklustre and disjointed Chelsea performance, there could be no such complaints about the new team put together by Neal and McNeill. On the contrary, it simply bubbled with energy, enthusiasm and commitment – qualities which reflected the personality and playing style of the recently installed coach, John Hollins. "We were a super-fit side," says 'Holly', "just like the sides I'd played in before at Chelsea."

By the beginning of December the Blues had risen to second place, three points behind leaders Sheffield Wednesday. However, a disappointing 1-0 home defeat by promotion rivals Manchester City saw Chelsea drop to third and, just as worryingly for John Neal, exposed a crack in the otherwise excellent team spirit. Surprisingly, given how well they were playing together, David Speedie and Kerry Dixon were the two players at loggerheads.

"I used to run about like an idiot, chasing, tackling and harrying defenders and that's what I expected Kerry to do as well," explains Speedo. "But he didn't. When he arrived he was primarily a goalscorer. Things came to a head during the game against Man City. Kerry ignored my instruction to run to the near post and it cost us a certain goal. I've never been afraid to speak my mind so I told him what I thought of him. It developed into a full-scale slanging match and carried on into the dressing room where we chucked tea at each other – tea urns at six paces you could call it. The gaffer, John Neal, banged our heads together and after that we started to appreciate each other's qualities. I remember thinking, 'Crikey, we've got a great thing going on here, we're going to have to start making the most of it or else we're going to be out on our arse.' We quickly became friends and that was reflected on the pitch where we were always on the same wavelength."

Kerry Dixon also realised that, the occasional tea-chucking incident aside, the partnership was developing into something special – and one that posed opposition defences all manner of difficulties. "I was capable of knocking balls down, but I could also go over the top with pace," he says. "Speedo was very good at going for a ball in the air. I would gamble when he went for a long clearance, perhaps from Eddie or a ball played up by a full back, that he would flick it on because I knew he had a better than average chance of winning it. He was very good in the air for his size, and he would deceive people into thinking he wouldn't win it. I would gamble that he would win it and more often than not he did."

Colin Lee, who played as a strike partner with both players, also has some interesting insights into why the Dixon–Speedie axis was so effective. "Kerry was a lot quicker than people realised, he was the quickest player at the club over a distance and we used that to our advantage," he says. "Dave used to like to come short to get involved in build-up play and Kerry used to like to go in behind. I would say that Kerry was just a natural goalscorer; whenever you spoke to him all he spoke about were goals. That's a goalscorer for you."

Dixon himself, though, emphasises that the contribution of Pat Nevin, Chelsea's street-urchin wing wonder, was an equally important element in the Blues' attacking strategy. "People talked about the telepathy, if you like, between me and David Speedie but Pat Nevin and I knew each other's games very well too," he points out. "Pat would come inside and leave a ball in behind the defender or chip the ball to the far post – there were plenty of options. As that first season wore on the three of us got to know each other's games very well and it gave us an edge."

Chelsea bounced back from the setback against Manchester City to thrash bottom-of-the-table Swansea 6-1 at the Bridge, left winger Paul Canoville claiming a hat-trick. But a sloppy 3-2 defeat in the next home game against Grimsby, after the Blues had led 2-0, suggested that Neal's young team were still a little naive. "We had too many people making forward runs when they should have been concentrating on containing the opposition," complained the manager in his next programme notes for the Boxing Day match against Portsmouth. "We lacked composure and discipline. Obviously there are some basic lessons still to be learnt and I hope they're picked up quickly."

The match against Pompey saw Chelsea take to the pitch with the name of their first ever kit sponsor, Gulf Air, emblazoned on their figure-hugging blue shirts in both English and Arabic. The national airline of Bahrain, Oman, Qatar and United Arab Emirates, Gulf Air was reported to have paid the club £100,000 to have their name on Chelsea's shirts until the end of the season. Not all the off-the-pitch news was so positive, however. Earlier in the season, the Mears brothers had sold their shares in SB Property to Marler Estates, a firm of property developers (see Chapter Fifteen, *The Battle for the Bridge*). Chelsea's future at Stamford Bridge, although not in immediate peril, was now in considerable doubt.

Back on the pitch, Chelsea could only manage a 2-2 draw with Portsmouth, Kerry Dixon missing twice from the spot to unleash a penalty phobia which would spread throughout the team over the coming years. Four days later Dixon saw another spot-kick saved by Brighton's Joe Corrigan, although the Blues still managed to collect all three points from an unconvincing display thanks to an opportunistic Speedie goal.

"When David scored it was a better feeling for me than getting a hat-trick," said a relieved Dixon afterwards.

The heavy winter pitches appeared to have extracted some of the early season zip from Chelsea's play, an impression underlined when the Blues lost their next two games, away to Middlesbrough and at Blackburn in the FA Cup third round. The mid-term blip persuaded Neal to make two changes to the team. First of all, he bought Mickey Thomas from Stoke to play wide on the left in place of the sometimes inspired, but frequently erratic Paul Canoville. The well-travelled Welsh international, who had played under John Neal at Wrexham before appearing for Manchester United, Everton and Brighton, was another tireless worker and added an extra dimension to Chelsea's entertaining brand of high tempo football. Like Joey Jones, Thomas would remain based in north Wales throughout his stay at the Bridge, requiring the pair to set their alarm clocks for 5am if they were to have any chance of arriving on time for training at Harlington.

The other change saw Colin Lee take over from John Hollins at right back.

"We'd struggled a bit over the Christmas period," says Lee. "It was as if the opposition were identifying John as being past his best and there was a lot of play, especially at Middlesbrough, arrowed at the right back position. John Neal spotted that and he knew I'd played right back a couple of years before when Gary Locke was out.

"But it was a bizarre situation. After we lost to Blackburn in the FA Cup we were preparing at Harlington for the next match at Derby. John Hollins took the training session and left myself and Clive Walker out of it but without explaining why. Clive and I were just left kicking a ball around and in the end I just said, 'I'm not having this!' I walked into John Neal's office and said, 'I don't deserve to be treated like this! When no one wanted to play last year, when we were bottom of the league, I held the team together and sweated blood. Now it's going well I don't deserve this treatment.'

"John looked at me and said, 'Let me ask you something – how do you fancy playing right back?' I said, 'Gaffer, I will play anyway for Chelsea. I don't care where, but I want to be part of this team.' And he said, 'Get yourself up, because you're playing right back on Saturday.'"

On a mud-clogged Baseball Ground pitch, Neal's re-jigged Chelsea won 2-1 at Derby, with Tony McAndrew, filling in for the injured John Bumstead, scoring the winner from the penalty spot. The victory set the Blues up nicely for the visit of table-toppers Sheffield Wednesday the following week, a match the home side could not afford to lose if they were to avoid being sucked into the chasing pack of clubs led by Manchester City, Newcastle and Grimsby.

Wednesday, managed by Howard Wilkinson, were prominent exponents of the increasingly popular long ball game which was also proving successful for Watford and Dave Bassett's Wimbledon. The Owls' reliance on high balls into the box, long-throws and near-post corners flicked on by mountainous defenders, allied to a well-drilled offside trap, did not make them easy on the eye, but there was no doubting that Wilkinson had created a highly effective outfit. Unlike Newcastle, their team included no household names, relying instead largely on journeymen pros such as future West Brom manager Gary Megson, former Everton defender Mike Lyons and straggly-haired right back Mel Sterland.

As part of his preparation for the big game John Neal organised a practice match between the first team and the reserves at Stamford Bridge. Among those playing for the reserves was Alan Hudson, who was shortly to return to Stoke for a second spell in the Potteries. "Soon after the game kicked off I dropped deep to pick the ball off the goalkeeper. John Neal just screamed at me, 'What are you doing? The team we're playing on Saturday won't be doing that – get it down the pitch!' That kind of thing summed up a lot of football at the time. I couldn't complain about not being in the Chelsea side, because they were winning every week, but they weren't playing my style of football."

The fans, though, were more than happy with the entertainment on offer. Watched by a full house of over 35,000 at Stamford Bridge, Chelsea and Wednesday produced an enthralling, heart-in-mouth contest. The Blues, sharper, quicker and more inventive throughout most of the game, raced into what appeared to be a decisive 3-0 lead thanks to two fine goals by Mickey Thomas on his home debut and a tap-in from Pat Nevin. Thomas, though, was lucky to stay on the pitch after reacting to taunts about the end of his turbulent marriage to a former Miss Wales runner-up. "Wednesday defender Andy Blair was dishing out loads of stick during the game so in the end I cracked and knocked him clean out with one punch," recalled the Welshman. "The ref and linesman didn't see it but the Chelsea fans were cheering and singing, 'There's only one Mickey Thomas!' That was the start of our special relationship." Two late goals by the Owls had the Chelsea fans howling for the final whistle, and when it finally came the home crowd erupted. "It was like the old days at the Bridge, tube trains bulging and an atmosphere that took you back more than a decade," reported Terry McNeill in the *News of the World*.

Victory over their closest rivals suggested that the Blues' promotion drive was back on course. Over the coming weeks Chelsea piled up the points, dispensing with lower and mid-table opposition with ease, and earning a useful draw at Newcastle with a good all-round team display capped by David Speedie's well-worked goal. The only poor performance came at Cardiff when the Blues were 3-0 down with six minutes to go and seemingly destined for their first league defeat in three months. Incredibly, goals by Lee, Dixon and a last-minute Spackman penalty salvaged an unlikely point.

The following week Chelsea were back to their best, hammering Fulham 4-0 at the Bridge. Crowd favourites Dixon, Speedie and Nevin shared the goals in another fine team performance. The game attracted another large crowd, just under 32,000, despite the fact that Ken Bates had recently announced a 20 per cent increase in admission prices to help fund the club's high legal costs in the battle with its landlords,

SB Property.

A scrappy 1-0 win at Crystal Palace, Pat Nevin volleying home a late winner from substitute Paul Canoville's flick, and a satisfyingly comfortable 3-0 victory over former bogey team Shrewsbury left the Blues on the brink of promotion. A win in the next fixture, a midweek game away to Portsmouth, would guarantee the return of regular encounters with Arsenal, Tottenham and Manchester United after five long years. Underneath a bright red sky, strikes by Nevin and Thomas put the 8,000 travelling supporters in party mood but a late Pompey rally produced two goals for the home team and sparked serious crowd trouble at the visitors' end. Ignoring a megaphone appeal by Ken Bates for calm, fans ripped up dozens of seats and threw them at the police cordon, injuring eight officers.

Four days later the Blues had another chance to wrap up promotion, this time against their old rivals from the Seventies, Leeds United. Amazingly, 14 years after the famous 1970 FA Cup final between the two clubs, the Yorkshiremen fielded two members of their losing side at Old Trafford, goalkeeper David Harvey and midfielder Peter Lorimer. Unsurprisingly, the veteran Tykes were no match for Chelsea's vibrant youngsters and Leeds were simply swept away by a blue tidal wave. Mickey Thomas started the rout, before Kerry Dixon helped himself to the classic centre forward's hat-trick – right foot, left foot and header. In the final minutes, with hundreds of fans encroaching onto the sides of the pitch, substitute Paul Canoville thundered home number five in gleeful fashion. The goal provoked a mass pitch invasion, during which referee Gilbert Napthine was knocked over by jubilant fans.

At the final whistle, in scenes reminiscent of the Blues' previous promotion campaign in 1977, thousands of supporters stormed onto the pitch, while the players beat a hasty retreat to the dressing room (see Chapter Sixteen, 'Here We Go'). Minutes later, champagne bottles in hand, the Blues' squad reappeared to take a bow from the middle tier of the East stand, and acknowledge the constant and ear-splitting chants of 'Chelsea are back!' from the blue-clad hordes below. Unsurprisingly, given their notorious reputation, these happy scenes did not go down well with the Leeds fans on the North stand terrace who promptly took out their frustrations on Chelsea's electronic scoreboard.

Once the initial excitement had died down, John Neal emerged to pay tribute to the side he and his staff had assembled. "It's one of the best seasons I've had in football," he gushed. "At this time it's the players who deserve the plaudits. They've gone out and done a marvellous job." Chairman Ken Bates, meanwhile, was confident that the best was still to come. "Of the 12 players who beat Leeds, eight are 23-year-olds or younger," he pointed out. "I have a feeling that like good wine, this team can only mature with age."

The first target had been reached, but there was more work to be done. Chelsea still had an outside chance of catching Sheffield Wednesday and pipping the northerners to the Second Division championship. The players were certainly keen to get one over their season-long rivals, as skipper Colin Pates pointed out: "I firmly believe we're a better footballing side than Wednesday and that we are better equipped than they are for the First Division," he wrote in the programme for Chelsea's last home game against Barnsley. "I shouldn't single out any players, but where is their Pat Nevin?"

However, Wednesday were five points clear with just three games to play and were clear favourites to win the title. Surprisingly, the Owls stumbled in their first two fixtures, picking up just one point while Chelsea won at Manchester City, in a match broadcast live on BBC TV on a Friday night, and then beat Barnsley at home to claim pole position with one game left.

Knowing that the Blues would be champions if they won at Grimsby, more than 10,000 Chelsea fans travelled up to Humberside, turning Blundell Park into a small-scale Stamford Bridge. After the kick-off had been delayed by crowd congestion the vital breakthrough came around the half-hour mark. The goal was typical of many scored by Chelsea that season, as Kerry Dixon recalls: "Pat Nevin put over a great cross, I got a good head on it and the ball powered past their keeper, Nigel Batch." Dixon's header, his 34th goal of a remarkable season, proved decisive and even a second-half Pat Nevin penalty miss couldn't dampen the celebrations. The news that Wednesday had won their game was immaterial; Chelsea's superior goal difference guaranteed that, for the first time in their history, they had won the Second Division title.

"It was brilliant to win the championship," says John Bumstead. "There were no medals for coming second and that spurred us on. The rivalry with Sheffield Wednesday was huge. We were more attack-minded than them. We almost played 4-2-4 with just myself and Nigel Spackman in midfield because both Pat Nevin and Mickey Thomas were always looking to get forward. Having said that, those two could run all day, and put in their fair share of work. So, for me and Nigel, it wasn't a problem because we were both very fit too."

"John Neal's basic philosophy was to get the ball out wide," says Kerry Dixon, looking back at the Blues' successful strategy in his first season at the club. "That's by and large what we did. Get it wide – or, when the opportunity arose, shove the ball through and leave it behind defenders, or whatever was on at the time. You wouldn't necessarily put it in behind for Pat to run onto because you wanted to get the ball to his feet."

The players celebrated their title in time-honoured style – with huge quantities of alcohol. "John Neal arranged for us to have a couple of drinks at the hotel we'd stayed at the night before," recalled Nigel Spackman later. "We were drenched in champagne and arrived in the middle of a wedding reception. The lads ended up getting their photos taken with the happy couple and playing pool with the bride. After leaving there, we must have stopped off at every off licence between Cleethorpes and London to refuel."

The only disappointment for the players – once they had sobered up – was that

Wednesday had successfully persuaded the Football League that they were still the more likely title winners, with the result that the trophy had been taken to Hillsborough on the final day. It was eventually presented to the Chelsea team at the first home game of the following season. As well as the cherished medals the players also received a gold pen each from the club to mark their achievement. "It was probably worth about £60," says Pat Nevin, "and I've no idea what happened to mine. We didn't get a bonus for winning the title."

No doubt the players would not have turned down a bonus had it been offered, but not even a barrow load of cash could compare to the thrill of promotion. The sense of excitement was especially acute for those in the squad who had never played in the First Division before. In fact, of the first team regulars in the 1983/84 season only Colin Lee, Mickey Thomas, Joey Jones, John Bumstead and John Hollins – who had, in any case, played his last game for the Blues at Grimsby – had any experience at all of the top flight. The rest could only imagine what it was like to play at Old Trafford, Anfield or White Hart Lane. How the novices coped with the step up in class from the Second Division would be crucial to Chelsea's prospects over the coming season.

CHAPTER NINE
'CHELSEA ARE WHITE' (AND BLACK)

On 12th April 1982 Chelsea won a Second Division match 1-0 at Crystal Palace thanks to a first-half header by Clive Walker. Just as significant as the result, though, was the fact that Paul Canoville replaced Walker in the dying minutes to become the first black player ever to represent Chelsea. In normal circumstances, a player making his debut for the Blues would be guaranteed an enthusiastic and welcoming reception from the Blues fans but Canoville – a fast, direct winger signed by Chelsea boss John Neal earlier in the season from non-league Hillingdon Borough – was not, as far as many of the travelling supporters were concerned, a 'normal' player.

A substantial section of the Chelsea fans that day made their feelings towards Canoville, and black players generally, very clear with a barrage of boos, jeers and racist chants. Among the supporters in the away end at Palace, although not one of those joining in the abuse directed at the new Blue, was Chris Ryan from Greenford. "When the Chelsea fans saw Canoville warming up, people were singing 'Chelsea are white!' and things like that," he recalls. "When he came on he got booed, and you couldn't say it was by a minority of Chelsea fans – it was more like 80-90 per cent of them."

Although racism was widespread at grounds around the country at the time, it was unprecedented for a black player to be booed by his own supporters. John Neal was shocked by the reaction of the Chelsea fans and made a point of speaking to Canoville about it two days after the game. "I had him in the office on the Monday," he remembered. "God, it hurt me, never mind him. I sat him down and said, 'Paul, well done, son, I'm proud of you. How do you feel?' He said, 'Boss, I've lived with it all my life.' I wasn't sure whether I should expose him to that again. But after talking to him, I made sure he was given every opportunity."

The other Chelsea players, too, were determined that the fans' antipathy towards Canoville should not affect the team's unity, spirit and performance. "Our attitude was that we were a team regardless of creed or colour and we had to get on with the job whatever the reaction of the fans," says Clive Walker. "Paul was the first black player to play for Chelsea and it was a big thing for him and the club. He was a very likeable guy and he came in for an enormous amount of stick from the fans at first, not just at that game at Palace but also when he made his debut at Stamford Bridge. The treatment he got was purely and simply because of the colour of his skin and it was very harsh. It was inevitable that a black player would make his debut eventually, and there was a section of fans who weren't happy about that. But it's also important to remember that, through his performances on the pitch, Paul won over the majority of the crowd."

The booing of Canoville had its roots in the widespread culture of terrace racism which had gained force with the arrival of the first wave of British black footballers in the 1970s. Players with Caribbean backgrounds like Nottingham Forest's Viv Anderson and 'The Three Degrees' at West Brom, Cyrille Regis, Laurie Cunningham and Brendan Batson, were idolised at their own clubs but, away from home, their appearance on the pitch would often provoke a chorus of boos, catcalls, 'monkey' chants and flying bananas.

At Chelsea, the distance between the Shed and the pitch made banana-chucking a pointless exercise but, nonetheless, opposition black players could expect a hostile reception. High-profile black players especially, like Regis and Anderson, were subjected to loud barracking which would greet their every touch of the ball and frequently last the whole of the match.

The racist chanting was usually instigated by the Shed, a bank of almost completely white faces where Chelsea's most loyal fans stood. Few supporters, in the climate that existed at the time, could resist adding their voices to the throng. "As a kid I'd join in the booing of black players," admits Scott Buckingham. "It was a way of having a go at an opposition player and, hopefully, putting him off. I didn't look at the significance of it from a wider angle. Whatever people were singing I joined in. We didn't have any black players at the time, so it seemed quite a natural thing for me. I didn't join in with the booing of Canoville when he first played, because he was Chelsea. That was probably the time when I thought 'hang on...' and, as I got a bit older, I also met more people from different racial backgrounds and that had an impact on me, too."

In the late 1970s and early 1980s racist attitudes at the Bridge were both encouraged and manipulated by the National Front, Britain's biggest far-right political party, who would sell papers outside the ground and, occasionally, in the Shed itself. Formed in 1967 following the merger of three groups – the Racial Preservation Society, the British National Party and the League of Empire Loyalists – the Front advocated the return of all non-white immigrants to their countries of origin, a policy which struck a chord with a section of the electorate in the late Seventies. In 1977, for example, the NF won 119,000 votes in local elections in London, beating the Liberals in 33 out of 92 constituencies. Despite this electoral success, which established the party as a serious force in British politics, the NF also had a street-level agenda which focused on exploiting racial tensions in areas of high immigration. Marches by the party faithful, typically led by bovver-boot wearing and Union Jack-carrying skinheads, would frequently lead to clashes with the left-wing Anti-Nazi League, most notably in Lewisham in 1977 and Southall in 1979. Around the same time, the National Front began targeting football grounds for new recruits, believing that disaffected, white working-class youngsters would be sympathetic to the party's avowedly racist stance.

One of the grounds on the NF hit-list was Stamford Bridge and, for a number of years in the late Seventies and early Eighties, fans attending matches at Chelsea had to run a gauntlet of about 20 shaven-headed NF newspaper sellers lined up along Fulham Broadway. The NF propagandists did brisk business outside the Bridge, particularly after the party launched a youth magazine in 1981, *Bulldog*, which aimed to appeal to young people through 'Oi' music (a racist branch of punk) and football. One of the magazine's most popular regular features was the 'League of Louts', a list of the most racist football fans in the country. Chelsea, along with West Ham, Newcastle and Leeds, invariably featured near the top.

The extent of the NF influence at Chelsea throughout this period is difficult to gauge and is still the subject of some debate. However, according to the anti-fascist organisation Searchlight, the Front would sell more papers at Chelsea than at any other ground in the country during the early Eighties. Even so, paper sales were in the low hundreds at the Bridge rather than the thousands. But these figures don't tell the whole story. Certainly there were times, especially when half the Shed indulged in chants of *Sieg Heil* accompanied by straight-armed Nazi salutes, when it appeared that a fascist rally had broken out at a football match. Generally, though, these outbreaks of apparent neo-Nazism were provoked by boredom and frustration rather than any deep-seated political conviction.

The ordinary supporters, though, were very aware of the neo-Nazi faction in their midst. "There were a lot of right-wing elements around at the time," says Cliff Auger. "The majority just went along with them, like sheep. I don't think they had strong right-wing or racist views at all. But there was a good percentage who were extreme right-wing. For other people booing black players was just the done thing then and not only at Chelsea. John Barnes had bananas thrown at him when he played for Liverpool at Everton, so it wasn't just a Chelsea issue, it was across the board."

While that was true, the booing of a black player by his own supporters was, as far as can be established, unique at the time. Even as the Blues surged towards the Second Division title in 1984 there were fans who were completely opposed to the idea that a black player like Paul Canoville could be a member of a Chelsea team, however successful. "I saw a few people who didn't get out of their seats if Canoville scored," recalls Chris Ryan. "They'd say if we won 1-0 and Canoville got the goal that it didn't count and really it was a 0-0 draw – which was stupid." Most fans, though, didn't share the racists' attitude and wanted Canoville to do well for the club. When the left winger scored a hat-trick for the Blues against Swansea at the Bridge in December 1983, for example, most of the Shed chanted Canoville's name as he proudly carried off the match ball.

Nonetheless, the perception that Chelsea fans were largely, if not wholly, racist persisted for a long time. Consequently, it was hardly a surprise that very few black fans were seen on the terraces at the Bridge during the late Seventies and Eighties. In fact, the club had a pool of black fans – the majority dating back to the glory days of the early 1970s – but a significant proportion of these supporters were extremely wary about actually attending a game at the Bridge.

"Lots of the boys I was at school with were Chelsea fans but I got the impression Stamford Bridge was the recruiting ground for the National Front," recalls Roger Cumberbatch, a Blues fan of West Indian origin who was then living in Hackney. "That was very off-putting. They used to come back singing really horrible songs and with stories about being given leaflets by the NF. There's no two ways about it, it worried me and put me off going. There were also rumours that Chelsea couldn't play Paul Canoville at the Bridge because of the amount of abuse he'd get from the home fans. They could only play him away. I don't know how true that is, but that was the rumour I was hearing and it was another reason why I didn't feel comfortable about going."

In fact, the statistics of Canoville's appearances reveal that there was no truth in the theory that he was left out of home matches to appease the 'Chelsea are white!' brigade. Certainly, John Neal is adamant that team selection was never dictated by the racism of a minority of fans – indeed, quite the opposite. "I bent over backwards to break down this barrier because there was National Front at Chelsea, which hurt me," he once said. "They were dragging the club down. We had a lovely team and 99 per cent were lovely supporters, it was just that one per cent that could destroy things."

When Chelsea played at Crystal Palace in April 1984 the 'one per cent' were to the fore again, loudly booing Canoville when he came off the bench to set up Pat Nevin's late winner. As ever, Canoville himself retained a dignified silence but Nevin, a committed anti-racist, was absolutely livid and gave vent to his feelings in his post-match press interviews. "When Paul's name was read out, certain sections of the crowd jeered him and I don't think they were Crystal Palace supporters," Nevin told reporters. "This kind of treatment towards Paul makes me ill. I think it's disgusting. It is up to the players to tell the fans to stop it."

Nevin's comments, at a time when the racism directed at black players by supporters was largely ignored by the media, was big news – simply because it was so unusual for anybody in football to stick their head above the parapet and take a stand on the issue. The headline in the *Daily Mail*, 'Nevin lashes the fans', was typical of the press reaction his words provoked.

It was, perhaps, slightly strange that the condemnation of the fans' behaviour should come from a 20-year-old in his first season at Chelsea, rather than a more senior figure at the club – but, for Nevin himself, there were no doubts that he had to act. "For me it was the most natural thing in the world to do because I was so angry they'd done that to Paul," says Pat. "I'd actually had a bit of a laugh with the hacks before because I'd told them my favourite band was Joy Davidson, rather than Joy Division, and that made a *Sun* splash headline. Another time they asked me for my phone number and I gave them a number I'd found at Earl's Court station for 'Big, Black and Busty'. But this time I came into the press room after the match and I was deadly serious."

The following week, back at the Bridge for the home game against Shrewsbury, the fans in the Shed appeared to have taken Nevin's fiery tirade to heart and chanted his and Canoville's names before any of the other players' when the Chelsea team came out onto the pitch. "There was a tear in my eye," recalls Pat. "It was a lovely, lovely moment. I felt good for Paul and I was proud of the Chelsea fans; they did extremely well that day."

Significantly, Nevin's outspoken attack on the fans who had booed Canoville was backed by Chelsea chairman Ken Bates. "The media decided to focus on Pat Nevin's rightful criticism of the people who booed Paul Canoville," he wrote in the programme for the match against the Shrews. "I applaud his open remarks, they endorse the club's official attitude that racism has no future at Chelsea. Pat was voicing the opinion of every other white player at the club."

It had taken a long time, but finally the club had decided to do something about racism in and around the Bridge. In the summer of 1984 Bates announced a new hard-line policy towards the National Front and their followers, saying, "I intend to persecute and harass them at every opportunity. They will be thrown out of the Bridge when identified."

Bates' tough comments were given wide coverage in the club newspaper *Bridge News*, which also featured reaction from some of Chelsea's younger black players, including midfielder Keith Jones. "I'm pleased the chairman made that statement," he said. "Something like that from a prominent person in football was long overdue. I got some barracking from a minority of Chelsea supporters when I played in the first team, but for every one of them there are a thousand Blues who are for the black players at the club. Basically, I think the National Front are a mindless bunch of idiots who live in a fantasy world."

Finally exposed, identified and targeted by the club, the Front soon disappeared from outside the Bridge, to be replaced briefly by the ultra left-wing Workers' Revolutionary Party selling copies of their daily paper, *Newsline*. The typical non-political or middle-of-the-road fan must have wondered why Stamford Bridge was such a popular stomping ground for extremist groups, and one answer was suggested by a private detective recruited by Ken Bates to investigate the root causes of hooliganism at the ground. "Political forces are at work, both extreme wings of the right and left see soccer hooligans as a means of furthering their causes," the un-named sleuth told the *Daily Mirror* in the wake of the trouble at Chelsea's match with Sunderland in March 1985. "The extreme right wing is the most dangerous. The National Front and the British Movement are well into soccer violence. They are not out to specifically discredit Chelsea or any other club. Chelsea's Milk Cup tie with Sunderland just happened to be the best target on that night." However, the investigator's conspiracy theory was largely ignored by the rest of the media, who instead blamed the riot on the broader community of 'Chelsea's notorious supporters'.

In the second half of the Eighties racism became far less apparent at the Bridge than it had been in the first half of the decade. Perhaps the most important factor in this development was that fans became more accepting of the idea of a mixed-race team as more black players – Keith Jones, Keith Dublin, Clive Wilson and Ken Monkou, in addition to Paul Canoville – played for the Blues. Certainly, Clive Wilson, who signed for Chelsea from Manchester City in the summer of 1987, claims he never experienced any racist abuse during his three years at the club. "Before I came Chelsea were notorious for the Chelsea Headhunters and I knew all about the problems Paul Canoville had had," he says. "But when I was signing Ken Bates emphasised that he was trying to get rid of the hooligan element at Chelsea and, fortunately for me, there weren't any problems during my time here.

"What helped me, I think, was that I had always played well for Manchester City against Chelsea so the fans were looking forward to seeing me play well for them. When I was at Manchester City places like Derby, West Ham and, to an extent, Newcastle were notorious for fans booing and jeering black players. Derby was particularly bad: I played one of my first games for Manchester City there and when I went over to take a corner I was showered with bananas. It was an unpleasant welcome to professional football. It's not nice, but you try not to let it affect you. The only thing you can do is play well, make a goal or score a goal. But deep down, nobody likes that to happen.

"The only time I got booed by the crowd playing for Chelsea was at Barnsley in 1988 when I got sent off. But that was more because of the incident with their player than

(*Above*) Driving force: Ray Wilkins, Chelsea's captain during the 1976-77 promotion season, with his Ford escort – blue and white of course.

(*Left*) Flare players: Garry Stanley and Ray Wilkins in full Seventies gear at the Bridge. The pair formed a successful partnership in midfield as Chelsea won promotion to the First Division in 1977.

(Top) The Wilkins brothers, Graham and Ray, with their mum, Winnie. A third brother, Steve, was also on Chelsea's books in the late Seventies but failed to make an appearance for the first team.

(Above) Garry Stanley lines up a blue on the snooker table. Nicknamed 'Starsky' for his striking resemblance to the TV cop played by Paul Michael Glazer, Stanley was a pin-up figure for Chelsea's young female fans.

(Right) Little Ian Britton and a very big Blues badge. Despite his lack of inches Britton was a key member of the 1976-77 promotion team, chipping in with 10 goals from midfield.

(*Above*) Fulham's George Best takes on Graham Wilkins, December 1976. Second Division leaders Chelsea won the match 2-0 in front of a crowd of over 55,000 at the Bridge.

(*Left*) Bad hair day: Clive Walker gets all frizzy. The fastest player on Chelsea's books, Walker injected some much-needed pace into the Blues team when he broke into the side in 1977.

MATCH MAGAZINE 50P
Chelsea

THIS WAS TO HAVE BEEN A COLOURFUL, COMMEMORATIVE FRONT COVER FOR TODAY'S GAME.
HOWEVER, DUE TO THE PROBLEMS CAUSED BY A SMALL LUNATIC FRINGE WHO PERSIST IN CAUSING TROUBLE FOR THE CLUB, WE HAVE BEEN FORCED TO ALTER THE DESIGN IN ORDER TO MAKE THE FOLLOWING STATEMENT:
IF YOU ARE HERE, MASQUERADING AS A FOOTBALL SUPPORTER, BUT YOUR SOLE PURPOSE IS TO CAUSE TROUBLE, THEN YOU ARE *NOT* WELCOME. YOUR BEHAVIOUR AS WITNESSED IN THE PAST, WILL NO LONGER BE TOLERATED. NOT ONLY WILL WE ENSURE THAT YOU ARE EJECTED FROM THE GROUND AND BANNED FOR LIFE FROM STAMFORD BRIDGE, BUT ALSO CHELSEA FOOTBALL CLUB WILL NOT HESITATE TO BRING A PRIVATE PROSECUTION AND CIVIL CLAIM FOR DAMAGES AGAINST YOU.

FA CUP ROUND SIX
TODAY'S MATCH SPONSORED BY BOVIS
Tottenham Hotspur
SATURDAY, 6th MARCH, 1982
KICK-OFF 3.00 p.m.

(*Left*) The programme cover for the Chelsea v Tottenham FA Cup sixth round tie, March 1982. The usual action shot was replaced by a stern warning to the hooligan 'lunatic fringe' among Chelsea's support.

(*Below*) Blues captain Mickey Droy tackles Liverpool's Ian Rush in the previous round at Stamford Bridge. The Blues beat the Reds 2-0 in one of the few highlights of the early eighties 'gloomy years'.

EMPICS

(*Top*) Groundbreaker: Paul Canoville, Chelsea's first ever black player. The pacy left winger was racially abused by a large section of Blues fans when he first appeared in the Chelsea team in 1982.

(*Above*) 'Kerrygoal': Kerry Dixon, shortly after his arrival at the Bridge from Reading, August 1983. In his first season with Chelsea Dixon scored 28 league goals to help the Blues win the Second Division championship.

JOHN INGLEDEW

(*Top*) 'You're nicked!': A Blues fan is nabbed by the police after running on to the pitch to celebrate Chelsea's promotion back to the First Division in April 1984.

(*Far left*) More (blond) highlights than *Match of the Day* in this Chelsea away crowd, 1984.

(*Left*) The top corner: blame Messrs Dixon, Nevin and Speedie for the wear and tear to the Shed end goal during the 1983/84 promotion season.

JOHN INGLEDEW

'Chelsea are back!': fans and players celebrate the Blues' promotion to the First Division, April 1984. John Neal's side went up in some style, beating old rivals Leeds 5-0 at the Bridge.

(*Above*) Shocking development: Ken Bates shows off his infamous electric fence, April 1985. The Chelsea chairman introduced this radical anti-hooligan measure after a riot at the Bridge during the Milk Cup semi-final clash with Sunderland, but safety officers at the GLC prevented the electric current from being turned on.

(*Right*) The odd couple: Chelsea mascot Stamford the Lion meets Culture Club singer Boy George after the group filmed a pop video at the Bridge, October 1984.

Cup glory: David Speedie, pursued by Kevin McAllister, celebrates his hat-trick goal against Manchester City in the Full Members Cup final, March 1986. Speedo's treble was the first in a Wembley final since Geoff Hurst's for England in the 1966 World Cup.

The happy Chelsea team pose with the cup
after their exciting 5-4 win over City. The
competition was derided as a 'Mickey Mouse'
cup by the media, but the Blues' victory was
one of the highlights of a largely barren decade.

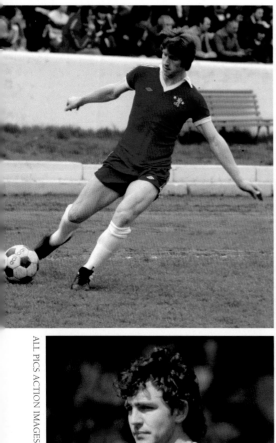

The changing colours of the Blues in the late Seventies and Eighties:

(Top left) Kenny Swain, whose strike partnership with Steve Finnieston helped fire Chelsea back to the First Division in 1977.

(Top right) England cricketer Ian Botham,

in the Chelsea away kit he wore in a testimonial game for Ron Harris at the Bridge in 1980.

(Above left) Mike Fillery, sporting the innovative le coq sportif kit of the early Eighties.

(Above) Kerry Dixon, in a shirt featuring the logo of Gulf Air, Chelsea's first kit sponsors.

(*Top*) Pat Nevin, posing in the short-lived 'Chelsea Collection' team kit.

(*Above left*) John Bumstead, in action in the red 'Commodore' away kit.

(*Above right*) Gordon Durie, in the home kit from the same season, 1987/88, which ended with Chelsea being relegated once again to the Second Division.

Bouncing back: the Chelsea team with the Second Division trophy, May 1989. Bobby Campbell's Blues stormed to the title with a record number of points, 99, and finished an impressive 17 points clear of runners-up Manchester City.

anything else. Otherwise, I didn't experience anything untoward while I was there. I think things improved during the 1980s and a lot of that was down to people like John Barnes, Ian Wright and Mark Walters. They were pioneers because they broke the mould and the stereotypes surrounding black players."

Another important factor in promoting a more tolerant atmosphere at the Bridge was the reduction of far-right activity around the ground. This was partly explained by Ken Bates turning up the heat on the National Front activists, but also by the decline in the party's political fortunes and the splits in the NF leadership which ripped the organisation apart from the mid-Eighties onwards. In particular, the Front's bizarre attempts to forge an alliance with and gain funding from Libya's Colonel Gadaffi did not go down well with the crude 'little Englander' racists among the rank-and-file members – many of whom were the party's recruiting sergeants at football grounds.

Whatever the reasons, Chelsea fans certainly noticed a change in atmosphere at the Bridge as the decade wore on. "The racism was just a phase to a large extent, and it died out on its own – I know there have been anti-racist campaigns but I think people just moved on and accepted different cultures into our country," says Cliff Auger. "Society moved on in the Eighties," adds Chris Ryan, "and people accepted that if you had a good black player at your club you supported him."

The more inclusive, but still fiercely partisan, atmosphere at Chelsea was recognised and appreciated by the club. "There really does seem to be a change of attitude amongst supporters, many of whom have come forward with information relating to troublemakers," Ken Bates pointed out during the 1985/86 season. "For our part we continue to do our best and it wasn't long ago that we dismissed a steward for making racist chants." In the same season, in a short programme article entitled 'Yids, Wogs and Nig-Nogs', Bates stressed "I must make it quite clear for the benefit of the people that use those terms, that they are not wanted at Chelsea."

Other clubs, however, were still stuck in a late Seventies time warp where racism directed at black players was the norm. In February 1986 Chelsea played a friendly away to Glasgow Rangers although, as Pat Nevin recalls, the atmosphere created by the home fans was far from welcoming. "I was getting a lot of stick because with my name and my coming from Glasgow I think all the Rangers fans guessed at my Celtic affiliations," he says. "Keith Jones was also getting terrible stick from the Rangers fans, who were chanting 'Get the darkie off!'. It was very embarrassing for me because I was from Glasgow and the game was supposed to be a friendly. I was gesturing to John Hollins to take Keith off because the abuse was so bad, and eventually John made the substitution. Keith ran down the tunnel but while the Rangers fans were cheering the stadium announcer called out, 'Coming on for Chelsea...Phil Priest!' Of course, his name provoked boos all around Ibrox and then the shout, 'Get the darkie back on!'"

Such blatant racism became increasingly rare at the Bridge in the late Eighties. There was a significant exception, however: any match with Tottenham would be guaranteed to produce a torrent of virulently anti-Semitic chants aimed at Spurs players and fans. For many Chelsea supporters, though, Spurs fans invited anti-Jewish taunting by styling themselves as 'Yiddos' and enthusiastically waving the Israeli flag. This excuse, though, did not impress Ken Bates. Time and again throughout the Eighties the Chelsea chairman would take Blues fans to task on this issue, reminding them that the club had as many Jewish fans, and indeed directors, as Tottenham. "It gave me no pleasure on Saturday to hear the idiots chanting anti-Jewish songs," Bates complained after a game at White Hart Lane in August 1987. "I am fully aware that Tottenham supporters describe themselves as 'Yiddos' and I am also aware, much to the Spurs chairman's concern, that there was an Israeli flag – the Star of David – suspended from the stand. These things are no justification for the racist chanting by some of our so-called fans."

The appeal had little, if any, effect. Probably because Tottenham are Chelsea's most hated London rivals, the Blues' most vocal fans have always been reluctant to let go of one of the chief weapons in their anti-Spurs armoury – although, at the same, it should be pointed out that in recent seasons chants celebrating Chelsea's tremendous record against Tottenham over the last 15 years have largely replaced anti-Semitic songs.

However, on the issue of general racism, and specifically the booing of black players, much progress was undoubtedly made at Chelsea in the Eighties. By the end of the decade racist supporters at the Bridge were very much on the back foot: publicly condemned and rejected by the club; opposed by the majority of fans, especially those who grouped together around the fanzines which appeared in the late Eighties; and increasingly monitored by the police, who were interested in the much-debated links between hooligan gangs and racist groups. As a political or terrace force, the Chelsea right-wing fans' heyday was well and truly over.

Undoubtedly, though, the biggest blow to the diehard racists and their dreams of a return to the days when Chelsea really were all white came at the end of the 1989/90 season. In the fans' poll to decide the club's 'Player of the Year' the most votes went to Ken Monkou, a composed Dutch defender signed from Feyenoord just one year earlier. For the thousands of fans who voted for Monkou it apparently didn't matter that that the player was not only a foreigner with an unusual surname, but that he was also black.

CHAPTER TEN
BACK IN THE BIG TIME
1984-85

helsea's title-clinching victory at Grimsby may have been a great day for the club, but for manager John Neal it was a rather more mixed occasion. Unbeknown to the fans or players, Neal had been taken ill during the match and was later diagnosed with a heart problem which required surgery during the summer. While he recuperated, a lot of his managerial duties during the 1984/85 season were delegated to his two assistants, Ian McNeill and John Hollins. "After John had his heart surgery we didn't see him so much, although we still appreciated what he had done for the club," says David Speedie. "Ian McNeill largely ran the team that season with the assistance of John Hollins and they did a very good job."

The squad was almost unchanged from the one which had won promotion, apart from the addition of rugged left back Doug Rougvie who arrived from Scottish champions Aberdeen for £150,000. Players leaving the club, meanwhile, included Shed favourite Clive Walker, who joined Sunderland for £75,000 and Tony McAndrew, who rejoined Middlesbrough early in the season.

Chelsea had stormed through the Second Division, but Neal and his players knew that the top division would be an altogether trickier proposition. As if to underline that obvious fact, the fixture computer provided the Blues with a daunting trip to Highbury on the opening day of the season. Backed by around 15,000 boisterous fans in the Clock End, Chelsea acquitted themselves well in the opening stages before falling behind to a goal by England striker Paul Mariner. Within minutes, though, the Blues were on level terms with a goal which was straight out of their back catalogue. Doug Rougvie hit a well-directed ball forwards, David Speedie flicked a header on and, although Arsenal keeper Pat Jennings blocked Kerry Dixon's first effort, the Chelsea centre forward bludgeoned home the rebound on the volley. The match finished 1-1, the result and the performance providing a huge confidence boost to the Chelsea team, of whom only Colin Lee had played in the English top flight before. "I knew after that game we would cope with the First Division," says Colin Pates.

At the first home game of the season, two days later against Sunderland, fans discovered that the jubilant pitch invasions at the tail end of the previous campaign had brought their inevitable consequence: blue fences had been erected in front of the West and East stands in addition to those already in place in front of the terraces. To the casual observer, Stamford Bridge now resembled a prison camp as much as a sporting arena, although Ken Bates did his best to put a positive spin on a depressing development. "Some newspapers made a fuss about the height of the fencing," he told fans in the club programme, "but it is identical to that used on other grounds throughout the country, such as Old Trafford and Wembley." Peering through the iron grilles, the Bridge crowd saw their team collect their first win of the season, an early goal by Paul Canoville settling the match.

Following a few weeks of adaptation to the higher league, the Blues soon found the First Division held no fears. Excellent home wins over Coventry (6-2), West Brom (3-1) and reigning champions Liverpool (3-1) pushed Chelsea up to sixth place in the league, inspiring thoughts of a possible UEFA Cup place come the end of the season. Three new faces appeared on the teamsheet during this period: Darren Wood, a compact right back signed from Middlesbrough for a bargain £50,000; Keith Jones, a neat passing midfielder promoted from the youth ranks; and Gordon Davies, a prolific scorer with Fulham over many years, signed to provide the squad with more striking options.

Davies made a startling initial impact, hitting a hat-trick in only his second game in a remarkable 4-3 victory at leaders Everton. In the longer term Davies was unable to break up the well-established Dixon–Speedie axis, although the Scot's not infrequent suspensions gave him more opportunities than he might otherwise have had.

Question marks about his temperament aside, Speedie was earning rave reviews for his thoughtful link-up play, decisive finishing and non-stop harassment of the country's best defenders. "David Speedie is about as difficult to mark as a handkerchief caught in a tornado," opined the *News of the World* after one typically dynamic display by the Chelsea number 10.

Meanwhile, Kerry Dixon was finding goals just as easy to come by in the First as in the Second Division, and would go on to share the Golden Boot with Leicester's Gary Lineker. A tabloid campaign for the blond striker to be called up for England gained mounting force and it didn't harm his cause that former national team boss Don Revie announced himself as a big fan. "Dixon is one of the best finishers in football," said Revie. "It doesn't matter where the ball is in the area, he always seems to be on the end of it." Eventually, England manager Bobby Robson responded to the clamour, taking Dixon on England's summer trip to Mexico.

Pat Nevin, too, also had a legion of admirers, England winger Chris Waddle among them. "It's not his speed that is his greatest asset, but his ability to catch an opponent off balance," reckoned the Newcastle star. "He has natural talent to wrong-foot a player when you least expect it and suddenly he's gone." *The Guardian*, meanwhile, was so impressed by Nevin's intricate footwork that, after one particularly dazzling display, its reporter suggested the little winger "could lift a corpse from his seat".

With their three main attacking players combining superbly, a hard-working midfield, a reasonably tight defence and a first-rate goalkeeper, Chelsea looked to have all the ingredients required of a trophy-winning team. The league championship was a step too far, but the Blues were strongly fancied in the cups. The FA Cup, though, ended frustratingly, Chelsea losing 3-2 at home to Third Division Millwall in the fourth round after Speedie sliced his last-minute penalty wide.

It was left, then, to the League Cup – or the Milk Cup as it was then called, in acknowledgement of its sponsorship by the National Diary Council – to provide much of the season's excitement. The competition, which at the time was taken deadly seriously by all clubs, didn't disappoint. Chelsea were paired in a two-leg tie with George Graham's Millwall in the second round and after a 3-1 victory at the Bridge in the first leg, Kerry Dixon scoring twice, travelled to the Den for the return two weeks later.

Again Dixon was on the scoresheet in a 1-1 draw, but the headlines after the match naturally concentrated on an appalling incident outside the ground when Chelsea reserve player Robert Isaac was stabbed by a group of Millwall fans half an hour before kick-off. "The Millwall gang asked him which team he supported," reported Nigel Freedman in *The Sun*. "He said 'Millwall' and was asked the name of their keeper. Isaac, Chelsea's youth team player of the year last season, could not remember. Seconds later, he was slashed across his back from his armpit to the base of his spine." Fortunately, Isaac was wearing a heavy leather jacket which gave him some protection against the knife attack, but even so doctors feared he may have punctured a lung. He was released from hospital after treatment the same night and recovered sufficiently well to make his full Chelsea debut later in the season.

Happily, the action centred on the pitch in the third round when the Blues survived a shock at Walsall before emerging with a hard-fought 2-2 draw. The replay at the Bridge was far more comfortable, with Dixon, Speedie and Keith Jones all on target in a straightforward 3-0 win.

Chelsea again avoided First Division opposition in the next round, when they were paired with Manchester City, who had narrowly missed out on promotion the previous season. On a muddy Stamford Bridge pitch, the Blues put in one of their finest displays of the season, a hat-trick by Kerry Dixon helping them to a spectacular 4-1 win. It should have been five, but the penalty hoodoo struck again, Pat Nevin bizarrely deciding to sidefoot his shot along the sticky, puddle-dotted ground. The ball barely reached City keeper Alex Williams, who was probably used to dealing with more firmly hit back passes.

For most players this would have been a head-in-hands moment, but Nevin, a maverick figure in many ways out of tune with the prevailing ethos of stern-faced pragmatism which valued results above entertainment, found it hugely enjoyable. "Brilliant!" he smiles. "We were 4-1 up, I'd played really well, I'd made a couple of goals and it was actually one of my best games for Chelsea. I'd been practising penalties the day before but I miskicked the ball and it just about reached the goalie. I was killing myself laughing, but I kept my head down because I knew the cameras were on me and if John Neal saw that I was laughing he would hammer me. He didn't think I took football seriously enough all the time; I took it seriously but I had it in perspective and I was laughing my head off!"

In the quarter-final Chelsea were held 1-1 at Stamford Bridge by their old rivals Sheffield Wednesday. The penalty jinx struck again with Wednesday keeper Martin Hodge saving Kerry Dixon's second-half spot-kick. At half-time in the replay it looked like an expensive miss: Chelsea, penned in their own half by an airborne Wednesday barrage, were 3-0 down and heading out of the competition. Within seconds of the restart, though, substitute 'King' Canoville waltzed through a sleepy Owls rearguard to give the Blues some hope. The goal stirred Chelsea into life and, during a period of intense pressure on the Wednesday goal, Kerry Dixon and Mickey Thomas pulled the Blues level. Then, incredibly, Canoville popped up on the end of an intricate team move to shoot past Hodge to make it 4-3. However, with an improbable victory just 20 seconds away, the Blues needlessly conceded a penalty. Doug Rougvie, once memorably described by veteran *Times* reporter Brian Glanville as being "as mobile as a telegraph pole but substantially less reliable," was the culprit and Mel Sterland accepted the gift, drilling home the spot-kick past Niedzwiecki. Extra-time produced no more goals and so the teams returned to the Bridge for a second replay.

Once again, the Blues started badly, going behind to a goal by Wednesday midfielder Gary Shelton. Urged on by the overwhelming majority of fans in the 36,395 crowd, Chelsea responded with incessant attacks down the wings and through the centre. The Owls, though, held firm until they were undone by an inspired piece of quick thinking by Nevin. Receiving possession after a Blues' free-kick had been blocked, the little Scot dinked the ball over the heads of the advancing Wednesday defenders, who were charging en masse away from their goal in an attempt to leave any stray Chelsea attacker offside. Having nipped through a small gap in the line of yellow-shirted bodies, Nevin then floated a delightful chip to the far post where the onrushing Speedie threw himself full length to head the ball past Hodge. The goal, which perfectly encapsulated the imaginative impudence of Nevin and the bravery of Speedie, was one of the most memorable of the era. To round off a great night, Mickey Thomas stooped low to head Canoville's corner through a crowd of defenders for a last-gasp winner.

Paired with Sunderland in the semi-finals, Chelsea were installed as the bookies' favourites for the trophy. The other tie, meanwhile, was an all East Anglian affair between Ipswich and Norwich. The first leg at Roker Park was a disaster for the Blues. Already without the suspended Speedie, they lost McLaughlin after just 11 minutes with a dislocated elbow. Substitute Dale Jasper, an inexperienced youngster more used to playing in midfield, was drafted into the middle of defence alongside Pates and promptly conceded two penalties, both of which were put away by Sunderland striker Colin West. Once again, Chelsea would need to call on their powers of recovery if they were to reach a first cup final since 1972.

Chasing the two-goal deficit at Stamford Bridge the Blues, reportedly on a £3,000 bonus each if they won the tie and roared on by a near-hysterical crowd, got off to a perfect start when Speedie turned sharply and slammed the ball past Sunderland keeper Chris Turner in the opening minutes. Shortly before half-time, however, old boy Clive Walker fired in a spectacular equaliser at the Shed end to put Sunderland back in control. Despite huge Chelsea pressure in the second half a goal just wouldn't come and when Walker broke away to slot his second past Niedzwiecki the tie was all but over. Predictably, some fans reacted violently to this *coup de grace*, spilling over the fences and on to the pitch.

One heavily-built fan, in particular, made a beeline for the villain of the moment, Clive Walker, and only the intervention of Joey Jones prevented an unpleasant incident. "I realised what was happening only when Joey yelled out," Walker told reporters. "The fan would have landed me one when I wasn't looking. He was throwing punches but Joey ran in to protect me. I'm grateful to him."

The match was stopped for five minutes as players and police were pelted with missiles, mostly hurled from the West stand benches. While the police struggled to regain order, Walker set up a third, killer goal for Colin West. Bizarrely, a police officer was chasing a fan inside the Chelsea penalty area as the Sunderland striker headed the ball in. In the closing minutes Chelsea's night deteriorated further when David Speedie was sent off, and had to be restrained from attacking Walker. "I did lose it big time against Sunderland," admits Speedo. "As I was trudging back to the dressing room, Clive Walker asked if I wanted to buy any tickets for the final. I just flipped and went for his throat. God knows what would have happened if I hadn't been pulled off him."

After the game, which finished 3-2 to the Wearsiders, Speedie and Walker clashed again in the players' lounge. "I was so angry I warned Clive not to come into the lounge but he wandered in and started chatting to Mickey Droy," remembers Speedo. "I went over to him and clocked him one. Then, Mickey stepped in to separate us."

Clive Walker, though, insists that Speedie's punch missed and that the whole incident was just a case of 'handbags'. Nonetheless, the fracas made the newspapers the following day after Sunderland's Chris Turner told reporters what had happened.

The press headlines the following morning made gloomy reading for Chelsea fans. "Savages!" screamed the back page of the *Daily Mirror*, above an account of the violence by Nigel Clarke which began: "Soccer reached sickening depths of savagery last night as Chelsea went out of the sordid Milk Cup semi-final." The paper went on to report that 104 fans had been arrested and 20 police officers injured during the disturbances. Sunderland quickly announced that they would be banning Chelsea fans from the league match at Roker Park later that same month, while the FA promised an inquiry into the events.

For Ken Bates, who was in the process of negotiating a £1 million shirt sponsorship deal with an electronics company from the Far East, the crowd violence could not have come at a worse moment. "Not only did we lose out on a trip to Wembley but the crowd trouble that evening cost us a very good sponsor," he recalled later. "The morning after I really felt like putting my head in the gas oven." Bates was soon in more upbeat mood, coming up with an innovative idea to prevent future pitch incursions: inspired by the electric fences which kept the cows on his Beaconsfield farm within their fields, he decided that the tops of the Bridge fences should be fitted with a 12-volt electric current which would give potential pitch invaders an unpleasant, but non-lethal, shock. "We're sorry to see it go up," he told fans in the club programme, "but it's interesting to note that of 200 letters received by us, only seven are critical."

The fans may have been behind him but, to Bates' dismay, his novel approach to tackling football hooliganism was opposed by the Minister for Sport, Neil Macfarlane. "I rue the day that the soccer grounds of our national game have to have this sort of installation," said the minister. Bates responded by calling for Macfarlane's resignation "for failing to solve the problem of hooliganism".

The electric fence was eventually given the thumbs down by safety officers at the Greater London Council and was never switched on. Simon Turney, chairman of the GLC's public service committee, summed up the body's opposition to the scheme by saying, "The idea is very unsavoury. The reaction I have had from my colleagues is 'What comes next?' – water cannons, guards, tanks, and consultant undertakers to ferry away the dead?"

The Blues' season might have been expected to peter out after their dispiriting Milk Cup exit, but to their credit Chelsea kept pushing on in the league in the hope of securing a UEFA Cup place. During the run-in John Neal tried out a number of young players, including powerfully-built left back Keith Dublin and central defender Robert Isaac. A victory in their last match against Milk Cup winners Norwich would have secured the Blues the last European slot ahead of Southampton, but they lost 2-1 on a waterlogged Bridge pitch. In the end it didn't make any difference: following the riot by Liverpool fans at the Heysel stadium, during which 39 Juventus fans died, all English clubs were banned from European football for five years. In one night a huge black cloud had descended over the domestic game, obscuring the memory of what had been a more than reasonable first season back in the top flight for the Blues.

CHAPTER ELEVEN
FOOTBALLERS' LIVES

C ompared with today's superstars of the Premier League, footballers in the late Seventies and Eighties had a much lower public profile. This was mainly because the saturation TV coverage of the game which armchair fans now enjoy didn't exist back then: with live games being few and far between, football followers mostly relied on the edited highlights packages of *Match of the Day* and *The Big Match* to feed their addiction. Aside from these two shows footballers rarely appeared on the small screen at all, although big names would occasionally pop up on *A Question of Sport*.

Lacking the millions that Sky has pumped into the game over the last decade, clubs were unable to afford the mega-salaries that star players receive today. Indeed, at Chelsea in the early Eighties first team players were earning annual sums which some Premiership reserves would reckon to easily double in a week. "We were on about £15-20,000 max a year," says Gary Chivers. "Win bonuses were around £200-300, with half that for a draw. So the bonuses were vitally important, they made a huge difference." Still, if fame and fortune were not as easily achieved then as now, there were compensations. Perhaps the chief one of these was that players could behave in ways which today would see them plastered all over the front pages of the tabloids, but back then wouldn't even make a small story on the inside pages.

Garry Stanley is a case in point. Among the Chelsea team of the late Seventies Stanley was something of a pin-up figure. With his mop of tousled black hair and strong chiselled features he bore a striking resemblance to the actor Paul Michael Glazer who starred in the hugely popular American cop show *Starsky and Hutch*. Inevitably, 'Stanners' became 'Starsky' in the dressing room and the nickname was soon picked up by fans, especially after the Chelsea star took part in a tabloid press shoot posing moodily by a fast car and wearing a big woollen jumper like the ones Glazer invariably sported on the TV show.

A firm favourite with female Chelsea fans, the fan mail for Stanley poured into Stamford Bridge by the sackful. The player himself didn't have time to plough through it all, so the task of sifting through the cards and letters fell to his best mate Mark Westwood, now the organiser of the Chelsea Old Boys team. "I used to go to the office to pick up his post and it was always a real sack-load – all from girls," recalls 'Westy'. "He'd get a lot of invites to parties on a Saturday night, mostly 18th and 21st birthdays, and I'd work out all the ones we could go to in the south-west London area after the game. We'd meet in the Lord Palmerston, round the corner from Stamford Bridge, have a few drinks then I'd pull out that night's list of seven or eight parties. The main core was me, Stanners and a couple of the other lads. We'd go to these parties, all at nice family homes in places like Putney and Southfields, the doors would open and the screeching when the girls saw us was unbelievable.

"These parties would make national headlines now, with some of the things that went on. All the girls were keen to meet or maybe even get off with a Chelsea footballer or just one of their mates. We'd often say to one of the girls, 'Let's go upstairs...' by which time one player would be behind the curtain and another would be under the bed – just for a laugh. Me and Stanners were in a wardrobe one time and a player came in and started doing the business with this girl. He was saying, 'Cor, I wish all my mates were here!' and we couldn't stop laughing. Stanners was kneeing me in the back and the wardrobe was wobbling and then it crashed onto the floor. Of course, then everyone else came out of their hiding places. There were 13 blokes in the bedroom and this posh girl just said 'Sod it, you can all have a go at me.'

"Streaking came into fashion," continues 'Westy'. "The party we were at in Putney was a bit boring so me and Stanners took all our clothes off, then we ran out of the house and round the whole block, completely naked. We got back to the party and half the people had copied us and were naked – it was like an orgy."

Stanley, while readily admitting that "I had an eye for the ladies", does not have a vivid recollection of individual events at these parties – but not, he points out, because he was drunk at the time. Unlike some of the other players interviewed for this book, he is happy to have his name mentioned in this chapter but he also stresses that Westwood's version of events are not necessarily correct and should, in some cases, be taken with "a large pinch of salt". On the other hand, while he disputes the details in some of Westwood's stories, Stanners has never been shy about his image as a top 'bird' puller. "I was courting from 17 to 21 then that relationship ended," he says. "That's when I might have earned my reputation a wee bit. I was let loose and felt like a free man. My attitude, and that of some of the other lads, was that we worked hard and we played hard, too – we needed a release from the pressure we were under trying to get Chelsea back into the First Division. But the things we got up to never interfered with the serious business of training or playing matches."

Occasional club functions at the Bridge, which often included a disc jockey pumping out smoochy ballads by the likes of the Commodores, the Bee Gees and Olivia Newton-John, were always a great opportunity for some of the players to, er, get to know their female fans a little bit better. "The girls would be all over the players," says Mark Westwood. "Quite often, they would pair off and go off together to the centre spot or to the back of the goal at the Shed end. These girls would come back all flushed saying, 'I've done it with a footballer!' At one of these discos I took a girl up in the lift to the third floor of the East stand where there was a settee in the corridor. I was shagging this bird in the pitch black when suddenly the lift doors opened and it was Ray and Graham Wilkins' mum and dad, Winnie and George. They must have pressed the wrong button on the lift. Winnie didn't seem too shocked, she just smiled and said, 'Goodnight, Westy!'"

In March 1977 Garry Stanley took a break from the Blues' ultimately successful promotion campaign to act as a judge in the Miss West London heat of the Miss Great Britain contest. Also on the judging panel at Stamford Bridge were Blues boss Eddie McCreadie, Brian Mears' wife, June, and the Mayor and Mayoress of Hammersmith. Naturally, though, it was Stanley who took centre stage when the winner was announced.

"I wasn't surprised that the girl who won was a brunette because Stanners was a brunette man," says 'Westy'. "He put the crown on her head and she sat on his lap. He took her home afterwards and I had her friend who was quite stunning too. Although I usually kept in the background because I wasn't a footballer, Stanners pulled most of his birds through me. He wasn't a cocky cockney boy from London; he was a quiet lad from Burton. I had all the talk and patter. We used to pretend we were plumbers and carpenters because if he told them he played for Chelsea the girls never believed him. But if we felt we weren't getting anywhere as a plumber and carpenter we changed the story a bit rapid."

Chelsea players' wedding receptions, which were often held at Stamford Bridge, would also see the talent-spotting duo working in tandem. "We had girlfriends but they were never allowed to come between me and him," says Westwood. "Stanners would get an invitation and it would say 'Mr Garry Stanley and girlfriend', but he'd always take me. There was normally a master of ceremonies as you walked through the door – so it was 'Mr and Mrs Ray Lewington!', 'Mr and Mrs Ian Britton!' and so on. But the other players knew Stanners was not going to bring a girl, so the master of ceremonies would go 'Mr

Garry Stanley and....?" And he would shout out 'Westy!' The place would erupt because they knew he wasn't going to turn up with a girlfriend. And, of course, his girlfriends over the years wouldn't talk to me. They just knew I was getting all the best invites."

Some of the pair's adventures were, it seems, straight out of the long-running sitcom *The Likely Lads*, with a dash of *Only Fools and Horses* thrown in for good measure.

"A lot of the players married early, in the 22-25 age range," explains 'Westy'. "I must have been to half a dozen weddings. Me and Stanners used to run into Argos on the morning of the wedding to buy a kettle or pots and pans as a gift. We were always running late and in a real hurry. Once we were driving over Wandsworth Bridge and I said, 'I've bought a toaster' and he said, 'So have I' – that's how stupid we were. So we walked in to the wedding with two toasters.

"We went to Gary Locke's wedding at Stamford Bridge. As usual, me and Stanners were looking around, wondering if any of the girls had brought their friends with them. Mickey Droy gave me a cigar and we were talking about his flashy new suit which he told us had cost him £500. I was a bit pissed and was waving the cigar around when suddenly this massive hole appeared in the sleeve of his jacket. He looked down at me, flicked the ash off and said 'It's just as well that I know you!' He was a man mountain but he's a gentle giant, a lovely bloke."

In the late Seventies and early Eighties, particularly, drink featured prominently in the players' adventures. On occasions the fact that Chelsea's training ground in Molesey had its own bar proved too much of a temptation for some of the squad. "One day after a training session me and another player stayed in the bar all afternoon," recalls David Stride. "We drove off in his Mini, we'd had a few and he made me a £10 bet. He said, 'I bet if I stop this car you won't jump in the Thames' so I got out and I dived straight in. I was in the water right up to my neck. Then some people threw a lifebuoy at me and hauled me out. I got back to my digs and the landlady looked at me sopping wet and said, 'What the fuck have you done?'"

Stridey's devil-may-care attitude was noted by some of the old guard at the Bridge, who knew all about having fun away from the prying eyes of the management. "I went a bit wayward," he says. "When I was 18 and still an apprentice Ossie and Ian Hutchinson said to me, 'We'll take you out today.' We went to a pub in Windsor and first thing they do is order three bottles of champagne at £25 a time, and I was thinking, 'Fuckin' hell, how am I going to pay for this?' because I was only on £16 a week as an apprentice. But, fair play to them, they always looked after me. They were good boys."

Another star of the early Seventies team, John Dempsey, also took the young Stride under his wing and provided him with some valuable advice. "Demps used to say to me, 'Play the game, but have a little niggle afterwards. Come in for treatment on Monday, Tuesday, Wednesday and Thursday, play the five-a-side on Friday and play the game on Saturday.' So I used to go in for treatment with John Dempsey on Monday. He used to lie there and take the piss out of the physiotherapist, Eddie Franklin, then we'd go up to the commercial department where Hutch was based and drink gin and tonics while the rest of them were running round the pitch."

Most of the players, though, were content to do their drinking after training rather than during it. "When we trained at Harlington we used to go out together afterwards on a Monday and Tuesday round the corner to the White Hart pub for lunch and a few beers," recalls Graham Wilkins. "We never got out of there until six o'clock at night. We'd eat a bit of food and then knock back seven or eight pints. We were always drunk. Johnny Bumstead, Trevor Aylott, Tommy Langley, Gary Chivers, Clive Walker, myself – we all used to like a drink. But because we socialised together it was good for team spirit." Other players, however, insist that Wilkins has exaggerated how much the players used to drink. "It was never eight pints," says Clive Walker. "We'd have a couple of pints and a game of cards. It was good for camaraderie."

However much the players drank, it was enough for some of them to feel somewhat worse the wear the following day in training. "I don't know about the others, but I used to feel the effects of the Monday afternoon drink the next day because Tuesday was our running day," says Graham Wilkins. "Seb Coe used to come down to training when Geoff Hurst and Bobby Gould were there. He'd do sprints and weights with us and he used to race us. He was in training for the Moscow Olympics at the time and I'd like to think we helped him. If it hadn't been for us he might not have won his medals!"

Post-match, pretty much the whole team would make a beeline for the players' bar at the Bridge. Originally, this was a room upstairs in the East stand but when Ken Bates took over as chairman he requisitioned the bar as a vice-presidents' lounge. When the players protested they were given a bolt-hole opposite the changing rooms which had previously been used as a tearoom by the Stamford Bridge groundstaff. "We'd definitely be in there after the game, and there was a brilliant atmosphere especially if we'd won," says Gary Chivers. "Clive Walker was usually behind the bar, and we had to pay for the beers – but everything we took went back into the players' pool."

The next stop, for some of the players at least, would be the bars and restaurants of the King's Road, the old stomping ground of the likes of Alan Hudson, Charlie Cooke and Tommy Baldwin a decade earlier. "There was a group of us who would go out on the King's Road after matches," recalls Colin Pates. "It was mainly the London boys – me, Johnny Bumstead, Jerry Murphy and Perry Digweed, who was a mad Chelsea fan even before he joined the club on loan. We'd meet a lot of fans while we were out and I think they related to us because we were much like them, working-class boys who wanted to play for Chelsea because we loved the club and not because we were on 50 grand a week. We were very approachable, too, fans would come up to chat to us and buy us a pint."

The players' favourite pub was the Magpie and Stump, which was converted into an up-market off-licence in 2004. Their other haunts included Leonardo's restaurant in

World's End and the Pheasantry, another King's Road eatery. After dinner the players would often head into the West End, ending the evening at a top nightclub. "We sometimes went to Stringfellow's but more often to Brown's in Great Queen Street because the manager, Jake, was a huge Chelsea fan," remembers Patesy. "There were always a lot of other footballers there, a few *EastEnders* actors and loads of musicians and DJs like Gary Crowley. George Michael was in there sometimes and so was Jimmy White, who was a big Chelsea fan. We always had an excellent time. It was a bit of a Chelsea tradition to enjoy yourself off the pitch. Ossie and Alan Hudson had been my tutors for that from when I was a youngster."

The routine following away games was, obviously, somewhat different but nonetheless having a good time featured high on the agenda. "Coming back on the coach from away games we'd have a few beers as well," says Gary Chivers. "How many we'd have depended on how well we'd done. We'd have a right few beers if we'd won and played well. Food was either fish and chips which we'd pre-order or else we'd stop off somewhere for a nice meal."

Apart from drinking, entertainment on the long coach trips home would consist of card schools and a video machine showing films and pop videos. Competition among the players to get their favourite videos shown was fierce, but all were pretty much agreed on one thing: on no account should Pat Nevin be allowed to put any of his music on. Once described as Britain's first 'post-punk' footballer, Pat Nevin was a huge fan of the indie scene and groups like Joy Division, The Jesus and Mary Chain and The Cocteau Twins. The other players, though, tended towards mellower tunes by the likes of Luther Vandross and George Benson and couldn't stand the discordant guitar sounds produced by Nevin's favourite bands.

"I did get my music played now and again but the reaction wasn't good from the others," admits Pat. "Most of the time I just put my headphones on. About the only one I got past them was *Relax* by Frankie Goes to Hollywood before it got popular. I put that on the video player and the video had girls dancing with very few clothes... the boys quite liked that one for some reason."

Another popular group at the time was Culture Club, led by the flamboyant androgynous singer Boy George. In October 1984 the chart-topping band recorded the video for their single *The Medal Song* at Stamford Bridge at half-time during the Blues' game with Watford. After the match the team met the group in the players' bar, an occasion which was recorded for posterity by *Bridge News*. "I thought one or two were a bit macho, especially the pretty one (John Bumstead) who asked me about my hair," Boy George was reported as saying.

"I was a bit surprised because he was a massive bloke," remembers David Speedie, "but he was a nice guy – not that I'm into the gay scene or anything. He was wearing his stage clothes, he had a big hat on which was similar to one of Pat Nevin's. In fact, I'd say he was better dressed than Pat." Other players, meanwhile, were pleasantly surprised that Boy George was not as 'soft' or 'effeminate' as they had imagined. "I must admit when I first saw him on *Top of the Pops* I thought: 'What a wally!'" said Joe McLaughlin. "But he's basically a normal bloke underneath that make-up and strange gear."

Another celebrity some of the players got to know quite well was cricket superstar Ian Botham, a Chelsea supporter from an early age. "As an up-and-coming player he was my hero," says Gary Chivers. "Both was great. His attitude was a bit like mine: this is my way and that's the way I'm going to do it. When he was at Worcester I went to see him play and I slid a note in to tell him that I was there and we went out on the champagne together. We had a great evening out in Worcester, just the two of us. We had a few glasses that night, I can tell you."

When he wasn't bashing a cricket ball around Botham could sometimes be found in panto and, bizarrely enough, the Chelsea team of the mid-Eighties also once appeared on stage, donning some outlandish outfits for a photo-shoot to publicise a charity performance of *Cinderella* at the Wimbledon Theatre. The 'cast' included Darren Wood and Dale Jasper as The Ugly Sisters, Colin Pates as the Coachman, Kerry Dixon as Buttons and Pat Nevin as Cinders.

"I was the only one who could fit into Bonnie Longford's dress so I ended up being cast as Cinders," grimaces Pat Nevin. "We just posed for a few pictures, we didn't act out any scenes from the play. There was a photographer there from a local newspaper and one from *Bridge News*, which was fine, but I made a point of saying that I didn't want the pictures appearing in any of the nationals – and that was agreed. I'd always said that I would only be photographed in normal clothes and I wasn't going to put on a top hat or whatever because I never wore one. I just felt that kind of thing was dumb. But, a day or so later, I saw the pictures on the back page of *The Sun*. The guy had been offered money to sell them and had gone back on the agreement. That annoyed me a bit, and for a while I refused to do stuff for *Bridge News*."

Taking such a principled stand on what others might see as a minor matter was just one of the ways in which the iconoclastic Nevin marked himself as an altogether different character from his team-mates. Apart from his off-beat musical tastes and trademark hats he was also a voracious reader, for example. "I used to read different things, it wasn't for affect it was just the person I was," he says. "Once I was up the back of the bus and reading some shorts stories by Anton Chekhov – as you do – and Dale Jasper said, 'I didn't know you were a Trekkie'."

Nevin may have been a cult hero for Blues fans in the Shed, but there was little doubt which Chelsea player of the Eighties had the biggest public profile: Kerry Dixon. The striker's superb goals record earned him a call-up to the England team two years after he joined the Blues and his new-found international status allied to his rugged good looks – he was once voted the second 'dishiest' footballer in Britain behind winner Bryan

Robson – ensured that he was much in demand for personal appearances.

"I was on *A Question of Sport* three times," says Kerry. "I was always on Billy Beaumont's team to cover the football side and on one occasion I had a nightmare. The question was 'Who was the last England player to score a hat-trick?' I dived in and pressed the buzzer, Billy said 'Go on, Kerry' and I said 'Luther Blissett'. Straight away the buzzer went on the other side – I'd dived in too quickly – and they got the right answer, which was Bryan Robson against Turkey. I was left a bit red-faced about that one but I learnt a lesson: not to dive in too fast."

Foiled by the injury-prone England captain not once, but twice, then. At least Kerry got his own back in April 1986 when his two fine strikes against Robson's Manchester United at Old Trafford pretty much ended the Reds' chances of winning a first title for almost 20 years. For a player who lived and breathed goals that had to be more satisfying than topping some silly poll in a teen mag or winning a TV quiz show.

CHAPTER TWELVE
TITLE CHALLENGE AND CUP GLORY
1985-87

n the summer of 1985, for the sixth time in a decade, Chelsea changed managers . On this occasion, though, there was a sense of natural progression rather than sudden rupture. John Hollins, having served as first team coach for two years, was promoted to the manager's position while John Neal was elevated 'upstairs' and appointed to the board of directors. Ian McNeill also remained at the club, in a role which largely involved scouting new talent and watching future opponents.

Speaking after his appointment, Hollins appeared thrilled to have landed the top job at a club he had first joined as a 15-year-old schoolboy. "I want Chelsea to be the best team in the land," he told reporters. "The best side for all reasons. The best defence, the best midfield, the best goalscorers. I have so much to thank John (Neal) for. He has helped me in so many ways – and I'm sure he will continue to do so. Undoubtedly I'll make mistakes. I just hope they aren't too costly."

Hollins made few alterations to the squad which had served John Neal so well. His one signing was free transfer Jerry Murphy, a languid left-sided midfielder from Crystal Palace. Another new face was tricky Falkirk winger Kevin McAllister, who had been signed by John Neal in May. Hollins also recruited former Crystal Palace manager Ernie Walley as his coach, who arrived from Selhurst Park with a reputation as a hard taskmaster. Players leaving the club, meanwhile, included former skipper Mickey Droy, who signed for Crystal Palace after two years in the reserves at the Bridge and Joey Jones, who joined Huddersfield Town.

Again, the Blues prepared for the new season among the sand dunes of Aberystwyth. "This time it was harder than ever," complained Colin Pates in the matchday programme, "as new coach Ernie Walley certainly knows some strenuous training routines. Ernie's a tough character who really puts us through it. Some of his sessions were murder at the time but we will be glad we worked so hard once the season is under way."

Chelsea, 20/1 outsiders for the title according to the bookies, began the season poorly, conceding a goal to old rivals Sheffield Wednesday after just three minutes at Hillsborough. But, playing in an unfamiliar all-red away kit, the Londoners hit back with a David Speedie goal to earn a useful point. Not that *Sunday Times* reporter Deryk Brown was at all impressed by the fare on show. "For football purists, this was a pie-and-peas start to the season," he whined.

Sporting a shiny new home kit, which included blue socks as opposed to the traditional white ones and the return of the V-neck collar, Chelsea opened their home campaign with a run-of-the-mill 1-0 win over Coventry. Again, Speedie was on target, converting a Pat Nevin cross. Slightly under 16,000 fans attended the game, the poor turnout possibly reflecting concerns about hooliganism in the aftermath of the events at Heysel. Surprisingly, Ken Bates announced himself to be 'very pleased' with the crowd figure, suggesting that the club had feared an even lower attendance. Generally, gates were down across the board during the 1985/86 season, a trend which was partly attributed to the post-Heysel effect but also to a dispute between the clubs and the TV companies which kept football off the small screen until a £1.3 million deal was negotiated in December.

Meanwhile, Chelsea's good start continued with just one defeat in the club's first nine league games. In September Hollins splashed out a club record £300,000 on Mick Hazard, Tottenham's creative and smooth-passing midfielder. In the same month Mickey Thomas was allowed to move to West Brom, partly because Hollins was unimpressed with the player's refusal to move from his north Wales home. Another player to quit the Bridge was Gordon Davies, who joined Manchester City after failing to break up the Dixon–Speedie striking duopoly.

The signing of Hazard was hailed as indicating a change in style in Chelsea's play, with less focus on long balls from the back and more emphasis on passing moves through midfield. "Chelsea looked vastly improved," noted Rick Shearman in the *Sunday Times* after Hazard made his debut in a 2-1 home win over Arsenal. "The addition of a good ball player in midfield was always likely to lift them from a hoof-and-hope outfit into a useful side."

Hollins, though, played down suggestions that Hazard's arrival would signal a complete rethink of the Blues' tried and tested methods. "I don't think anything has changed," he said the following month. "Mick is a very good passer of the ball who adds a new dimension to our play and it will take a while for everyone to get used to his style, but we shall continue to play the way that has worked for us in the past couple of years."

An eventful 2-1 win over champions Everton at the Bridge in October – both teams missing penalties and Kevin Ratcliffe ending the game in goal for the Toffees after Neville Southall was sent off – kept Chelsea in the chasing pack behind leaders Manchester United, who were 10 points clear at the top after a storming unbeaten start. The Blues, though, had a chance to reduce the deficit when Ron Atkinson's men visited the Bridge at the end of October.

Chelsea's biggest game of the season so far attracted London's first capacity crowd of the campaign, 42,485. Hollins surprised many by leaving Hazard out of the squad, the first public sign that the manager already had severe doubts about the mercurial midfielder. "His strength was being on the ball, using the ball and keeping the ball," says Hollins now. "That's what we wanted him for. But his awareness of closing a little hole down or whatever wasn't up to scratch and his fitness levels weren't good, so at times he was a good sub to bring on to change the game. In the end that's what they did at Tottenham with him."

With both sides playing two wingers, Nevin and McAllister for Chelsea and Jesper Olsen and Peter Barnes for United, the match at Stamford Bridge was an open affair. Olsen put the Reds ahead with a low shot on 41 minutes, but almost immediately United defender Graeme Hogg was sent off for a second bookable offence. When Joe McLaughlin equalised for the Blues in the second half the game seemed to be turning Chelsea's way, but after Kerry Dixon's shot struck the bar United broke away and won the match thanks to a thunderous effort by Mark Hughes. The defeat seemed to signal the end of Chelsea's slim championship hopes.

However, over the next two and a half months, the Blues put together a magnificent unbeaten run of nine wins and two draws which, allied to a spectacular loss of form by United, thrust them back into the title race. Highlights of this period included an exciting 4-2 victory over Brian Clough's Nottingham Forest at the Bridge and a first win at Newcastle for 15 years. Kerry Dixon, demonstrating the power, pace and finishing skills of the classic centre forward, was in especially prolific form at this time, notching 21 goals in all competitions before New Year.

The last of those goals, a header in a raucously received 2-0 home triumph over Tottenham just after Christmas, lifted the Blues to second place in the league behind the rapidly disintegrating men from Old Trafford. Liverpool, Everton and – unlikely though it sounds – West Ham were also keenly involved in a title picture which had changed from being a procession to a closely-fought dogfight in just a matter of weeks.

Chelsea were now being discussed as serious championship contenders in the press, but the prospect of blue and white ribbons fluttering from the league title trophy did not enthuse all commentators. "It is a profoundly disturbing thought that Chelsea might yet climb up the steps to the English throne," declared Stuart Jones in *The Times*. "If the young pretenders succeed, it will make a significant and regrettable change in the ancient lineage. The crown will have been placed not so much on the head of talent but more on that of effort." Despite this sweeping critique, Jones did have the good grace to praise the Blues' attack. "No one would dispute that Chelsea are led by a front line of genuine class," he added. "Dixon and Speedie are arguably the most potent weapons in the country and Nevin, when the mood takes him, can be an irrepressible supplier of ammunition."

The widespread criticism of the team's playing style did not, understandably, go down well in the dressing room. "I heard some comments after the match that we play a 'Watford style' up-and-under game," said Colin Pates after a 3-0 win at West Brom in January left the Blues just two points behind United with a game in hand. "It amazes me that people should say this. Watford play the ball up into space, whereas we play directly to our forwards, either in the air or on the ground. Just because we move the ball upfront quickly we seem to be bracketed with the less attractive clubs."

Kerry Dixon is also adamant that the Blues' style was more sophisticated than it was given credit for. "The team could play the long ball to myself or David Speedie, who was very good at leaping, looking for the flick on to the other one if we had to go Route One," he says. "Failing that, we played it wide to Pat Nevin who was more than capable of holding play up, beating players and setting up play for us. So we could play both ways." John Hollins also took issue with the critics, saying, "I believe the best teams can play a bit of everything. Whizz-bang one day, careful construction the next."

The knockers may have carped, but the results continued to come. After Chelsea beat Shrewsbury on a snow-covered pitch at Gay Meadow in the FA Cup third round, optimistic Blues fans began daydreaming about a possible domestic treble. But Chelsea lost 2-1 at home to Liverpool in the next round, their cause not helped by a serious stomach muscle injury to Kerry Dixon which put him out of action for six weeks. Three days later, the Blues also went out of the Milk Cup, losing 2-0 at home to QPR in a quarter-final replay at the Bridge.

The league remained the top priority and in February Chelsea had a chance to go top when they played at home to Leicester on a muddy, rain-splashed surface. With Dixon injured and David Speedie suspended – or, as Ken Bates put it, 'taking his customary mid-season holiday' – a patched-up side, featuring a front two of reserve team striker Duncan Shearer and Kevin McAllister, were held to a 2-2 draw. The following weekend, the Blues' lack of depth in their squad was further exposed when they lost 4-1 at home to Oxford. Even the fans seemed unconvinced by their team's title credentials, with under 29,000 turning up in total for the two home games.

The poor weather got worse, especially in the south of England, and icy conditions caused the cancellation of Chelsea's next three games. By the time the Blues returned from practice games in Scotland and, bizarrely, Iraq (see Chapter Thirteen, *Chelsea on Tour*) they were 11 points behind new leaders Everton, although they had four games in hand.

Two wins and two draws in the first three weeks of March kept the Blues hot on the heels of the Toffees, who were now joined at the top of the table by their Merseyside rivals Liverpool. However, the 1-1 home draw with QPR brought more bad injury news when goalkeeper Eddie Niedzwiecki, who had been enjoying an outstanding season, suffered a cruciate ligament injury which would eventually end his career.

"I just went to catch the ball and landed awkwardly," Eddie recalled later. "Big Steve Wicks was off balance too and fell on top of me. It was all completely accidental. After three or four minutes the pain went away so I played on. But when I tried to take a goal-kick my knee went completely." Surprisingly, the pint-sized David Speedie took over the gloves for the remainder of the match and was promptly lobbed by David Kerslake for Rangers' equaliser.

Three days later, with Steve Francis filling in for Niedzwiecki, the Blues won 1-0 at Southampton thanks to a long-range goal by Colin Pates. Incredibly, Chelsea were back in action the following afternoon at Wembley for the final of the Full Members Cup, a competition originally conceived by Ken Bates as an extra revenue-raiser for clubs not competing in Europe. Of course, after Heysel that now meant all English clubs, but very few showed any interest in the new tournament. Indeed, of the 21 teams who entered only five – Chelsea, Manchester City, Coventry, West Brom and Oxford – were members of the First Division.

At least the final, between the Blues and Manchester City, promised to be an entertaining match. The early rounds of the competition had seen some pitiful attendances – only 3,714 fans, for example, watched Chelsea's 3-1 victory over Charlton at Selhurst Park in October – but a huge crowd of 67,236 crammed into Wembley for a final between two of English football's great under-achievers.

Having stayed overnight at the Posthouse Hotel, Heathrow, the Chelsea party arrived at the Twin Towers to be mobbed by excited fans – many of whom had never seen the Blues play at the home of English football before. The team chosen by John Hollins showed just one change from the side which had won at The Dell the previous day, Colin Lee reverting to his old striker's position in place of the injured Kerry Dixon.

"I'd not played for a while and I wasn't 100 per cent fit," says Lee. "But David Speedie got a massive lift because he knew we had this understanding and he loved playing up front with me. We were determined to win it – it was one of those cups nobody initially wanted to be in, but once you got to the semis everyone wanted to be in it."

Unusually for a Wembley final, both teams took to the field in a change strip: Chelsea in their third-choice white kit and Manchester City in black-and-red stripes. After conceding an early goal to a City side that had played in a Manchester derby the previous day, Chelsea completely dominated the game. Speedie scored a hat-trick – the first in a Wembley final since Geoff Hurst's slightly more famous trio in the 1966 World Cup final – and Lee twice as the Blues cruised into an apparently unassailable 5-1 lead. Three City goals in the final minutes including one at the wrong end by Doug Rougvie, though, had the Chelsea fans anxiously checking their watches. After the final whistle, life-long Blues fan Sir Richard Attenborough presented the cup to Colin Pates. As well as their medals the players also received a £1,000 bonus each for winning a trophy which was largely derided by the media as a 'Mickey Mouse cup'.

It may not have been the FA or even the Milk Cup but, for the fans, victory at Wembley was a huge thrill. "The Full Members Cup final in 1986 was a hilarious highlight of the period," recalls Tim Harrison. "It was a great game with an absurd, ludicrous number of goals and a fantastic atmosphere. Rougvie scored an own goal and there were great chants of 'Rougvie scored at Wembley!' I took my missus to the match, and she never came to another game for 10 years because she was terrified of a police horse that backed into her and nearly crushed her against a wall. But it was a terrific day."

The following week, on a high after their Wembley triumph, the Blues approached the Easter programme in fine spirits. "We feel we have a very good chance of winning the league title if we can come through our two Easter matches without dropping any points," announced Pates. As it turned out, the Blues didn't pick up a single point from the games and effectively dropped out of the title race.

Worse than that, they were humiliated in both games against London rivals. Still lacking Dixon, Chelsea were thrashed 4-0 by fellow championship challengers West Ham on Easter Saturday on a bumpy, rutted Stamford Bridge pitch. "Surely, Chelsea can forget about championships, after this," wrote Deryk Brown in the *Sunday Times*. "They began this derby as London's favourite sons; they ended it in pieces." Two days later, the Blues suffered an even more devastating defeat, 6-0 on the plastic at QPR.

Writing in the programme, Colin Pates, who somewhat strangely had been named 'Man of the Match' at Loftus Road, summed up the mood in the dressing room by admitting that he was "still in a state of shock". The Chelsea skipper accepted that West Ham had won "fair and the square" but the psychological damage inflicted on the Chelsea camp by the drubbing at Loftus Road was still evident. "Frankly, to analyse that defeat would create enormous self doubts, and we could do without them at the moment," Pates told fans. For his part, Hollins preferred not to talk about the games, instead concentrating on the magnificent support of the fans at QPR: "I won't go into details about why things happened as they did," he wrote. "I will just say that this kind of support gives us all the determination we need to make us ensure that results like last week's never happen again."

Unsurprisingly, the chairman also had his say about the games, admitting that Easter had been "an unmitigated disaster". But he also called for a sense of perspective. "These are the same players that caused people to talk of us achieving the treble two months ago," he pointed out. "Frankly, we were never that good, but neither are we as bad as last week's results suggest."

With Steve Francis' confidence shot to pieces by the maulings, Hollins moved swiftly to sign goalkeeper Tony Godden on loan from West Brom. Two good 2-1 wins at Manchester United – Kerry Dixon scoring both goals to get on the scoresheet for the first time since his return from injury – and West Ham raised hopes that the Blues could have some say in the last month of title race, but it was not to be. Chelsea picked up a just a single point from their last five fixtures and finished in sixth place. "We had a chance but it was a lot to ask to actually win the championship," says Hollins. "We lost important players right through the middle of the team. Our squad wasn't particularly big: we had young players, but not of the quality of the players that were missing." Gallingly for Chelsea fans, a lone Kenny Dalglish goal at Stamford Bridge at the beginning of May was enough to give Liverpool the title in front of the Blues' highest home crowd of the season, 43,900.

For the last game of the season, at home to mid-table Watford, Hollins handed debuts to rookie goalkeeper Les Fridge, signed from Highland club Inverness Thistle; John McNaught, a dishevelled-looking midfielder with an equally untidy playing style signed from Hamilton Academicals; and Gordon Durie, a fast and direct striker recruited from Hibs for £381,000. Predictably, the mix of old and new faces played like strangers, the 17-year-old Fridge endured a nightmare and the Blues crashed to another heavy defeat, this time by five goals to one.

Among the players to make way for the debutants was Kerry Dixon, and he wasn't happy about being dropped. "To be honest, the cast was set after that game," he says. "OK, you might say it's only an end of season game but to me it was absolutely important. To me it was a hurtful decision, the World Cup was coming up and I wanted to go to Mexico. John Hollins said, 'I'm resting you' and I said, 'But I want to play,' but he insisted I was being rested. Fine, it's the manager's decision, but it told me what I needed to know."

Hollins didn't know it, but Dixon's disenchantment was a foretaste of the full-scale player discontent which would erupt the following season. The signs for the coming campaign, however, looked promising. After two consecutive top-six finishes the Blues were established as one of the First Division's better teams, although still not on a par with the league's two dominant forces, Liverpool and Everton.

In an attempt to bridge the gap, Hollins strengthened his squad by signing a number of players over the close season. After seven years away from the Bridge, Steve Wicks rejoined Chelsea from QPR for a club record £450,000. The player seemed impressed by the changed set-up, saying, "When I was last here there were a lot of moaners. Many of the people weren't happy. It's a lot more professional now." Another arrival was Roy

A SERIOUS CASE OF THE BLUES

Wegerle, a flamboyant South African forward who had been playing in American football with Tampa Bay Rowdies. With Tony Godden's loan move being made permanent and Durie and McNaught also relative newcomers, Hollins had added competition to every department of the squad. Meanwhile, players on the move included Paul Canoville, who joined Reading for £50,000, and Dale Jasper, who moved to Brighton on a free transfer.

As many managers have discovered, a big squad brings with it its own inherent difficulties – a fact Watford manager Graham Taylor alerted listeners to on a Radio Two season preview programme. "One of Chelsea's biggest problems will probably be deciding what is their best team," he argued. "You do have to have strength but when you have too many players it is very easy to make changes and you sometimes lose sight, or stop recognising, what your strongest 11 or 12 is. It could be that Chelsea might fall into that trap."

Off the pitch, meanwhile, Chelsea announced the termination of its contract with kit suppliers le coq sportif. "We were far from satisfied about having to wear a red away strip last season, which came about because le coq were not able to supply the more familiar yellow," explained Ken Bates. Instead, the club decided to produce its own kit as part of the Chelsea Collection – 'a fashionable range of clothes and accessories for fashionable people' according to the publicity material, although whether the gaudy and lurid designs could ever be described as 'fashionable' was a moot point. The range, which featured a lot of bluish-green 'jade' after the colour was strangely chosen for Chelsea's second-choice kit, also included a new club badge. To the dismay of traditionalists, the famous rampant lion was no more, replaced instead by a snarling feline leaping out from the letters 'CFC'. Nonetheless, the Chelsea Collection of replica kits, T-shirts and tracksuit tops sold well, with the club taking £300,000 worth of orders in the first four months.

In a change from previous pre-seasons, the squad did only two days of running before embarking on a protracted series of warm-up games. "The new approach has proved quite successful," said Hollins. "The players have looked hungry for the ball and their control is better." The results, though, were dire: after victories over local teams in Wales and Ireland, the Blues lost four consecutive friendlies to Hibs, Plymouth, Torquay and Crystal Palace.

Summer games are a notoriously poor indicator of future success or failure, but on this occasion Chelsea took their unimpressive pre-season form into the league season. For the opening game of the campaign against Norwich, Hollins tried out a three-pronged strike-force of Dixon, Durie and Speedie and left Nevin on the bench. The new alignment failed to gel, the Blues created few chances and had to settle for a dull 0-0 draw. After a draw at Oxford and defeat at Sheffield Wednesday, Nevin returned for the second home game against Coventry. Again, the Blues lacked spark and the result, another 0-0 draw, was greeted with boos by a poor attendance of under 12,000.

Four days later a 3-1 defeat at home to Luton generated even fiercer terrace criticism and plunged Chelsea into a relegation zone which, as part of a plan to reduce the First Division to 20 teams inside two years, had been widened to include a 'play-off' position. The idea, which was inspired by the 'Test matches' of the late nineteenth century, was that the side finishing fourth from bottom in the First Division would compete with three Second Division teams for the last remaining top flight place as a tension-soaked postscript to the normal league season.

While the Blues' home form remained a worry, away results picked up. Excellent wins at Tottenham and Manchester United, a game in which Tony Godden saved two penalties, sandwiched a numbing 6-2 home defeat by Nottingham Forest – the first time Chelsea had conceded six goals at home since 1967.

As Graham Taylor had predicted, the Chelsea line-up had already seen numerous changes. For example, three players - Colin Pates, youth product John Millar and Doug Rougvie – appeared at left back in the opening two months of the season; Bumstead, Hazard and Spackman were disputing the two central midfield roles; while the number 11 shirt seemed to be rotated on a Buggins' turn basis. But, after a 1-0 home defeat by Charlton at the beginning of October, Hollins decided to give the team a real shake-up.

To the surprise of the fans, three established figures – Joe McLaughlin, David Speedie and Nigel Spackman – were left out for the visit of York City in the Milk Cup. All three players reacted to being dropped by asking for a transfer, although Speedie's absence from the teamsheet was more of a catalyst for his request than the prime cause. The Scot's main gripe went back to the summer when he was informed by the football agent Dennis Roach that Spanish giants Barcelona, then managed by Terry Venables, were interested in signing him. "I told Dennis that I had a six-year deal with Chelsea and I didn't want to leave," says Speedie. "But I also said that he should speak to John Hollins about it. I asked Hollins to speak to Ken Bates and then, two weeks later, I went to see the chairman. He told me that John Hollins hadn't spoken to him which I felt showed a lack of respect, and after that I couldn't see myself staying under that regime. Then the story came out that I was trying to negotiate my own deal with Barcelona, which was bullshit."

John Hollins, though, strongly disputes this version of events. "It's absolute rubbish!" he claims. "I brought Speedie into the office – Bates was there as well – and I rang Terry Venables and he'd never heard of it. He'd already got Steve Archibald, Gary Lineker and Mark Hughes – so no chance! Dixon and Speedie had the same agent and if I didn't play one of them, after Durie came in, the player was always off to play for someone else. If I didn't play one of them there was discontent. The players, which they always do, think of themselves first – they don't think of the team. But if the players are playing well they don't have to worry; the trouble is they weren't at that point."

Apart from the Barcelona business, Speedie was also fed up with the coaching style of

Ernie Walley. "I didn't dislike him as such," he says, "but I thought his methods, the way he coached and the way he treated players were all wrong. I told the chairman that I couldn't play for this guy and that one of us would have to go. He said he was backing his manager.

"We called him Sergeant-Major Walley. He had a squad of players who were disciplined and professional and very fit. Yes, we went out sometimes and painted the town red but at the appropriate time. Ernie changed everything when he came in, the whole coaching and training regime we'd been used to. He was a disciplinarian. We weren't allowed to swear in training – if we did we got sent off. It was the same if we argued with decisions in practice matches. At times we felt he was winding us up in training by making controversial decisions which were designed to make us argue with him. It got to the stage where I didn't want to get out of bed in the morning to go to training. Everyone who had played in the Second Division championship-winning team felt the same, Kerry Dixon, Pat Nevin and Nigel Spackman to name three. They all had issues with Ernie but I was probably the one who was most outspoken about him at the time."

"Ernie Walley was very strict," confirms Spackman who, according to press reports at the time, was also in dispute with the club over his salary. "He was completely the opposite to what John (Hollins) was when he was coaching. So players inevitably became disgruntled and disheartened. I was one of them."

All of which raises the question of why the Chelsea boss appointed Walley in the first place. "I needed someone strong and disciplined," says Hollins. "At the time that's what I felt we needed. It had been very casual before I got there; you've got to have discipline. You see that now: if anyone steps out of line they get jumped on, perhaps we were a little bit too early with that attitude. At the time that's what was needed and that's what we did."

As if a mutinous squad wasn't bad enough, Hollins was also unhappy about John Neal's role at the club. In the summer the former Chelsea manager had stepped down from the board of directors only to return to the club as a 'consultant' on a salary of £40,000 a year. This development did not go down well with Hollins, who felt that Neal's continued presence at the club undermined his own position. "One of the major problems was having the manager and the assistant manager still at the club," he says.

"They did more damage to me than anybody. When someone says 'Boss' and two people turn round you can't have it. Perhaps after the first year I should have moved on, but you're always wiser in hindsight."

Results in the autumn of 1986 did not improve with the controversial team changes made by Hollins. Three days after a first home win of the season over Manchester City, Blues fans attending Chelsea's shock 2-1 Littlewoods Cup exit at Fourth Division Cardiff City chanted for their manager to resign. Even Hollins himself admitted that this defeat, after a Keith Jones penalty had put the Blues a goal up, represented a new low. "This was the most disappointing performance since I became manager," he said. "We just didn't compete."

At least there was better news for the Chelsea boss two days later when Ken Bates sacked John Neal from his consultancy position for a 'lack of loyalty'. The former Blues manager paid the price for publicly criticising his successor and the chairman, telling the *Evening Standard*: "I left the club in perfect shape and I don't know how they have managed to let it go wrong."

"I think Hollins wanted me out of the way because I was the one with all the respect from the players still," Neal observed later. "They'd all come to me and it was a bit embarrassing because he wasn't consulted. When John came in he changed things round. He got a coach in who I didn't rate and these people tried to rule with an iron fist. But you can't throw a fist at someone like Pat Nevin!"

With Neal finally out of the picture, Ken Bates issued the dreaded vote of confidence to his manager in his programme notes for the visit of Watford. "To the avoidance of any doubt John Hollins has my full support and also that of most players despite the unsettling influence of a few people both inside and outside the club," he wrote. There were also harsh words for some players who "seek scapegoats elsewhere rather than examine their own inherent weaknesses". Those weaknesses were again on show, as the team struggled to break down a well-organised Watford defence and were held to yet another 0-0 draw.

Struggling in the relegation zone with a batch of clubs including Alex Ferguson's Manchester United, Manchester City and Newcastle, Chelsea were now in full-blown 'crisis' – at least according to the media. It didn't help that negative news stories seeped out of the Bridge on an almost daily basis. First, fans were informed that a behind-closed-doors practice match between the first team and a reserve side featuring many of the malcontents had been stopped prematurely by Hollins with the stiffs 3-0 up. Then came news that the electronic Bridge clock would in future be turned off after 80 minutes to stop the players nervously checking how much time was left.

The Blues desperately needed a home win to lift the spirits of the players and fans and the visit of bottom-of-the-table Newcastle in late November seemed to offer the ideal opportunity. The Geordies hadn't won in London for two and a half years and looked to be heading for another defeat when Gordon Durie put Chelsea ahead. Once again, though, the Blues could not hold their lead and ended up losing 3-1. Throughout the second half fans called for the return of David Speedie, Nigel Spackman and Mick Hazard, all of whom had been left out, and there were further demands for the head of Hollins. Even Newcastle skipper Glenn Roeder admitted to being surprised by the Chelsea line-up. "Right back Darren Wood was in the centre of midfield, central defender Colin Pates was on the left side of midfield – a position I know he hates – and left back Doug Rougvie was at right back," he pointed out. "They gave everything, but I didn't think they looked comfortable."

On the same day as the Newcastle defeat a strong Chelsea reserve side, featuring Speedie, Spackman, Wicks and Hazard, won 9-2 at Reading to put the Blues top of the Football Combination. The squad's strength in depth was clear, but the lack of cohesion in the first team was equally apparent. The grumblings among certain players continued, with Mick Hazard publicly criticising Hollins' team selections. Another player to have grave reservations about the manager's overall strategy was Colin Lee, who spent most of the season watching from the sidelines with a hamstring injury. "I felt that John wanted to produce his own side and change what I thought was a fantastic team too early," he says. "I felt that when certain players were fit they played, because they were the best. But John tried to change that; I'm sure that he wanted to say over a period of time he was going to produce his own team. I think that was a major mistake at Chelsea. I think the team was well good enough, it was capable of holding its own because there was a magnificent understanding throughout the team."

On the advice of Gordon Taylor, the secretary of the PFA, Chelsea's disgruntled players met Hollins for a frank discussion in the build-up to the Full Members Cup tie at West Ham. The upshot was that Speedie and Spackman were restored to the side, while John Bumstead also returned from injury. With eight stalwarts from the Second Division championship team reunited, the Blues put in an excellent performance and deservedly won 2-1.

Hollins had emerged from the 'clear the air' meeting saying, "All differences have been resolved in as much as everyone knows what they have to do, which is to win as many matches as possible." That, though, proved easier said than done. In their next home game the Blues crashed 4-0 at home to long-ball specialists Wimbledon, after Doug Rougvie was sent off in the opening stages for head-butting the Dons' abrasive striker John Fashanu. "I'm at rock bottom," admitted the normally chirpy Hollins afterwards, while Ken Bates issued a veiled warning by saying, "It may be a hiccup. Let us hope it doesn't develop into whooping cough."

Two weeks later, following a 3-0 defeat at Anfield in a televised match, the Blues emerged from the Stamford Bridge tunnel for the London derby with Tottenham with their shirts bearing a new sponsor's name. Marketed as 'the weight conscious cuppa', Bai Lin tea was the creation of the notorious Australian conman Peter Foster, who in years to come would shoot to prominence in the long-running 'Cherie-gate' saga. The so-called 'slimming aid' was soon revealed to be entirely bogus so it was, perhaps, fortunate for Chelsea's credibility that the club's association with the product only lasted a handful of games. Later in the season the names of Ken Bates' Grange Farm and the sportswear company Simod also featured on Chelsea's shirts for selected matches, finally providing the club with some sponsorship income fully three years after the short-lived deal with Gulf Air.

The programme for the game against Spurs made fascinating reading. While Hollins bemoaned a long injury list and Ken Bates admitted "some of the performances this season have made me feel like swearing", skipper Colin Pates lambasted the press criticism of his manager. "Some sections of the media have gone way over the top recently with regard to John Hollins," he wrote, referring specifically to a 'Shall-we-sack-John?' phoneline poll in *The Sun*. "It is disgusting. In some ways it is laughable; the kind of thing you expect to read in *The Beano*. You just can't take it seriously. Such trash doesn't affect the way we play but it does grind you a bit when every time you pick up a paper you read the same old rubbish."

The following day's papers made equally unpleasant reading after a 2-0 defeat, the Blues' sixth home reverse in 10 league games, sent them to the bottom of the table.

Questioned about his future at the club, Hollins responded passionately. "Chelsea are my blood," he declared. "I am not going to resign or run away from this – I am going to get it right."

Chelsea had been slightly unlucky against Spurs – a Nigel Spackman shot had hit the bar and clearly bounced down over the line, but to the players' dismay the referee waved play on. The Blues desperately needed a break and they got one at Southampton on Boxing Day, where John Bumstead popped up to lob the winner in the 87th minute. Victory at The Dell provided a massive confidence boost and comprehensive wins over the festive period against Aston Villa and QPR lifted Chelsea out of the danger zone.

The three consecutive victories kick-started Chelsea's season and the Blues were eventually to pull comfortably clear of the relegation area. "The difference in the second part of the season was the players forgetting about themselves and getting their mind on the job," says Hollins. "It's like anything else, if they concentrate on what they're doing the spirit at the club comes through."

The atmosphere at the Bridge may have been improved but it was far from perfect. Speedie, McLaughlin, Wicks, Hazard and Rougvie were all playing while on the transfer list, while Kerry Dixon was unsettled by Arsenal's reported interest in him. Chelsea's attempt to lure Leicester striker Alan Smith to the Bridge by offering Mick Hazard and Kevin McAllister in part exchange also suggested Dixon's future at the Bridge was uncertain. Asked if he had informed Dixon of his interest in Smith, Hollins replied curtly: "Why should I? It had nothing to do with him."

The Smith deal fell through, but the Blues did manage to sign versatile St Mirren defender Steve Clarke for £422,000 and his calm assurance at the back was an important factor in the team's much improved goals against tally. Clarke, however, was nonplussed by the poor team spirit he encountered at the Bridge. "I couldn't quite believe the atmosphere when I got down to Chelsea, cliques here, cliques there," he said later. "The discipline was poor. They must have had arguments before I signed because there were people who just didn't talk to each other."

A SERIOUS CASE OF THE BLUES

Following a fourth round FA Cup defeat at Watford, Hollins again made significant changes to the side. Nigel Spackman was sold to Liverpool for £400,000, fringe players Steve Francis and Robert Isaac joined Reading and Brighton respectively, 18-year-old goalkeeper Roger Freestone was recruited from Newport for £95,000 while Roy Wegerle and young reserve striker Colin West were both given extended run-outs up front. For the first time in his Chelsea career, discounting the end of season game against Watford, Kerry Dixon was dropped and found himself playing in the reserves along with a number of other big names.

"Eddie, Pates, McLaughlin, Speedie and myself went down to Ipswich for a reserve game," recalls Kerry. "John McNaught, who was renowned for not having the best taste in clothes, turned up in a blue suit and bright red shoes. He got the mickey taken out of him by everyone. Then, Speedo came out in the warm-up. The Ipswich fans were laughing but we didn't know what about until we saw McNaught chasing Speedie who was running around the muddy pitch with his red shoes on. It was a hilarious sight.

"It doesn't sound a very professional attitude but it probably summed up the mood of the players at the time. It was hard to get your enthusiasm up for playing in the reserves, there was a lot of disappointment, things weren't going right for us and we tended to show our displeasure in that sort of way. It wasn't ideal but, I'm afraid, that's what happened."

All in all, it had not been a season to remember with any pleasure: player discontent, a manager under siege from the press and a section of the fans, and a brush with relegation. Yet, in the second half of the campaign the Blues had showed top six form to climb up the table, losing just once at home in 12 matches. As they settled back to watch the cricket and tennis over the summer months, Chelsea fans could have been excused for thinking that the worst was over and their club was back on an even keel. The coming season would reveal just how misguided that complacent assumption was.

CHAPTER THIRTEEN
CHELSEA ON TOUR

G iven the violent history of Iraq in the first few years of the new millennium it now seems extraordinary to think that the country was once safe enough for Chelsea to go there on a mid-season trip. Safe, though, is perhaps a relative term as when the Blues travelled out to Baghdad in March 1986 the Iran-Iraq war had been raging for six years and showed no signs of ending. The hostilities had been triggered by a dispute over the borders between the two countries, and a fear within each country of interference by the other in its internal affairs. The fighting that followed, much of it on barren desert terrain, would eventually cost half a million lives on both sides. And if the bloody conflict itself wasn't enough to cast doubts about the wisdom of the Blues' jaunt, there was also the small matter that Iraq's President was one Saddam Hussein – then little known outside the Middle East, but fast acquiring a reputation as a brutal and ruthless dictator.

Surprisingly, or perhaps not, when the players were informed about the trip few of them thought twice before packing their bags and heading off to the airport. "Only Pat Nevin had reservations about going," says John Bumstead, "because he was the only one up on the news." In the event, the sole player who stayed behind was Nigel Spackman, but that was because his wife was expecting the couple's first child.

The tour, which was sponsored by Chelsea's first kit sponsors Gulf Air, took place during a period of appalling weather in England which had led to the postponement of the Blues' last three fixtures against Manchester United, Arsenal and Watford. In the previous four weeks the team, which was challenging strongly for the First Division title, had managed to play just one game, a hastily arranged friendly away to Glasgow Rangers. As well as providing some much-needed cash for the club, the trip to Iraq would give the players some equally welcome match practice. In addition, the Blues' opponents in Baghdad, an Iraqi national selection, were expected to provide John Hollins' men with a suitably stern test as the country had qualified for that year's World Cup finals in Mexico.

The squad arrived in the Iraqi capital via Jordan. "Baghdad was the weirdest place I've been to," recalls John Bumstead. "Pat Nevin announced that he was going to the local market to see what it was like, and he was back inside five minutes looking as white as a ghost – he didn't say anything, but we reckoned it was because he'd had his bottom pinched."

Nevin, though, insists that he spent half a day marvelling at the intricately woven carpets and ornate hubble-bubbles in the labyrinthine Baghdad bazaar. "I was out for hours with John Millar," he says. "We may have come back looking a wee bit frazzled but that was because there were so many guys around with machine guns."

At least on this point, Bummers and Patsy are in agreement. "Baghdad was just full of army blokes," remembers Johnny B. "On every street corner there were blokes in army uniform carrying machine guns. They all had black moustaches and looked like Saddam Hussein, so I can easily believe those stories about him having body doubles.

"One of the weirdest things was just watching the Iraqi TV. I was rooming with Colin Pates and we were flicking through the channels on the TV. The Iran-Iraq war came on and it was pretty gory, bodies lying everywhere. Then we flicked over and it was Leslie Crowther presenting *The Price is Right* with sub-titles in Arabic..."

"It was a wonderful, fantastic trip," continues Pat Nevin. "I missed the bus from the hotel to the ground and ended up getting this Mercedes with these three shady-looking characters driving me through the middle of Baghdad. I remember thinking, 'They could be kidnapping me' – I didn't have a clue what was going on. Anyway, I got there and we had to wait an hour and a half in the middle of the pitch in the baking sun for Saddam to turn up. In the end he didn't show, but he sent his brother. While we were waiting it was time for prayers so all their team and the whole stadium knelt down and faced Mecca. We didn't know what to do – whether to get down on our knees as well or carry on doing keepy-uppy. We kind of just sat there and felt out of place."

The game eventually kicked off in front of 15,000 spectators and Chelsea took a first-half lead through Joe McLaughlin. The Iraqis equalised in the second half and the match finished in a diplomatic 1-1 draw. "Iraq's national players were a keen bunch," reported Colin Pates in his captain's programme notes, "and gave us a good work-out. Although not having the technical ability of a Football League player, they couldn't be faulted for enthusiasm."

After the game the touring party was invited to a reception at the British Embassy in Baghdad. "They laid on a decent spread for us and some drinks," remembers John Bumstead. "The Embassy building was a great big place and, at one point in the evening, me and Dale Jasper were both trying to find the toilet. We opened this door and it was just a cupboard, but it was filled from the floor to the ceiling with crates of Johnny Walker whisky. It was a bit like stumbling over Arthur Daley's lock-up in *Minder*! I don't think the Embassy staff were boozing the nights away, I think they used the whisky as currency with the local Arabs."

For many of the players the Embassy party was one of the few highlights of the trip. To say that they were unimpressed with what they saw in Baghdad would be a major understatement. For David Speedie, in particular, the flight back home couldn't come soon enough. "Iraq was a shit-hole," he says. "Our hotel was alright but the rest of the place was a dump. It was the worst trip I've ever been on. We went to a local English bar for the expat workforce, had some beers there and played darts and pool. That was OK, but Baghdad as a whole was a shit-hole. We only went there to make some money for the club."

If the Iraqi trip was the most exotic undertaken by Chelsea during the period covered by this book, the most enjoyable was probably the Blues' tour of North America in 1977, a few weeks after Eddie McCreadie's young side had won promotion back to the First Division. The 10-day itinerary included games against Seattle Sounders, Vancouver Island All Stars, San Jose Earthquakes and Los Angeles Aztecs and, more importantly, allowed the squad to unwind after an arduous and tension-filled season.

On a high from their successful campaign, the players were in buoyant spirits from the word go and it didn't take long for them to get up to the usual footballers' pranks. "David Hay had a set of false teeth and he lost them within three hours of take-off," remembers Tommy Langley, who made the trip at the last moment after another player dropped out injured. "I don't quite know how it happened but he and Ronnie Harris were mucking around, he went into the toilet and his teeth fell out. Although he looked everywhere, he couldn't find them so he was toothless for the rest of the trip, which was a laugh."

The Blues kicked off their tour with a 2-0 defeat against Seattle Sounders, who included former Tottenham and Wales defender Mike England and future Manchester City manager Mel Machin in their line-up. From there the party travelled the short distance over the Canadian border to Vancouver, where they had an easy 3-0 victory over the All Stars. Four days later goals by Steve Finnieston and Bill Garner secured a 2-1 victory over San Jose Earthquakes before the team moved on to the final tour destination, Los Angeles.

"We had a great game against the Aztecs in the Los Angeles Coliseum," remembers Graham Wilkins. "Robbie Resenbrick, the great Dutch striker, was playing for them but we beat them 3-1. After the game a few of us were in a bar in LA. Me, Steve Finnieston and another player who shall remain nameless were all as drunk as anything. Steve went for a piss and, while he was away, the other player pissed in Steve's drink. When Steve got back he drank the whole lot. We started cracking up but we didn't know the woman behind the bar had seen what had happened and had called the police. All of a sudden we got a tap on the shoulder, we turned round and saw two big American policemen. They pulled us over to one side and took all our names and UK addresses. They were about to book the player who had pissed in the drink but one of the policemen was a rugby player and he found the incident so funny he told him, 'This time, I'll let you off.' Then, motioning to Jock, he said, 'You go and wash your mouth out.' Steve was gutted; in fact, I think he was sick."

The trip also saw some of the *Carry On*-style bedroom antics which some of the younger players had first got up to on an earlier Chelsea tour to Australia. Again, Graham Wilkins is the narrator and again the identity of the player at the centre of the drama must remain cloaked in secrecy: "Me and another of the lads spotted this Chelsea player trying to pull an Australian girl in the bar. We could see where things were leading so we went up to his bedroom and locked the door from the inside. Then we hid in the wardrobe behind the player's clothes. He wasn't the smartest of men and, although we were out in Australia for a month, he had just one shirt there and a pair of trousers. When the player came in with the girl we could see everything, because the wardrobe had slats in it. We couldn't stop laughing so in the end we just burst out of the wardrobe. The woman looked shit scared and rushed straight out of the door; the player was horrified, panicked and jumped naked straight out of the window. Fortunately, the room we were in was only one floor up and was above the swimming pool."

Such side-splitting japes were generally reserved for post-season tours – pre-season trips, with their emphasis on rigorous training and lung-bursting cross-country runs, were more serious affairs. Throughout the late Seventies and Eighties, Sweden was the preferred venue for Chelsea's pre-season preparations, the club making half a dozen trips to the country that gave the world Abba, Ikea and the Volvo.

"One pre-season we went to a training camp in Sweden," recalls Mickey Droy. "The complex had great facilities but it was in the middle of nowhere, stuck in a forest about 20 miles from the nearest town. Geoff Hurst and Bobby Gould had chosen it specially because there would be no distractions for us.

"When we got there, we thought 'Oh, shit!' because there was absolutely nothing to do in the evenings after training. There wasn't even a TV and there was no bar. All you could do was read or play snooker. But what Geoff and Bobby didn't know was that the Swedish Women's Olympic team was staying there as well. When they saw them their faces dropped, they weren't too happy. They'd done all that secret planning but they'd overlooked that 40 or 50 super-fit Scandinavian women would be staying at the same place as us. We were training three times a day so it was nice to chat to the girls in the evening and have some female company. They all spoke English so there were no communication problems. There were a lot of good-looking girls in the group and they all looked fitter than us. We were banned from going into the town – but we managed to arrange with a cab driver to bring us in a few beers. We didn't have a big drink up with the girls, but we felt we deserved a couple of beers after the hard work we'd put in."

The following year Chelsea toured south Sweden under new manager John Neal and then, in 1982, returned to the country for a third year running. This time, the Blues based themselves in northern Sweden, playing three matches against local opposition and one against Finnish side IFK Mariehamn. The tour was unexceptional enough, except for one thing: it saw the birth of the classic Chelsea chant, 'One man went to mow'.

Only a handful of Blues fans were following the team, but one of the supporters out in Sweden was the legendary Mick Greenaway, the creator of the famous 'Zigger Zagger' Shed chant back in the late Sixties. Devoted Chelsea supporter Punky Al was another member of the small party. "We were at a train station going to a place called Stroemsund, where Chelsea where playing, and Greenaway produced this tape of himself singing *One Man Went to Mow*," recalls Al. "I've no idea what inspired him to do the tape, I'm not even sure he intended it to become a football chant. He may just have done it for a laugh. But the rest of us who were on the tour picked it up and it carried along from there. Then, it spread the following year onto the terraces.

"We toured south Sweden in 1981 and there were about 150 Chelsea fans on that trip," continues Punky Al. "In 1982 the club toured north Sweden and a lot of people turned their noses up at going to Sweden again so we were down to about 30. We were struggling for money because a beer there was about three quid a pint when back in England it was 50p or whatever. I think the players knew it was expensive for us because, after one game, Mick Fillery and Gary Chivers came over to our table and put a load of beers in front of us. That was a nice gesture by them."

Meanwhile, the small band of fans was attracting the attention of the local Swedish population, few of whom could quite understand what the motley crew was doing in a remote part of the country which attracted few overseas tourists. "The reaction from the locals was curiosity," says Punky Al. "There was no hooliganism, nobody went for a row or anything like that. They couldn't believe we'd come all that way to watch what they thought were just training games. We were interviewed on one local radio channel and we had to sing a few songs for them after we'd answered their questions."

After a seven-year gap, Chelsea returned to Scandinavia in 1989 for four pre-season matches against Swedish and Norwegian opposition. On a roll from their successful promotion campaign a few months earlier, the Blues made light work of their part-time opponents, banging in a total of 18 goals while wracking up four comfortable victories.

As was usually the case on these trips, Chelsea manager Bobby Campbell had booked the team into an isolated hotel many miles from the nearest sizeable town. "We were staying in a hotel in the middle of nowhere," confirms Clive Wilson, "but on the Wednesday or Thursday night the whole of the nearest village came to the hotel for a disco or pop concert. We were staying at the top of the hotel, and the entertainment was down at the bottom. There was a normal way down the stairs but Bobby Campbell used to have Gwyn Williams or Ian Porterfield on sentry duty, looking out for us. However, there was also another way down through the fire escape which took you through the kitchens. We went down that way to see what was going on, mingle for a while and then go back up again. I don't think anybody got caught and it was good fun. There were a lot of nice looking women, so we'd have a beer or three and have a dance. The Scots were the keenest, because they liked their drink. One night we raided the kitchens. Dave Beasant had just arrived from Wimbledon via Newcastle and brought a bit of the Crazy Gang spirit with him. We were in the kitchens at four o'clock in the morning and Dave was trying to cook something, because we all felt hungry after being up so late."

The night owls avoided detection on that occasion but, nine years earlier, Chelsea's pre-season trip to Scotland resulted in a major falling out between players and management after some of the touring party broke a curfew imposed by Blues boss Geoff Hurst.

"We went to Scotland and stayed in a lovely hotel at one of the famous golf courses, St Andrews or Gleneagles," recalls Tommy Langley. "We had a pre-season game against Hearts the next day. We had our meal and then we went out to a pub about half a mile away. We weren't stupid enough to go out and have loads of beers but as we went to the bar Geoff and Bobby popped in to the pub and went 'Got yer! You're all fined two weeks wages.' We'd only just walked in, although some of the other players were already in the pub drinking, and they didn't know if we were going to have an orange juice or a beer. I was actually going to have a beer. Looking back, they were within their rights. There wasn't a curfew per se, so it may have been a slight grey area; but it was pre-season and when you have a game the next day, you don't have a beer the night before. But the way they did it upset a lot of people." Not that the players took the telling off lying down. According to one of the many accounts of this incident, young midfielder Timmy Elmes spoke for many of the players when he asked the management duo, "What do you expect us to do at night, play ping-pong?"

However, Hurst and Gould were livid at what they saw as the players' irresponsible behaviour and, the following day before the game with Hearts, made an unexpected announcement. "Geoff called us all together and said, 'Bobby and I are having nothing to do with this game, so it's down to you,'" recalls Gary Chivers. "Harry Medhurst, our physio, kind of took the team, saying 'We've got to do this and we've got to do that', and

Mickey Droy, Clive Walker and I spoke. Everyone who wanted to pretty much had their say and we went out there as normal, played quite well and won the game." Indeed, the 1-0 victory, with Colin Viljoen scoring the only goal in the second half, was the best result of the tour, which also included a 3-2 defeat by Raith and a 0-0 draw with Dundee United.

According to Chivers the players' fine was revoked, but Tommy Langley insists that he was docked two weeks wages. "I actually left the club the next month," he says, "and I remember going to get my last month's wages and finding out I'd been fined two weeks pay. Looking back, it was probably deserved because it was a bit of stupidity and it wasn't the thing to be doing, even though I don't think the boys would have gone mad if Geoff and Bobby hadn't showed up in the pub."

Hurst's hard-line approach to pre-season discipline contrasted with the somewhat subtler methods of his successor, John Neal. In 1983 the Chelsea boss took his revamped squad, which included new signings Kerry Dixon, Pat Nevin, Nigel Spackman, Joe McLaughlin and Eddie Niedzwiecki, to Aberystwyth for some vigorous pre-season training among the sand dunes which litter this part of the Welsh coast. The team's accommodation was spartan to say the least, as Neal had arranged for the club to hire halls of residence at the town's university.

"There were only four or five baths so there used to be long queues after training," remembers Pat Nevin. "We developed a rule that the once you'd turned the bath on it was yours. Anyway, Paul Canoville started running a bath then disappeared to get his various lotions. While he was away, Kerry Dixon must have nipped in and got in the bath because when I went past the door I could see the pair of them standing in the bath together completely naked and trading punches. It was a weird scene and got me wondering what I'd let myself in for. In the end big Mickey Droy went in there and kicked them both out."

After their hard training schedule and a couple of warm-up games against Aberystwyth and Newport the players looked forward to a Saturday night booze-up they'd been promised by their manager. "On most nights in pre-season we had to be in by 11.30," recalls John Bumstead. "But on the Saturday we played an evening game and John Neal announced there was no curfew and we could go and have a drink. What we didn't know, but he did, was that all the bars closed right on the dot of midnight because the pubs in Wales were dry on Sundays for religious reasons. So, we were in the pub after the game having just had a couple of drinks and looking forward to a 'lock in' when we were all kicked out. The next time, we knew what the score was so we made sure we got double rounds in."

Even when the league season started and the team went off on their travels around the country there was rarely a dull moment. "We had to be really careful whenever we stayed at a hotel," recalls David Speedie. "I would always bribe the receptionist not to give my room key to any of the others. If they ever got hold of it, you could guarantee that your room would be totally trashed. My speciality was turning over people's beds in the middle of the night – when they were still in them. Eddie Niedzwiecki and Nigel Spackman used to stitch each other up all the time – they were always wrecking each other's rooms, turning beds over, filling socks and shoes up with shaving foam and putting toothpaste in underpants. One evening, I walked along the ledge connecting my room to Nigel's and wrecked his room knowing he would blame Eddie for it. Sure enough, Spackman came in, discovered his room in a right state and marched straight to Eddie's. He turned the wardrobe upside down and chucked the mattress out of the window. I think he'd forgotten we were three floors up. Imagine that landing on top of you! In an odd way, though, it all helped to build team spirit."

And, that surely was the point. All the smashed up rooms, the juvenile giggling in wardrobes, the occasional illicit drinks in the early hours forged a camaraderie which could not be created simply on the training ground or in the dressing room. Ultimately, it didn't really matter whether the players were in Iraq, the USA, Sweden or in the less glamorous surroundings of Wales or Scotland: while they were together the bonds that united the team could only be strengthened, even if sometimes the way the players expressed that togetherness didn't go down well with the Chelsea management.

CHAPTER FOURTEEN
DISASTER!
1987-88

During the course of the turbulent 1986/87 season no fewer than 30 players had turned out for the Blues. Flux and change was a theme of the Hollins era and the high staff turnover continued during the close season. The most significant departure was that of David Speedie who joined Coventry for a (tribunal set) fee of £750,000. It wasn't quite the dream move to Barcelona that Speedie had hoped for, but all the same it brought to an end a frustrating and troubled final year at the Bridge for the Scottish international.

Other players to move on, meanwhile, included Doug Rougvie, who dropped down two divisions to play for Brighton in a deal worth £73,000; Colin Lee, who left for Brentford where he combined playing with a role as the club's youth development officer; Keith Dublin, who joined Rougvie on the south coast at the Goldstone Ground; goalkeeper Tony Godden, who was signed by Birmingham for £35,000; and Keith Jones, sold to Brentford for £40,000. A few weeks into the season straggle-haired midfielder John McNaught became another departure, personal problems prompting his return to Scotland where he briefly worked as a nightclub doorman before finding a new club.

Hollins used the money generated by these transfers to bring in three new players, all of whom arrived at the Bridge with good reputations. England Under-21 international Tony Dorigo, a fast and attack-minded left back, came from Aston Villa for a club record £475,000 to fill the gap left by the departures of Rougvie and Dublin. He was joined on the left flank by Manchester City's Clive Wilson, a skilful midfielder who could also play in defence. Finally, Kevin Wilson, the moustachioed Northern Ireland international striker, joined from Ipswich for £335,000.

As part of his overhaul of the team Hollins also appointed a new captain, passing Colin Pates' trademark red armband (Pates believed that a black one was 'morbid') to his central defensive partner Joe McLaughlin. "I'm quite looking forward to it," said McLaughlin, shortly after signing a new six-year contract with the club. "There's more to the job than just tossing the coin up. John has not given me any specific instructions. He has just asked me to keep everyone going in the game, give them plenty of encouragement and work to create the atmosphere we used to have." Pates, though, was less than happy with the way the switch was handled. "I'd told the gaffer, John Hollins, if he was going to change it, to let me know," he says. "But when I came back from holidaying in Spain I read in a paper at the airport that I wasn't skipper anymore, that Joe had taken over. John and I had strong words over that, although this cleared the air. Still, I never enjoyed it after that and I started to pick up a couple of injuries to my knee."

In a break with the routine of previous summers, pre-season training took place at Harlington rather than Aberystwyth. If the players were anticipating an easier time – Middlesex, after all, is not famed for its sand dunes – they were in for a rude surprise.

"Ernie Walley was hard on us," says Clive Wilson. "It makes you cringe to think what he had us doing that pre-season compared to what players do now. He would have us doing runs with people on our backs, for example. He was very strong, he wouldn't take any shit from the players. He was a sergeant major type, very old school; but that's what he knew and it was his way, or no way."

Chelsea's pre-season results – seven wins out of seven – suggested that Walley's lung-busting, muscle-straining sessions were already paying dividends. However, as the opposition included non-league sides Aldershot and Maidstone United as well as Colin Lee's Brentford, Blues fans were not getting too carried away. There were, though, other reasons for optimism, not least the fact that Steve Clarke and Pat Nevin played for a Football League side in a pre-season friendly at Wembley against a Rest of the World XI and did not look out of place in the company of Diego Maradona and Michel Platini.

A week before the season started 10,000 fans turned up for a 'Fun Day' at Stamford Bridge – a sign that expectations were high for the coming campaign and, more generally, that football was beginning to win back lost supporters after the post-Heysel dip in attendances. Encouragingly for the club, more than double that number were back at the Bridge the following Saturday for the opening game against Sheffield Wednesday.

Hollins, as ever, appeared upbeat about Chelsea's prospects in the club programme. "I sense that the players are keener than they have ever been before and I'm really optimistic about our chances this season," he wrote. "The new faces we have drafted in have added a new aspect to our game. We have brought in skilful players whose style I'm sure will get you tingling with appreciation." Ken Bates, writing in his always readable column, was equally optimistic. "I think it will take a good team to stop us," he said. "You should also be surprised by a more attacking style of play that should be more entertaining."

With so many changes at the Bridge, it was fitting that Chelsea should emerge from the tunnel for the game against Wednesday sporting a new strip. While it continued as a brand of leisure wear, the Chelsea Collection no longer included the team kit in its 'fashionable' range. Instead, the club had signed a new contract with Umbro to supply the kit. The company's design for the home strip was an eye-catching one, featuring a multitude of criss-crossing thin white lines across the navy blue jersey, which together created a patchwork of small diamond shapes. In an echo of the controversial le coq sportif shirts of the early Eighties, a dash of red appeared on the side of the shorts and again in the lion motif on the club crest. Meanwhile, some supporters were none too happy to see that the blue socks of the previous season had been retained, leading those organised around the new *Chelsea Independent* fanzine to begin a long-running campaign for the return of the traditional white ones. Strangely, remembering how le coq sportif's failure to provide Chelsea with a yellow away kit had cost them dear, the Blues opted for all-red as their second-choice colours for the season. Again, this decision did not go down particularly well with many supporters.

The fans, though, were happy enough with the result and the performance against Wednesday. A late penalty by Durie, awarded when Pat Nevin was brought down in the box, gave the Blues the points after Lee Chapman had cancelled out Kerry Dixon's well-taken opener. There was much to savour, too, in the displays of the new boys: Dorigo and Clive Wilson combined intelligently down the left, while Kevin Wilson was lively when he came on as a second half sub.

Three days later Clive Wilson scored his first goal for his new club as the Blues trounced newly-promoted Portsmouth 3-0 at Fratton Park – the first time since 1966 that Chelsea had won their opening two top flight fixtures. Few newspapers bothered to print a league table at this early stage of the season but those that did showed the Blues sitting proudly at the top.

Chelsea maintained their good start over the following two months, reaching a high of second place after another emphatic 3-0 away win, this time at Watford, at the end of September. By now the Blues were bearing the name of a new sponsor on their chests, Commodore, after Ken Bates announced "the biggest club sponsorship deal in the history of English football" with the computer company at the beginning of the month. The deal, worth £1.25m over three years, was certainly a significant improvement on the £100,000 a year Gulf Air had paid a few seasons earlier.

But Chelsea's campaign, which had begun so brightly, started to turn sour in October. First, the Blues were knocked out of the League Cup by Second Division Reading. Having lost 3-1 at Elm Park in the first leg, a Gordon Durie hat-trick at the Bridge looked to have put Chelsea in command of the tie. However, on a night of incessant rain in West London, the Berkshire side pulled two goals back to pull off a shock aggregate victory.

Apart from the disappointing result, the match also provided some of the first signs of the internal strife which would soon become the season's theme. "I had an argument with Joe McLaughlin on the pitch and the ref threatened to send me off," recalls Clive Wilson. "It was just something petty, but we were arguing for the rest of the half. At half-time, John Hollins, took me off. I started thinking, 'What have I let myself in for here?' That's maybe when the rot started for me."

Yet, on the surface, nothing appeared seriously amiss. Ten days after their League Cup exit, a Kerry Dixon goal at home to Coventry lifted the Blues to within three points of the joint leaders, Liverpool and QPR. Two weeks later Pat Nevin, having denied rumours that he was interested in playing in France when his contract ended, cemented Chelsea's place in the top six with a late winner at home to Oxford. However, the victory was marred by a recurrence of Eddie Niedzwiecki's knee injury which resulted in him being carried off and replaced in goal by midfielder John Coady, a former postman signed by Hollins from Irish side Shamrock Rovers at the tail-end of the previous season. This time, there was to be no comeback for Niedzwieki. "It was a terrible shame that Eddie's career was ended by injury," says Peter Bonetti, who coached the Welsh keeper for many years. "In my opinion, if he hadn't been injured he would have taken over from Neville Southall, who was one of the best keepers in the world at the time, as the Wales goalkeeper."

Niedzwiecki was replaced by Roger Freestone, a capable but inexperienced goalkeeper who had just half a dozen First Division games under his belt. Although it would be unfair on Freestone to make a direct causal link, it's an undeniable fact that Chelsea's results began to dip from this point. The club's away form was particularly bad, a televised 2-0 defeat at Derby in November being the Blues' fourth consecutive loss on the road. "We had a lot of the ball but didn't show what we can do with it and that was very disappointing," said Joe McLaughlin after the game at the Baseball Ground.

Meanwhile, back at the Bridge, the Blues became the pools punter's friend, drawing five consecutive home games in December and January. At least Kevin Wilson, who had struggled to find the net in the opening months of the season, managed to break his duck with a goal against West Ham in one of these games, but the series of away defeats and home draws saw Chelsea slide down to mid-table. The early season optimism had now vanished, but there still seemed no reason to panic: the Blues were, after all, comfortably clear of the relegation zone.

The FA Cup promised some relief from the disappointing league run. Given a tricky draw away to Derby, the Blues responded with their best performance for some time.

Key figures in the excellent 3-1 win were Roy Wegerle, who ran half the length of the field before scoring a fine solo goal, and Roger Freestone, who saved a penalty. The result raised hopes that it might re-energise Chelsea's season, but instead Blues fans were rapidly cast into an even deeper depression.

Following a 3-0 defeat at Sheffield Wednesday, Chelsea then visited Swindon in the Full Members Cup, now sponsored by the Blues' former kit sponsors Simod. The competition was still low down the priority list of those clubs who deigned to take part, but nonetheless John Hollins put out his first choice side at the County Ground. The result, a 4-0 defeat against the Second Division side, was bad enough but the Chelsea performance was even worse.

"At Swindon we had a back four which didn't really know what it was up to," admitted Colin Pates afterwards. "We had people pushing up, people sitting off, the back four all had different ideas on how to defend." The shambolic display persuaded Hollins to completely redesign his defence, with Steve Clarke acting as a sweeper between two central markers for the next game at home to Portsmouth.

The sweeper system worked reasonably well against Pompey, and Clarke appeared to enjoy his new role as the free man at the back. "Obviously it will take us a few weeks to get it sorted out properly but if the manager perseveres with it I think it will prove very effective," he observed after the game. The 0-0 draw, however, did not impress the fans and at the final whistle there were loud chants for Hollins' dismissal – much to the dismay of some of the players. "They wanted Hollins' head again which is totally out of order," said Pates afterwards, "and to be frankly honest I'm sick of it. When we don't create chances then the fans are entitled to moan but we are creating chances and missing them and the last thing people need is for the crowd to tell them they are missing goals, then be subjected to jeers and boos."

Hollins retained the sweeper system for the next game, away to Manchester United in the fourth round of the FA Cup, but again risked incurring the wrath of the 10,000 travelling supporters by leaving fans' favourites Pat Nevin and Mick Hazard on the bench. Without their two most creative players and struggling to adapt to a new defensive formation, the Blues went down to a limp 2-0 defeat. Indeed, but for another penalty save by Freestone United's victory would have been even more emphatic. "On the day's play we have to be honest and admit that we didn't really deserve much better," admitted Joe McLaughlin. "We sat back far too much and in the end got our just reward."

The following week Hollins changed tack again by fielding a 4-2-4 formation away to Nottingham Forest. The four attackers, Nevin, Dixon, Wegerle and Kevin Wilson, caused Forest numerous problems and the Blues easily won the corner count, 14-3. Unfortunately, Chelsea lost the only score that counts, going down 3-2 in an exciting match. But even Forest manager Brian Clough acknowledged that the visitors had played well, saying, "I saw a Chelsea team packed with talent and Hollins deserves credit for that."

Still, the pressure was building on Hollins and for the visit of Manchester United the following week he was beginning to sound a little desperate. "I have tried everything this season, sweepers, three across the middle, and so on to try and find the best blend," he told fans in his programme notes. Yet, maybe the constant change in personnel and formations were part of the problem. Colin Pates certainly seemed to think so. "Liverpool have such a consistent side with everyone used to each other's style," he said. "At Chelsea it's been quite the opposite – we've never been able to settle into a certain pattern."

Clive Wilson also felt that Hollins' Ranieri-style tinkering unsettled the players. "John Hollins was chopping and changing the team and the tactics and sometimes, if you're not winning, you're better off doing what got you success before," he says. "You might do that with slightly different players but I don't think it helped that we had a different team virtually every week."

The 2-1 defeat by United, Chelsea's first home reverse for ten months but also their 14th league game without a win, proved to be a watershed. Ken Bates, well aware of the players' dissatisfaction with the coaching style of Ernie Walley, sacked Hollins' unpopular assistant and installed former Fulham manager Bobby Campbell, a close friend of the Chelsea chairman, as his replacement. Unsurprisingly, Walley's departure was unlamented by the players. "Ernie was a very hard taskmaster," says Clive Wilson. "Normally, the second in charge is in a no-win situation because he has to be the buffer between the manager and the players, but it seemed like John Hollins became the buffer between the players and Ernie if anything ever happened. It was either Ernie's way or the highway and that approach didn't go down well with the players – although I don't recall anybody falling out with him to the extent that blows were going to be exchanged."

Bates' appointment of Campbell, a manager with a proven track record, led to feverish speculation in the tabloid press that Hollins was on borrowed time. The future of Kerry Dixon also filled many column inches on the back pages, with Arsenal and West Ham leading the chase for the £1 million-rated striker. Dixon himself seemed to feel that it was time to move on from Stamford Bridge, and had formally handed in a transfer request. "When I asked for a transfer it was because I felt I needed to get away to make a fresh start," he told reporters. "I don't know whether John Hollins rates me as a player, and sometimes the uncertainty just kills me."

However, with Dixon apparently on his way to Highbury or Upton Park, Ken Bates returned from a three-week holiday in South America to put the mockers on any move. "Why should we sell off our best player to Arsenal and let them get the benefit of his goals?" he declared. According to press reports, Dixon reacted with 'stunned disbelief' when he heard that his 'dream move' to Highbury had been blocked. Now, looking back at the long-running transfer saga he says, "There was talk of me going to Arsenal. If the situation had become intolerable I would have looked at leaving and it was heading that way. But I never had to make that decision because Ken Bates made it for me."

The news that Dixon was staying was just one point to emerge from a three-hour crisis meeting held on Bates' return. The press, fully expecting to hear that Hollins had been sacked, instead were amazed to discover that he would be kept on as manager until the end of the season, although his contract would not then be renewed.

Mick Hazard, strongly linked with a move to QPR, would also be staying at the Bridge according to the statement issued by the club. "We did have a board meeting and it was confirmed that all that has happened since I went away is that Chelsea have changed their coach," added Ken Bates.

Having predicted the end for Hollins and a player exodus from the club, the press turned on Bates. 'Blue Joke' screamed the headline in the *Daily Mirror*, above a report from Nigel Clarke which began: "The goings on at the Bridge have been a joke for too long. Now they have become a farce. Chelsea has reached rock bottom. Their credibility as a club has been destroyed." The hack's main gripe was that there was no clear indication from the club as to who was really running the team: Hollins or Campbell?

For the players, the intense media speculation that Campbell was the designated manager-in-waiting added to the pressure in the dressing room. "It was destabilising," says Clive Wilson. "We had John and Ernie who were a team, and then we had John and Bobby who were two individuals, and you felt that Bobby was vying for the position of manager."

The fans were equally perplexed. The club appeared to be in limbo, facing a possible relegation struggle with a manager who it was known would be packing his bags in the summer. How long could that situation be tolerated? Was it true, as the papers were saying, that Bates was reluctant to sack Hollins because he would then have to pay him compensation? Was Campbell already the de facto manager? The appearance of Ken Bates on TV's *Football Focus* before the 0-0 home draw with Everton in March suggested some answers might be forthcoming, but the Chelsea chairman performed a passable impression of a cagey government minister, neatly sidestepping all of Bob Wilson's pertinent questions.

The following week Chelsea threw away a 3-0 half-time lead to draw 4-4 at Oxford, the fourth winless game under the Hollins-Campbell 'partnership'. Press reports, once again, were damning. "Still reluctant to sack Hollins before the end of the season, they have a lame-duck manager to go with their lame-duck team," chortled Brian Glanville in the *Sunday Times*. Four days later, though, the widely predicted demise of Hollins became a reality, with the Chelsea manager receiving a reported £150,000 pay-off from the club after Gordon Taylor of the PFA had acted as a mediator between the parties.

The club issued a short, and not very revealing, statement which read: "After an amicable discussion, Chelsea and John Hollins have agreed it would be in both parties' best interest if they end their association. Both parties are disappointed that the association has not been more fruitful. Bobby Campbell has been appointed caretaker-manager until the end of the season."

The news could hardly have been a shock for the players but, despite the dressing room unrest which marked the latter part of Hollins' period in charge, some at least were sad to see him leave the club. "Holly was great," said Tony Dorigo later. "I really liked John and he was one of the reasons I joined Chelsea. He was a very honest man, always chirpy, but looking back he was working under very difficult circumstances."

There was, though, little or no time to look backwards. With eight games left, six of them at home, Bobby Campbell still had every chance of saving the Blues from disaster. His first move as manager was to buy Mansfield's promising young goalkeeper Kevin Hitchcock on transfer deadline day, and the new signing was thrown straight into the first team for the home game against Southampton.

Writing in the programme, Campbell told fans: "There is a lack of confidence in the side at Stamford Bridge, even a blind man can see that. The lads are so keen to do well that they are afraid of taking chances in case they make mistakes and I have to try to encourage them to be a little more positive, to go out there and grab the game and take it away from our opponents."

The game-plan sounded positive enough, but it didn't work. Chelsea lost 1-0 and, according to Southampton scorer Graham Baker, gave little impression of being a united team. "After only 10 minutes of the match they were effing and blinding at each other," he said afterwards. "There was a lot of back-chat. I think they are in trouble, because they are playing without spirit, and under the pressure they are facing, you have to pull together. If they don't start to do that soon, I think they will go down."

However, four draws and, finally, after a club record 21 matches, a league win – Mick Hazard scoring the only goal of the game at the Bridge against Derby – looked to have pulled the Blues away from the drop zone. By now, the three automatic relegation places had been taken by Oxford, Watford and Portsmouth. Only the play-off position needed to be settled, and Chelsea's final two opponents, West Ham and Charlton, were the favourites to fill it. Much, though, would depend on the Blues' pressure-cooker games away to the Irons and at home to the Addicks.

Two years earlier West Ham had virtually ended Chelsea's championship hopes with a crushing 4-0 victory at the Bridge. Now, the East Enders delivered another hammer blow to the Blues' future prospects, cruising to a 4-1 win which plunged Campbell's team into the dreaded play-off position for the first time. Following this disastrous setback, only a victory against Charlton at the Bridge would enable Chelsea to escape an unpredictable four-way dogfight for First Division status with three Second Division sides.

In front of a tense crowd of 33,701 the Blues got off to a good start against the Addicks, taking the lead through a Gordon Durie penalty after Steve Clarke was brought down in the area by Charlton defender John Humphrey. The killer goal proved elusive, however, and as the clock ticked away the Blues became increasingly edgy. Charlton weren't playing particularly well, either, but they were seasoned relegation fighters who had just held onto their First Division position the previous season by beating Leeds in the play-off final. At 1-0 the Addicks knew they only needed to produce a single moment of inspiration or one stroke of luck to save themselves. They got the latter: a bouncing ball in the Chelsea area deflected off Paul Miller and past Kevin Hitchcock. The 1-1 draw meant Chelsea finished in the play-off position, behind both Charlton and West Ham on goal difference.

Drawn against Blackburn in the play-off semi-finals, the Blues spent five days in Blackpool preparing for the first leg at Ewood Park. The sea air clearly suited the team as Chelsea controlled the game and, thanks to goals by Nevin and Durie, took a well-padded 2-0 cushion back to Stamford Bridge. "When we beat Blackburn the spirit came back," says Kerry Dixon. "We were really confident of getting out of it." The second leg was even more comfortable, the Blues strolling to a 4-1 win with the three-pronged strike-force of Dixon, Durie and Kevin Wilson all appearing on the scoresheet. "That 6-1 aggregate mirrored our class," suggested Steve Clarke. "We gave them a bit of a lesson over the two matches."

Chelsea's opponents in the two-leg final were Middlesbrough, 3-2 aggregate conquerors of Bradford City in the other semi-final tie. Boro', who were enjoying a remarkable renaissance after almost going out of business in 1986, promised to be a tougher nut to crack than Blackburn. Their defence, which included future England internationals Gary Pallister and Colin Cooper, was strong and well drilled, while leading scorer Bernie Slaven, winger Stuart Ripley and former Reading hitman Trevor Senior gave their attack a sharp cutting edge.

The Blues were again drawn away in the first leg and prepared for the midweek match at Ayresome Park by spending a couple of days training at the Gateshead international athletics arena. Again Chelsea performed well and created a number of good opportunities, but were unable to reply to Boro' goals in each half by Slaven and Senior. If the Blues were to stay in the First Division they would have to win the return by three or more goals at the Bridge – something they had only managed twice all season, against Luton and Blackburn.

Nonetheless, the players seemed confident of pulling the tie around. "Boro' are a good, well-organised team with a lot of ability but we know that on our day we can match the best teams in the First Division," said Joe McLaughlin in the matchday programme, "and by this evening we hope we have earned our right to do just that again next season." Bobby Campbell was equally bullish, telling fans, "This is only half-time and we shall go out this afternoon and continue to play our football. If we make as many chances as we did on Wednesday night then I think you will see us hit the back of the net."

Campbell made just one change to the team which had lost in the north-east, replacing the injured Clive Wilson with his namesake, Kevin. In front of the Blues' biggest home attendance of the season, 40,550, the Blues almost got off to the perfect start when Pat Nevin, from just five yards out, struck his first-minute shot against a post.

Less than 20 minutes later the same player tricked and jinked his way into the penalty area before passing the ball to Gordon Durie, who cracked a right-foot shot past Boro' keeper Stephen Pears.

With 70 minutes left, Chelsea looked to have every chance of grabbing at least another goal. At half-time, with the score still 1-0, fans scanned the programme for details of what would happen if the tie finished level after 90 minutes at the Bridge: no extra-time would be played, but there would be the added drama of a penalty shoot-out to determine the venue for a third match. As the second half wore on, the Blues would have gladly settled for that scenario but the Boro' defence, superbly marshalled by the impressive Pallister, was proving difficult to penetrate. Chelsea upped the pressure, the crowd increased the noise, Campbell tried to set Boro' new problems by bringing on his subs, youth product Gareth Hall and Kevin McAllister, but it was all to no avail – that vital second goal just wouldn't come.

The final whistle signalled delight for Boro' and despair for Chelsea. As the players trooped off, a group of Boro' fans climbed over the fences at the North stand end and ran onto the pitch to celebrate. This sight proved too much for many grieving Blues fans who stormed over or round their own fences to engage the Boro' supporters in full-scale battle. Prolonged fighting inside and outside the ground followed before, having made 102 arrests, the police eventually managed to restore some semblance of order. (See Chapter Sixteen, *Here We Go*).

Inside the Chelsea dressing room the mood was, unsurprisingly, sombre. In an attempt to turn thoughts to the future, Ken Bates gave the shell-shocked players a simple message. "He came into the dressing room and said, 'Right, nobody's leaving, you lot got us relegated, next season you'll have to get us back up,'" recalled Steve Clarke. "We accepted that because, obviously, nobody sets out to be relegated. It's probably the worst feeling a professional footballer can have, because you're branded a failure and, basically, that's what you are." Having pointed out a few home truths to the players, the Chelsea chairman then returned upstairs to fire a quick broadside at the press, telling the hacks, "I'm off to my 300-acre farm. You lot can bugger off to your council houses."

The humour, though, could not disguise the despair Bates must have felt. A return to the Second Division, where Chelsea had slumbered for so many years in the early Eighties, was not part of the chairman's masterplan. So, how had it come to this? How had a team which regularly featured half a dozen current or future internationals ended up in such a desperate plight?

Bates himself, having pointed the finger at the players in the dressing room, also blamed himself for promoting Hollins so quickly. "The appointment of John Hollins was a mistake," he said later. "He has a very strong wife. It might have been better if I'd made her manager."

The players, though, are altogether less convinced that Hollins should be made the scapegoat for Chelsea's sudden decline from championship contenders to relegation fodder. Pat Nevin, for instance, explains the club's demise by pointing to two unrelated factors. "I'm big on psychology," he says, "and the group dynamics in the squad at the beginning were great, although I don't think the Chelsea fans understood at the time that they were held together by one person who was admired, respected and was the perfect pro. That was Tony McAndrew. It didn't matter that he wasn't always in the team. He was in the reserves some of the time but he made sure the right attitude was there. For example, I remember him absolutely slaughtering some of the reserve players for moaning when they heard the first team had won. The other thing that killed us off was Eddie Niedzwiecki getting injured. The difference between being a decent side and being a side in trouble was losing Eddie. I've no doubt at all about that."

John Bumstead, meanwhile, points to a combination of unnecessary changes to the playing squad and inflated egos as the prime causes of the Blues' nosedive down the table. "Too much happened too quickly," he argues. "We were trying to run before we could walk. New players came in but, to be honest, I don't think they were any better than the ones we had. At certain times, too, it wasn't a great place to work. I think some players made the mistake of believing what was written about them, and started thinking they were better than they really were."

Tony Dorigo makes a similar point. "I felt that sometimes all the players weren't singing from the same hymn sheet," he said. "That was always a problem throughout the time I was there, and so were the off-the-pitch problems which always seemed to get through to the players. It was never a settled team, either, which was a real shame, because I think we had some very good players and we could produce a great run – but we could also produce a great run of defeats. To a certain extent, that inconsistency seemed to be the image of the club."

In Chelsea households around the country the post-mortem continued long into the summer. Yet, ultimately, it mattered little who was blamed for the club's failure: the players, who had underperformed so badly throughout the season; the two managers, neither of whom had got the best out of the squad for any length of time during the campaign; or the chairman who, by his own admission, was now ruing some of his past decisions. The plain fact was that the Blues, having apparently re-established themselves as a genuine First Division force in the previous seasons, were once again facing life in the lower tier with the likes of Shrewsbury, Bournemouth and Walsall for company. For the fans, especially those who remembered the aptly-named 'Gloomy Years', the prospect of day trips to Gay Meadow, Dean Court, Fellows Park and other similar backwaters was distinctly unappealing. True, everyone expected Chelsea to bounce back at the first attempt – but what if they didn't, and instead became mired in the Second Division for years and years again? For most supporters, that nightmare scenario just didn't bear thinking about.

CHAPTER FIFTEEN
THE BATTLE FOR THE BRIDGE

Relegation back to the Second Division was a huge blow to Chelsea, as was the return of the terrace violence which accompanied the Blues' demise. Yet the prospect of life in the lower tier and an FA Inquiry into the events at the Middlesbrough play-off match were not the greatest of the club's worries in the summer of 1988. Overshadowing everything was the ongoing threat to Stamford Bridge which, to varying degrees throughout the Eighties, had blighted the whole of the decade.

The story of how football at the Bridge was almost consigned to the history books is a long, complex and convoluted one. The tale begins in 1979 when the club was struggling with massive debts of £3 million, largely incurred as a result of the inflated costs involved in the building of the East stand some five years earlier. Rather than go into receivership, which in any case was dismissed as unworkable, the board transferred the debts, the ownership of the ground and the 14 acres that surrounded it to a specially-created company called SB Property. In business-speak, SB Property was a 'holding company' as it simply 'held' and controlled the assets (or, in this case, liabilities as well) of another company.

While the Mears family retained control of both the club and the ground, Chelsea's future at the Bridge appeared secure enough – provided the debt could slowly be whittled down through the cost-cutting measures introduced by chief executive Martin Spencer.

A SERIOUS CASE OF THE BLUES

Events, though, began to move quickly after Brian Mears resigned as chairman in June 1981 following a terrible season on the pitch.

Ten months later, in April 1982, Ken Bates, the 51-year-old former chairman of Oldham and director of Wigan, bought Chelsea FC from the Mears family. Described in the press as a 'property tycoon', Bates in fact had a colourful and varied business background which included a good number of controversial episodes. His career, which included running a building firm in Burnley, property development in the Caribbean and banking in Ireland, led him eventually to the comfortable environs of Monte Carlo where he put his feet up while planning his next move. It was here that Bates had renewed an old acquaintance with Brian Mears, a regular visitor to Monaco. Naturally, the subject of Chelsea came up in conversation. The prospect of owning one of the most distinguished names in English sport appealed to Bates and, in early 1982, he made his famous offer of £1 for the ailing club.

Negotiations between Chelsea's new owner and Brian Mears' brother, David, for the sale of SB Property, in which the latter held a sizeable stake, continued and looked to have reached a conclusion on New Year's Day 1983. On this date, according to Bates, the two main protagonists shook hands on a deal which would see Mears sell his shares in SB to the new Chelsea chairman for around £450,000 as long as Bates managed to arrange to fund the company's £1.6 million overdraft. This proviso appeared to present no stumbling block to completion when Bates agreed a phased repayment with Barclays Bank of no less than £200,000 per annum. As part of the deal Mears would also be given a three-year consultancy role at the club on a salary of £12,000 a year and the use of a Volvo estate car.

Bates was expecting to complete the deal early in the 1983/84 season but, two days before a scheduled meeting to finalise the matter, he was informed by Chelsea vice-president George Thomson at a reserve game at Stamford Bridge that Mears, in company with a property developer, had been to see Crystal Palace directors to discuss the possibility of Chelsea groundsharing at Selhurst Park – the idea being that the Blues would move out of the Bridge while the ground was 'redeveloped'. The Chelsea chairman was horrified to hear this news as Mears had given him no indication that he was involved in other discussions. Bates promptly telephoned Mears and, at the end of what Bates later described as a "very acrimonious conversation", decided he had no option but to remove both Mears and Viscount Chelsea, another leading SB Property shareholder, from the Chelsea board of directors.

With the Mears–Bates deal now dead, the Mears brothers and Viscount Chelsea sold their SB shares instead to a firm of property developers with longstanding roots in west London, Marler Estates, in September 1983. As a result, Marler gained a 70 per cent interest in SB Property as part of on overall agreement worth £1.25 million. This was very disturbing news for all Chelsea fans. Marler now owned a prime piece of real estate in south-west London and, it had to be assumed, their main interest in the site was to maximise profits regardless of the effect on the football club.

When they first took over SB in 1983, Marler's stated intention was to work with Chelsea while retaining a smaller stadium in a development which would also include flats, offices and a supermarket. "A much smaller and more compact stadium could be one answer," said Marler's chairman, David Bulstrode. "The old ground is too large and deteriorating. We would like to create a much more controlled environment. The ground is all wide open spaces and difficult to police."

Marler valued the Bridge at around £4 million yet, as press reports pointed out, this figure would rise substantially if the stadium was not rebuilt and all 14 acres were used solely for commercial development. "The main supermarket groups would compete vigorously for such a site," reported *The Times*, which quoted 'a leading property analyst' as saying that "the site would be worth around £50 million fully developed".

For the moment, though, Marler maintained that Chelsea would remain part of a redeveloped Stamford Bridge. While the work was undertaken on the site, however, the team would have to find another ground "for at least two seasons", according to Bulstrode. Initially, and to the dismay of Chelsea fans, Selhurst Park in deepest south London was mooted as a temporary home for the Blues. QPR, Fulham and even Brentford were also named as possible landlords.

Horror stories soon appeared in the press suggesting that Chelsea were in immediate danger of being turfed out of Stamford Bridge, but these rather ignored the fact that Bates had earlier signed a seven-year lease with SB Property which ran until 19th August 1989. Chelsea also had an option to buy the ground at any time before that date. The club, Bates pointed out in his programme notes on numerous occasions, could only be moved from the Bridge before that date if suitable alternative accommodation could be found. The club's requirements in this case, he stressed, would be 'exacting'. At the same time as reassuring fans, behind the scenes the Chelsea chairman began waging a guerrilla campaign against Marler, buying up a minority stake in SB Property and testing his enemies' patience with a series of court actions.

By January 1984 Chelsea owned or influenced 20 per cent of the shares in SB Property, not including those belonging to former Chelsea director Sir Richard Attenborough who had promised to fight the club's corner with the chairman and George Thomson, whose loyalty had been rewarded with promotion to the position of president. "The good news is that Marler's Chief Executive claims to be a season-ticket holder and lifelong Chelsea supporter and the Marler chairman has said on two separate occasions that he wants to see Chelsea remain at the Bridge," Bates wrote in the programme for the home match against Brighton. "Let us hope that 1984 shows that they are both men of their word."

But could Marler be trusted? As Bates himself revealed to fans later in 1984 there were many things about the company that were "odd and worrying", specifically the fact that the company was controlled by an offshore entity called Blade Investments, about which little was known other than it was based in Jersey.

Meanwhile, Bates upped the pressure on his opponents by launching a High Court injunction on 27th January 1984 to prevent any SB Property shareholders from selling their shares to Marler. This was essentially a stalling tactic designed to delay Marler's takeover of SB and to give Bates more time to increase his shareholding in the same company. By the time Chelsea discontinued their action at the beginning of March the club had increased its shareholding in SB to 24 per cent, while Marler had 70 per cent and Attenborough 6 per cent. These figures were significant, as until they held 75 per cent of shares Marler were unable under company law to dispose of their chief asset – the freehold of Stamford Bridge – without taking account of the interests of the minority shareholders.

Soon, the early skirmishes turned into full-scale war as Marler gave up the pretence that the football club had any part to play in their plans for Stamford Bridge. In the autumn of 1984 Shaw Associates, an international firm of architects retained by Marler, submitted a planning application for the complete redevelopment of the site to Hammersmith and Fulham Council. The proposals showed the ground being turned into houses, flats and offices, killing off football at the Bridge once and for all.

In response, Chelsea put forward their own plan for redevelopment, which included a 42,000 capacity stadium with all fans under cover, a multi-purpose community centre under one of the stands, a hotel and a low-cost residential complex for first-time buyers.

The club also launched a petition against Marler's proposals, which was signed by 17,868 fans before it was handed in to the council in January 1985. Bates seemed confident of victory, saying, "Chelsea are stubborn in their determination to fight this threat all the way."

The first round, though, went to Marler when their plans were approved by the council's Planning Policy sub-committee by five votes to three. According to an 'insider' quoted in *Bridge News* the councillors were split along party lines. "The Labour councillors were very pro-Chelsea," the source said. "Unfortunately, they were in a minority. There were only three of them, compared with five Conservatives. The Labour councillors were concerned that Chelsea are part of local history and had been here since 1905, longer than the current residents." Despite Chelsea's protests, full planning permission to develop the site without a stadium was approved by the council in March 1986.

Two months later Marler added another element to the equation when they bought Fulham and Craven Cottage for £9 million, suggesting that their plan was to squeeze both the Cottagers and the Blues into one ground while selling off the other site at a huge profit. The scheme might have worked but for the intervention of the local council, which changed hands from Conservative to Labour in May 1986. To the delight of fans of the local teams, the new administration swiftly announced a policy to preserve football at all three grounds in the borough: Chelsea's, Fulham's and QPR's.

Still, the threat to Chelsea remained. With the deadline fast approaching, the question remained how the club could afford to pay the soaring asking price for the Bridge when its option to buy the ground ran out in August 1988. "In just three years, Marler have said the value of the ground has gone up from £4 million to £12, £18, £25 and now £40 million," Bates fumed in February 1987. "These claims are absurd. I have asked them to produce the basis on which these claims are made, and I am now issuing an open challenge to them. Chelsea are substantial minority shareholders in SB, and yet we cannot get any information at all from Marler about its assets." In response, Robert Noonan, a Marler Estates executive, insisted that the ground's value had doubled in the last year. "The price will continue to go up because that area of west London is better than docklands," he added.

In February 1987 Marler further expanded their portfolio by buying Loftus Road for £6 million. Rather like a devious Monopoly player scooping up a set of highly-valued properties, the company now owned all three football grounds in Hammersmith and Fulham. In a shock move, David Bulstrode, recently installed as the chairman of QPR as well as Marler, announced plans to merge his club with Fulham to form a new entity, Fulham Park Rangers FC. There was even a suggestion that Chelsea would move to share Loftus Road with the hybrid club. However, the Football League, under pressure from outraged fans of all three clubs, vetoed the proposed merger.

In a bid to involve the fans further in Chelsea's battle, Bates launched the 'Save the Bridge' campaign in April 1987, with the aim of raising £15 million – the amount the Blues chairman thought Marler could be persuaded to sell the ground for – before the club's lease ran out. The campaign was spearheaded by the former Wimbledon chief executive, Colin Hutchinson. "This is potentially the top club in London," said Hutchinson on his appointment, "and even the thought of bulldozers wiping out 82 years of Stamford Bridge pride, passion and history – and replacing it with a concrete jungle for property-dealing profit – makes my blood boil."

Bridge News billed the ensuing fight as the 'Match of the Century: the Chelsea Lion v Marler Bulldozer'. In 1987 huge blue-and-white billboards imploring supporters to 'Help! Save the Bridge' sprung up inside the ground. Over the next two years fans, celebrities and politicians of all parties put their weight behind the campaign. All contributions, great and small, were recorded with thanks in the programme: the actor Tony Curtis donated one of his paintings, Sir Harry Secombe provided an autographed diet book, a female fan had her head shaved on the pitch just before kick-off, the club organised race days, pro-celebrity golf tournaments and star-studded luncheons while, outside the ground, volunteers collected supporters' loose change in blue buckets.

A SERIOUS CASE OF THE BLUES

In the autumn of 1987 Bates presented his vision of the new Stamford Bridge to the council. Now including a redeveloped 40,000 stadium in which only the East stand remained of the existing ground, 260 flats, a 150-bed hotel, a leisure centre and a pedestrian walkway linking Fulham Broadway underground station to the ground, the overall scheme was broadly similar to the Chelsea Village development which eventually appeared in the late 1990s. The proposals were initially put forward for public consultations and, predictably, drew complaints from the well-heeled 'Nimbys' who lived near the Bridge.

December 1987 was a tense month for Bates and the fans as the final decision of the council's Planning Committee loomed. Mike Goodman, a member of the committee, made it perfectly clear that in the event of Chelsea failing to get planning permission there would be little future for football at the Bridge. "If Chelsea's plan falls through, the bulldozers will be in by August 1989," he said, referring to the date when the Blues' lease expired. "If the plans do not satisfy us then it will probably be too late for Chelsea to do anything more."

But, by a majority of six to two, the plans were approved by the Planning Committee and Chelsea were given outline planning permission for the development of Stamford Bridge, including the all-important stadium. Naturally, Bates was thrilled by this momentous decision. "All the uncertainty that has hung over the future of Chelsea is now removed," he declared, a trifle prematurely. "I can now predict that we are well over halfway to securing the safety of the ground."

The next stage was to negotiate a selling price with Marler – but the two parties were as far apart as ever in their respective valuations of the Bridge. "It will seem reasonable to assume that it is unlikely we will agree a price on the ground without arbitration unless external financial pressure brings Marler to the negotiating table," predicted Bates on Boxing Day 1987.

Two months later Chelsea's plans were dealt a blow when the Department of Environment announced it would hold a public inquiry into the club's scheme to redevelop Stamford Bridge, following a letter-writing campaign among local residents organised by the Fulham Conservative Association. As ever, Bates took this latest development in his stride, saying, "This twist in the saga certainly hasn't dented our resolve." The public inquiry was held in the summer of 1988, shortly after Chelsea's relegation to the Second Division in the play-offs. The inquiry was a drawn-out affair, lasting 21 days rather than the expected 10, but at the end of it Chelsea's plans were approved within certain conditions.

Shortly after the start of the 1988/89 season David Bulstrode died, having already been succeeded as Marler chairman by Robin Turner, another QPR director. Press talk of a possible deal between Marler and Chelsea was dismissed by Turner, who instead insisted that the club would soon be leaving their ancestral home. "There is no hope for

Chelsea at Stamford Bridge," he said. "A deal has already been done and we have received a £2m deposit."

The deal Turner hinted at was with Cabra Estates, another firm of property developers, who bought out Marler for £82 million in April 1989. Four months later, in August 1989, Chelsea's lease at Stamford Bridge expired but Bates managed to keep the legal wranglings ticking over to buy more time. By now, Fulham were in an even worse plight than Chelsea, as the Cottagers only had a licence from Cabra to play at Craven Cottage until May 1990, whereupon they had to vacate without notice. If, at that point, Fulham could not convince the Football League that they had a viable ground they risked losing their league status.

Thus, in November 1989, Fulham chairman Jimmy Hill approached Ken Bates about the possibility of the Cottagers groundsharing at Stamford Bridge. Knowing that Cabra had promised Fulham a juicy £5 million to leave the Cottage, Bates agreed in principle to a groundsharing arrangement and a third dressing room was installed at Stamford Bridge – even though the council's planning consent for the new Bridge specifically ruled out another team playing there. Meanwhile, Jimmy Hill attempted to mollify Fulham fans who were opposed to moving to their neighbour's home. "It is fundamental and vital to our future that we go to Stamford Bridge," he announced. "The address of Stamford Bridge is Fulham Road, Fulham Broadway, so why not have Fulham there?" But Bates and Hill couldn't agree on the details, and the groundshare scheme was dropped in May 1990.

Still the saga dragged on, preventing Bates from setting into motion his plans to redevelop the ground. In June 1991 the High Court ruled that if Chelsea were going to buy Stamford Bridge, the price would be set according to its value back in August 1988. Bates reckoned that would be £6-£10 million; Cabra chairman John Duggan's estimate, however, was £40 million. The two sides were still poles apart, but the tide was turning against Cabra whose shares had just collapsed from 110p to 11p after announcing pre-tax losses of £11 million. In November 1991, the independent valuation of the Bridge was set at £22.85 million, roughly halfway between Bates' and Duggan's two very different estimates.

By now, Cabra were struggling with debts of £50 million. Another High Court action gave Bates seven days to produce the £22.85 million but instead, in March 1992, the Chelsea chairman became a substantial minority shareholder in Cabra, investing £3 million in the ailing company with the intention of influencing policy from within. Six months later, though, Cabra's assets and Bates' shareholding were finally wiped out by the collapse of the property market and the fall-out from 'Black Friday'.

Cabra's main creditors, the Royal Bank of Scotland, took over the Bridge's freehold and on 15th December 1992 the bank granted Chelsea a 20-year lease with an option to buy the ground at any time within that period for £16.5 million, less than half the figure

A SERIOUS CASE OF THE BLUES

Marler had quoted four years earlier. At this point the battle to safeguard football at the Bridge was essentially won, as a bank was much less likely to throw a club out of its ancestral home than a firm of 'get-rich-quick' property developers.

   Thanks to the determination, ingenuity and resourcefulness of Ken Bates, supported by the fans and the local council, Stamford Bridge had a future to go with its rich past. The victory, though, had come at a cost. Bates estimated that it had cost £2.5 million in legal fees to defeat Marler and Cabra, while planning matters and the public inquiry had eaten up another £1 million. On top of these expenses, Bates had lost his £3 million investment in Cabra when the company went bust. Then there were the less obvious costs. Chelsea's uncertain future at the Bridge affected all aspects of the club: delaying, for instance, much-needed ground improvements and, quite possibly, influencing the thinking of some players who might otherwise have moved to west London. Yet, in the end, there was no question that the fight had been worthwhile: against the odds, the bulldozers had changed course and Stamford Bridge, one of the most illustrious names in English football and the home of Chelsea since the club's foundation in 1905, had been saved.

CHAPTER SIXTEEN
'HERE WE GO'

Football fans didn't have it easy in the second half of the 1980s. After the Heysel disaster, supporters were seen by the authorities as a public nuisance at best or, at worst, a threat to the very fabric of society. The police, in particular, could barely contain their contempt for fans, especially those who travelled to away matches. Clubs, too, often regarded their followers as a necessary evil rather than valued customers, and the nineteenth-century facilities at most grounds were an obvious reflection of this disdainful attitude. Nor did the terrace fashions of the day do fans any favours: with their expensive designer label 'casual' gear and bouffant 'mullet' hairstyles, many home ends looked like a convention of Duran Duran-loving golfers.

Yet, for the Chelsea fans who had followed the club during the 'Gloomy Years', the revival of the Blues' fortunes during the mid-Eighties more than made up for any inconveniences or fashion disasters off the pitch. Having stood by a team that couldn't win – or at least not consistently – and had in recent memory gone months without scoring a single goal, the sight of Kerry Dixon, David Speedie and Pat Nevin tearing opposition defences to shreds on a regular basis was something to savour. The team's success meant that, after years of being mocked by supporters of other clubs, Chelsea fans could hold their heads up high at work, at school and down the pub. In the words of the chant, which accompanied many a Blues victory during the 1983/84 promotion season, 'Chelsea were back'.

A SERIOUS CASE OF THE BLUES

Although a celebratory atmosphere was the dominant one throughout that campaign, at times a more menacing tone was detectable. As in the club's previous promotion year, in 1976/77, the season was marked by outbreaks of violence, especially at away games. Although Chelsea fans, their reputation for hooliganism doing them few favours, were generally blamed for these incidents in the national media they were just as often on the receiving end of unprovoked attacks by home supporters.

The club's first away league game of the season, at Brighton, set the tone. During clashes between rival fans 125 arrests were made and 40 people, including seven police officers, were treated in hospital. Ian Macfarlane, now revelling in the long-winded title of under-secretary of state at the Department of the Environment with responsibility for Sport, immediately called for a report on the disturbances and appeared to pin the blame on Blues fans before the full facts were known.

"We spent the whole of the summer liaising with the football authorities to try to ensure that these disastrous scenes would not be repeated," he complained. "We especially concentrated on the flashpoints where known troublemakers would be appearing, particularly matches involving Chelsea, to make sure that the police and the club took the most stringent precautions to eliminate the sort of violence that seems to have occurred."

A month later, the rarely acknowledged fact that Chelsea fans could be the innocent victims of football violence as well as the perpetrators was illustrated in the starkest and most tragic way possible. Following Chelsea's victory at Huddersfield, Richard Aldridge, a 20-year-old Blues fan, was attacked by Huddersfield supporters as he returned to his car 300 yards from the ground. He died from his injuries and a Huddersfield man was later sentenced to four years' imprisonment for manslaughter.

There were few, if any, away grounds Chelsea fans could attend at this time and feel entirely safe. The so-called 'scourge of hooliganism', which the media liked to present as infecting a small number of big clubs including Chelsea, Leeds and Birmingham, could in reality be found at every ground in the country. Even a sleepy old university city like Cambridge was not immune.

Indeed, Chelsea's visit to the Abbey Stadium in February 1984 sparked some of the worst violence of the season. In all, 92 people were arrested after vicious clashes between the two sets of fans, many of them instigated by local supporters determined to put on a big show against what they perceived as the cocky 'Cockney' visitors from the capital. Once again, however, the national media twisted events to suit their own agenda and put the blame fairly on the shoulders of Blues fans. "Chelsea's crazy 'fans' went on the rampage again and turned United's Abbey Stadium and the nearby streets, into an area of fear," reported the *Sunday Express,* which was by no means alone in pointing the finger at the visiting supporters. Yet, a very different picture emerged from the *Cambridge Evening News'* man on the spot. "Cambridge United supporters have been blamed for a day of violence in which a man's throat was slashed, another was stabbed and two policemen were attacked," the paper announced on its front page. The report of the day's events also quoted Chief Supt Harry Gelsthorpe of the Cambridgeshire constabulary, whose 450-strong force had been on 'maximum alert' for the game, as saying: "The Chelsea supporters deserve some credit. They were well-behaved and well-marshalled. Most of the trouble came from Cambridge supporters."

Six weeks after the ugly scenes at Cambridge, Chelsea fans were again on the receiving end at Cardiff. This time the local police were less sympathetic as Patrick Kenny remembers: "I was attacked by Cardiff fans, but I was arrested at the station after the game and put in the police van. I had to go down to the court in Cardiff three times because I pleaded not guilty and the case was adjourned twice. Even though the policeman who arrested me had been suspended it didn't make a difference; if you were a football fan, you were guilty. I was given a £60 fine."

Blues fans were generally on safer ground at Stamford Bridge, which bubbled with anticipation at every home game. A new powerful rallying call, 'Here we go, here we go, here go!' echoed around the Bridge in the seconds before kick-off, signalling the fans' almost uncontrollable excitement at the prospect of seeing John Neal's side burst into action again.

The Shed, of course, led the singing but the northern section of the East stand lower also became a meeting point for some of Chelsea's most vocal fans. Over the next couple of years this section, known as 'Gate 13' after the entrance number on the East stand concourse, developed a reputation as one of the noisiest and most passionate parts of the ground. One of the many fans who upgraded from the Shed to Gate 13 around this time was Cliff Auger. "We went in there mainly to be near the away fans and have a bit of banter with them," he explains. "There wasn't any fighting because you couldn't get near them – you were fenced in and there were police in between the two sets of fans. If there hadn't been any police it might have gone off, but there was little chance of that happening.

"Gate 13 was pay on the day, unreserved seating and, at the time, there wasn't a big difference in price between standing up and sitting down. Not that there was any sitting down, because we used to stand up for the whole game. A lot of the fans brought along the 'Millwall brick' with them. This was a rolled up newspaper which, if you whacked somebody over the head with it, was like being hit with a brick. You were searched when you went in but the police couldn't complain if you had a newspaper stuck in your back pocket. I can't remember if a particular paper was the preferred choice, but I'm sure the *Sunday Times* would have worked a treat."

The club was aware of the new terrace-style culture developing in the lower East stand and, surprisingly perhaps, didn't discourage it. "The vocal support from this area of the stadium is tremendous and a great help to the team," wrote Ken Bates in the programme, while reminding the Gate 13 fans of the ground rules (although, interestingly, not the one about spectators remaining seated throughout the game).

As Chelsea surged towards the Second Division title in the spring of 1984, Gate 13, along with the Shed and West stand benches, provided an ear-splitting soundtrack of support which reached a crescendo for the promotion-winning home game against Leeds. "It was a steaming hot day and the Bridge was brimming with chaps in Lacoste, Fred Perry's and le coq sportif home tops," remembers John Ingledew. "At half-time, 3-0 up, Ken Bates implored us by megaphone not to come onto the pitch during the game for fear of the match being abandoned, promising us we were all welcome on after the final whistle. The 50p gate from the Shed to the benches had been left open and with loads of others I squeezed into the West stand and down to the front. By the time Dixon had his hat-trick we'd spilled over the wall onto the track around the edge of the pitch. When Paul Canoville smacked in the fifth it proved too much for many of the younger supporters who joyously rushed on to celebrate with the players. The playing area was eventually cleared of fans although the rest of the game was played with a sort of 30 deep human touchline surrounding the pitch. At the end, the whole of the West stand poured onto the pitch.

"The Leeds fans, perhaps inspired by the huge A & J Bull Demolition sign at the away end, decided to do a bit of demolition of their own and, as if to erase the result, smashed the score board. Meanwhile, John Neal came out to salute the crowd from the centre of the East stand and I took pictures standing near the centre spot holding the camera above my head through an ocean of cheering fans. The East stand looked amazing – no adverts just the old crest above the tunnel and tens of thousands of ecstatic Blues. For those of us who started coming to the Bridge in the late seventies, which looking at the pics now seems to be the whole crowd, this was simply the greatest game and the best team we'd ever seen."

The press, however, took an altogether dimmer view of the day's events which resulted in 41 arrests and injuries to four policemen after missiles were hurled by rival groups of supporters. One of the injured policemen, PC Ray Cole, was given the kiss of life on the pitch after being struck in the throat by a missile. In *The Times*, Stuart Jones condemned both sets of fans, suggesting that "the scenes rivalled anything seen on the continent for violence that was sickening and potentially lethal... The First Division will be a richer place for Chelsea's players and the poorer for some of their followers." Ken Bates, though, defended the conduct of his club's fans, saying, "Our supporters were not badly behaved, they were just boisterous."

The following evening comedian Jimmy Tarbuck complimented Chelsea on gaining promotion in a theatre show. Asking if there were any Blues supporters in the house, a few voices called back. Tarby's quickfire response, "Are you out on bail?" was not exactly gag of the century, but it probably summed up the poor image many people had of

Chelsea fans at the time. Among those to suffer from this negative reaction to the club's name were the members of the Chelsea Supporters Club football team, which was forced to disband after rival teams refused point blank to play them.

More significantly, the hostility to football fans in general spread to Margaret Thatcher's government, which increasingly viewed supporters as a branch of the 'enemy within' along with striking miners, inner-city street rioters and Greenham Common peace protesters. Determined to reduce the incidence of crowd trouble, the government set up a Working Party on Hooliganism. Reporting in the summer of 1984, it made a number of proposals to tackle hooliganism, including admission to matches only by an electronically-read membership card and, as an ultimate sanction, the withdrawal of clubs' licences to play matches. There was also a suggestion that local derbies should not be played on Bank Holidays.

The Working Party would, presumably, have been pleased that Chelsea's first home derby of the following season, against West Ham, was played on an ordinary Saturday rather than a public holiday. It made little difference, because there was still a lot of trouble at the game, as John Kiely recalls: "I had an East stand lower ticket and the West Ham fans all came in chanting from different sides. Somehow they'd got home supporters' tickets – they should have been in the North stand terrace. I spent the whole game just running up and down the East stand trying to get away from the West Ham fans. They were chasing everybody. I ended up in the upper tier; there was so much disarray the stewards were just letting anyone up there to get away from the trouble."

Nor were Chelsea fans any safer on the terraces. "Throughout the Eighties West Ham would always take the Shed," says Tim Harrison. "The stupid idiots would open the gates at the Shed end with 15 minutes to go and you'd see the away end emptying. The West Ham fans would come sprinting round and march in to the Shed. Suddenly, you were aware of West Ham chants all around you, people would start moving away, and a few would turn back and say, "C'mon, Chelsea, stand and fight!" It seemed extraordinary that the police never stopped the West Ham fans getting into the Shed. It happened season after season.

"It was still that era of fighting. I wasn't involved in it, I was a typical coward, but I could sprint and you needed to sometimes. Certainly the games at the Bridge against West Ham. On one occasion I was chased past the Britannia pub outside the ground and through the back streets and, amazingly, managed to outrun them. I wasn't wearing my old scarf that my sister had knitted me but they just knew I was a Chelsea fan. Maybe it was the way I walked or because I didn't have a spider's web tattoo on my face, but somehow they knew. Millwall were terrifying as well, but the biggest fear I always felt was for West Ham."

A month after the chaotic scenes at the Bridge when West Ham visited in September 1984, though, it was the Chelsea fans who were hitting the headlines again following violent incidents during a 1-0 defeat at Southampton. The south coast club announced that, as a result of the crowd behaviour, it would be banning Blues fans from future games at The Dell. "With Chelsea it is not a minority who cause trouble, it is a hell of a lot," argued Southampton secretary Brian Truscott. "We would rather have a lower gate and lose money than have this repeated." However, Ken Bates, who made a point of defending Chelsea fans when he believed they were being victimised, brushed off the comments, saying, "I think it's a bit of sensation-seeking for domestic consumption."

Bates was far less sanguine after the riot at Stamford Bridge during the 1985 Milk Cup semi-final tie against Sunderland. The violence, which resulted in injuries to 20 police officers and 23 members of the public, put Chelsea on the front pages of the tabloids for a couple of days. Much of the attention focused on John Leftley, a 29-year-old bricklayer who attempted to assault former Blues player Clive Walker. The fan was bound over to keep the peace for a year, a slap on the wrist which outraged the players' union among other bodies. Chelsea chairman Ken Bates was equally unimpressed by the sentence, saying, "If George Best got three months for being drunk and disorderly, the supporter who tried to attack Clive Walker should be jailed for six."

Bates, though, was less unhappy with the sanctions against the club announced by the FA Commission of Inquiry. The Chelsea chairman feared the worst, but the club was let off relatively lightly with a £40,000 fine and warned that the Bridge terraces would be closed if there was another outbreak of violence. "We decided not to make an example of Chelsea, just to please the public," said Les Mackay, the FA commission chairman. "We did consider shutting the ground, or having Chelsea play some matches behind closed doors. Both ideas were rejected."

Nine days after the incidents at Stamford Bridge, Millwall fans went on the rampage at Luton in an FA Cup tie. The violence made the so-called 'riot' at Chelsea look like a slightly rowdy summer picnic: hundreds of Millwall fans ripped up plastic seats, hurled them on the pitch and used others as shields or weapons as they engaged in a full-scale battle with 200 police officers. The players were taken off for 25 minutes, but the match could easily have been abandoned. After the game finished, Millwall fans ran amok through the town, causing thousands of pounds of damage to shops, houses and cars. To cap off a fun night out, they then wrecked their train back to London. In all, 47 people, including 31 police, were injured during the events. Afterwards the Police Federation Chief, Alan Eastwood, called on chief constables to revoke the licences of clubs with violent fans – a move which would have shut down certain grounds including, quite possibly, Stamford Bridge. "We are sick and tired of endless inquiries by official bodies which lead nowhere," he complained. "We don't want to wait until a police officer is murdered at a match." The fact that Millwall's game at Brentford a few days after the Kenilworth Road riot was called off on police advice illustrated that the threat to clubs with a hooligan following was a very real one.

Margaret Thatcher was, according to press reports, "appalled, angered and outraged by the violence" at Stamford Bridge and Kenilworth Road. The government's immediate response was to establish a 'war cabinet' on football hooliganism: having seen off General Galtieri in the Falklands War and miners' leader Arthur Scargill, the Prime Minister now turned her beady eye on fans in the Shed and the Cold Blow End.

On 28th March 1985 Thatcher chaired a long ministerial meeting on hooliganism. Four days later football chiefs were summoned to Downing Street, where Ted Croker, the FA Secretary, shifted the blame away from football's door. "These people are society's problem and we don't want your hooligans at our sport," he told a visibly irritated Thatcher. The government was unimpressed with this line of argument, however, and instead prepared a bill banning the sale of alcohol at football grounds. It also set in motion plans for a national identity card scheme for fans: all supporters, not just the hooligans, were the clear target.

Ken Bates, for one, thought the government was barking up the wrong tree. "If shutting Chelsea solved the hooligan problem I would do it tomorrow, but it wouldn't," he pointed out. "We have shown the country that it is not only a Chelsea problem but a national one. Every football club has its hooligans and so does every society. Eliminate the hard core and much will be solved."

The police, for their part, attempted to follow this logic. New technology increasingly played an important role in detective methods and Stamford Bridge was often a testing ground for counter-hooligan measures which were then introduced at other grounds. For example, in 1983 Chelsea became the first club to install CCTV cameras in their ground, while the Hoolivan – a mobile surveillance unit featuring a periscope-style video camera with a zoom lens which could film and identify suspects from a distance of 150 yards – had its first outing outside the Bridge in the spring of 1985. Later that year, in November 1985, a Chelsea fan was jailed for life at the Old Bailey and another sentenced to eight years for offences committed after the home match with Manchester United the previous December. The life sentence passed on 25-year-old Kevin Whitton for riot and assault by Judge Michael Argyle QC was the heaviest ever passed on a football hooligan. Incredibly, Whitton was punished more severely for his role in the riot – "waving his fist in a menacing manner and lashing out with his feet" outside Stamford Bridge, according to the prosecution – than for his part later the same day in the grievous wounding of the manager of Henry J. Beans on the King's Road.

Fans around the country were shocked at the severity of the sentence, but no more so than at Stamford Bridge where one supporter was quoted in *The Times* as saying, "I feel like fighting but I won't do it because I'm scared." Civil liberties groups were appalled by the life sentence, which was later reduced on appeal, but the football authorities and politicians of both main parties applauded it. "At last we have a judge with the courage to step forward and say the sentences must fit the crime," was the gleeful response of

A SERIOUS CASE OF THE BLUES

Conservative MP Geoffrey Dickens. "Judges have been demeaning their own currency by imposing woeful sentences."

Post-Heysel especially, fans who got into trouble were unlikely to be given a sympathetic hearing. Even perfectly well-behaved supporters were frequently targeted by the police, who appeared to adopt a blanket policy of viewing all fans as potential, if not actual, hooligans. Occasionally, and satisfyingly for those fans who had suffered from their heavy-handedness, the police were caught out. In April 1984, for instance, Blues fan Robert Connor was awarded £2,658 damages for an assault by a police constable at a Chelsea match way back in 1979. Then, in 1985, Chelsea fan and Oxford student Paul Marples won his appeal after being convicted of conduct likely to cause the breach of the peace at the Milk Cup semi-final first leg in Sunderland. He later announced his intention of pressing for damages for wrongful arrest.

The police, though, continued to conduct their operations around grounds almost as though they were in a Balkan war zone. "You were heavily policed when you came out of the tube at Fulham Broadway," says Nick Worger, who attended many home games at the Bridge in the mid-1980s. "You were corralled along Fulham Broadway, and if you stepped off the pavement they'd shout at you through a loud hailer. For some games there would be a police helicopter flying overhead. It was a military-style operation.

"It all added to the sour atmosphere which developed around football after Heysel. It certainly wasn't a family atmosphere. The people going were nearly all lads, the 18-30 crowd. But the violence was exaggerated by the press. I didn't feel unsafe at all at Chelsea and can't remember seeing any trouble.

"What was annoying was that the pubs near the ground were open before the game but not after, because the police set up an alcohol-free exclusion-zone around Stamford Bridge. So you'd have to trek down the King's Road to find the first pub that was open, which I think was the Chelsea Potter. Most people seemed to just go home after the games, so there wasn't much of a post-match atmosphere in the pubs. There would be a few fans in, but not loads."

Other fans, especially those who travelled away with Chelsea, knew that behind the apparently peaceful veneer of the crowd, violence was always a possibility. "The Eighties seemed to be a lot more violent, it was more planned and people knew what they were doing," says Dave Johnstone. "The police really started clamping down on it. I think the violence in the Eighties put the mockers on things. In the Seventies it was more like thousands of kids going up north to cause a bit of anarchy and to run around, more than looking to slash people up. In the Eighties the violence went a little berserk and it did put people off – attendances went down." Patrick Kenny makes a similar point. "Originally, the violence was all about giving someone a slap and taking their territory, it wasn't supposed to be about people being taken away in bodybags," he says.

In the press a lot of the violence at Chelsea matches was attributed to the 'Chelsea

Headhunters', allegedly the club's foremost hooligan group. The police, though, were on their case and managed to infiltrate six undercover officers into the gang in a sting called 'Operation Own Goal'. In March 1986 seven 'Headhunters' were rounded up in dawn raids across the south-east and, the following year, were put on trial. According to the prosecution, the gang had a "well-oiled organisation" which met for "board meetings" in pubs around Stamford Bridge to plan attacks on rival fans. It was also alleged that victims of the gang would be presented with a 'business card' which read 'You have been nominated and dealt with by the Chelsea Headhunters'. At the trial much was made, too, of 'a diary of terror' one of the defendants kept of violent incidents at Chelsea matches. A sample entry from November 1984, the court heard, read, "We done a pub load of Geordies. We done well against the Geordies, they were terrified outside the pub."

In May 1987 the evidence collected by the police team resulted in five 'Headhunters' being jailed for up to ten years each for offences committed over a six-year period. Passing sentence at Inner London Crown Court, Judge Shindler QC described the five as "ruthless, violent and nasty men" who had used football as "a vehicle for violence". In November 1989, however, three of the convicted 'Headhunters' were freed by the Court of Appeal because of inconsistencies in the police evidence. Lord Lane, the Lord Chief Justice, was damning in his condemnation of the police operation. "These statements are unreliable and the creditworthiness of the officers has been destroyed," he declared. Operation Own Goal, it seemed, couldn't have been more aptly named.

With fans worried about being hit with draconian sentences, the old days of mob aggro were over. There was, though, time for one last outbreak of terrace violence when Chelsea met Middlesbrough in May 1988 in a high-stakes shoot-out to decide which of the two teams would play in the First Division the following season.

"The first leg up at Middlesbrough was hairy," recalls Chris Ryan. "Our coaches got bricked, we were kept in after the game and the Middlesbrough fans were trying to break through police lines to get at us. So that experience carried over into the second leg." Meanwhile, for those fans who were unable to get a ticket to go to Ayresome Park, there was the option of watching the game live in a number of cinemas in London. "We sold out our away ticket allocation very quickly so I watched the first leg in Odeon Leicester Square," remembers Scott Buckingham. "There was chanting to start with, then frustration as the game went on and we were losing. We just sat there in silence. But there was no trouble, no ice creams being thrown at the screen or anything like that."

There was, though, plenty of trouble at the second leg after Chelsea failed to pull back the two-goal deficit from the first leg. "At the end of the match about 20 Boro' fans ran on the pitch to celebrate," recalls Scott. "Lots of Chelsea supporters felt that they were taking the mick – it was bad enough watching them celebrate behind the goal – so Chelsea fans went from the Shed to confront them. I'm not sure they how got on, whether they went round through the benches on the West stand or just went over the fences. That sparked a lot more coming on the pitch, maybe around 1,000 altogether. The police were stuck in the middle, trying to push Chelsea fans back in to the Shed."

Dave Johnstone was among the fans who ran on the pitch after the initial invasion, storming through a gate that had been opened by stewards to enable press photographers and disabled fans to leave the ground. "I ran across from the Shed," he says. "I just thought, 'This is shit, the end of the world.' I just followed everybody else. I don't know what I've had done if I'd run into any of their fans. I was quite pissed off and not thinking clearly."

Other fans were equally devastated at the team's relegation. "That was the third time I'd seen us relegated and it was the only time I've sat on the terraces and cried at the end," admits Scott Buckingham. "The other times, in 1975 and 1979, we were useless. That 1988 side was a good one and should have stayed up. I just sat on the terraces crying until the stewards made me leave."

The authorities' response to the events at the Bridge was a familiar one from past episodes of hooliganism over the previous decade. Colin Moynihan, the government's diminutive sports minister, immediately called for a 'full and urgent' inquiry into the disturbances, saying, "Clearly every such incident is a major step backwards on the road to re-admission to Europe." Margaret Thatcher, meanwhile, was said by a Downing Street source to be "deeply distressed" by the violence.

Deputy Assistant Commissioner Paul Condon, Scotland Yard's senior commander at the scene, who had been forced to order 10 van loads of reinforcements to contain the fighting, described the clashes between fans as "predictable, but nonetheless disgusting." Tom Pendry, the chairman of the all-party parliamentary football committee, also put in his penny-worth, saying: "These people are a disgrace to football. They are not soccer fans. They are just hooligans. It is an element which attaches itself to one or two clubs, and Chelsea is one of the great clubs that is being marred by them." However, Ken Bates, while not condoning the violence, turned his fire on the police operation. "We pay an awful lot of money," he fumed. "We are the second-highest fee-payers to the police in the country. I think we are entitled to service." Once the talking stopped, Chelsea were hit with a stiff punishment: a £75,000 fine and the closure of the Stamford Bridge terraces for the first six games of the following season. Reports in the press suggested that the fences at the Bridge would be fitted with revolving spikes to deter pitch invaders but, happily, this speculation proved to be wide of the mark.

The last two years of the decade were relatively trouble-free at Stamford Bridge. The violent encounters that took place between rival 'firms' tended to take place well away from the grounds, out of sight of the police and often arranged in advance by that handy new invention, the mobile phone. Meanwhile, after the Hillsborough disaster, the football authorities' focus swiftly moved away from the obsession with hooliganism, and turned instead to stadium redevelopment and ground safety. The days of the Shed, and other vast terraces, were well and truly numbered.

Initially, Chelsea fans were overwhelmingly opposed to the proposal to turn Stamford Bridge into an all-seater stadium. A survey conducted by the club immediately after the Hillsborough disaster revealed that only 6 per cent of fans in the Shed supported the move to make the area all-seater, although only 4 per cent said they would stop watching football at the Bridge if future legislation outlawed standing areas. Some fans, though, were less attached to the club's ancient crumbling terraces. "Hillsborough had a big effect on me," says Patrick Kenny. "I just thought they were normal football fans and that could quite easily have been me. When you had the terraces I remember being squashed up against the barriers trying to get into the ground and sometimes you couldn't breathe because of the crush. You knew potentially it could be lethal."

Other fans, too, felt little affection for the old stadium and its inadequate facilities. "Stamford Bridge was a shit-hole," says Ron Hockings. "The only grounds worse than ours were Luton, Millwall and Wimbledon." Among the many grumbles fans had concerned the poor view from the Shed, the disgusting state of the toilets and the unappetising refreshments. "The view from the Shed was, quite often, of backs of heads and a bit of the pitch," says Dave Key from Peterborough, who was a regular at the Bridge in the late Eighties. "I'm short-sighted so I couldn't see the far end very well, but you'd be aware that the opposition had scored because you'd see a few hundred fans in the distance jumping up and down.

"The food wasn't great. The Shed tea-bar sold crap hamburgers, sausage rolls, tea, coffee and the occasional pasty. I used to nip up there a couple of minutes before half-time to beat the queues, because when the whistle blew there would be a great exodus. You didn't really expect to miss a goal in the 45th minute, and normally you didn't.

As for the toilets, there were running streams of piss everywhere. You couldn't stand in the dry anywhere. The toilets were to be avoided if possible. Sometimes I'd sneak off somewhere under the stands and just have a piss there."

Yet these were all minor inconveniences in the great scheme of things. When the Blues pulled off a great victory or put a smile back on their fans' faces by winning promotion back to the First Division, it really didn't matter that you couldn't see who had scored that vital goal at the North end or that you felt slightly queasy after eating a dodgy half-time hamburger.

It helped, too, that the fans didn't have to fork out the vast sums of money they now do to see their side in action. "I suppose you got what you paid for," says Dave Key. "Compared to now, it was a cheap day out: £4 or whatever to get in, £1 for the programme, a few quid on beers and food. I suppose the whole day came to about £15."

Throughout the 1980s Chelsea fans put up with appalling facilities and, at times, a team that wasn't much better. But their support for the club never wavered. "A lot of

A SERIOUS CASE OF THE BLUES

Rangers fans support Chelsea but I've always thought that Chelsea and Celtic fans are very alike," says Pat Nevin. "They follow the team manically everywhere, they support the team well even when they're getting beaten and through the tough times – they're the best two sets of supporters I've come across in my life."

CHAPTER SEVENTEEN
BOUNCING BACK
1988-89

The summer of 1988 will surely go down as the most miserable in Chelsea history. Two months after the event, the melancholy reality of relegation was beginning to sink in for fans and players alike. No more London derbies with Arsenal, Spurs and West Ham; instead the Blues' main local rivals would be Crystal Palace or, at a pinch, Watford. Either way, these were hardly encounters to set the pulse racing. Then, there was the fall-out from the violent scenes at the end of the play-off match with Boro'. Back in 1985, after the pitch invasion against Sunderland, Chelsea had got away with a slap on the wrist from the FA. This time round, the Blues' 'previous' would certainly be taken into account and a much tougher penalty was widely predicted.

All the same, few fans were prepared for quite how harsh the FA's disciplinary commission punishment turned out to be. Meeting on 13th July, the commission announced that Chelsea's terraces would be closed for the club's first six home games of the 1988/89 season. In addition, no tickets would be on sale to visiting supporters, while Blues fans would not be able to buy tickets on the day of the match. The loss of revenue to the club from the closure of the terraces was estimated to be in the region of £200,000. As if that wasn't enough, Chelsea were also fined £75,000 for failing to control their fans.

Days after the commission's decision, Blues fans suffered another blow when cult hero

A SERIOUS CASE OF THE BLUES

Pat Nevin joined Everton for a tribunal set fee of £925,000, the highest ever paid for a Chelsea player. It was widely reported that, with a World Cup approaching, Nevin wished to stay in the First Division to enhance his international prospects but, says Pat, that was not his motivation for heading north: "I would definitely have stayed, despite relegation. But it was my time to leave with the management and stuff, because I really didn't see eye to eye with Bobby Campbell. So while it looks like my decision, it wasn't. But I have no complaints: I had five years there and it was absolutely brilliant."

Nevin's departure, though, did not spark the predicted player exodus from the Bridge – although a number of fringe players, including Jerry Murphy and Roy Wegerle, also moved on. Instead, Bobby Campbell, who had been confirmed as the club's manager in the summer, bought two experienced players with well-earned reputations as fierce competitors. First to arrive was central defender Graham Roberts who joined the Blues from Glasgow Rangers for £475,000. "Chelsea are the only Second Division club I would have considered joining," 'Robbo' told reporters at his unveiling at the Bridge. "They are a big club and do not deserve to be in Division Two." The former Tottenham star was followed down south by ball-winning midfielder Peter Nicholas, who arrived from Aberdeen for £350,000.

A third significant new face was Ian Porterfield, famously the scorer of the winning goal for Sunderland in the 1973 FA Cup final, who Campbell appointed as his assistant. The dynamics of the Campbell–Porterfield partnership were, according to the players, very different from the Hollins–Walley era. "John Hollins was a calm fellow," says Clive Wilson. "Whatever was going on, he would never seem to lose his temper. Bobby Campbell was the opposite – he would rant and rave, so we had two extremes. Again, Ian Portfield was very different to Ernie Walley. He was the buffer between the manager and the players and he was very good at it. He was a really nice guy. When we went away he would come out for a drink with us, which was unusual. I don't know if the stories we told him would go back to Bobby Campbell but some of them were for Bobby's ears anyway."

Campbell, who was hugely experienced having coached at Arsenal and QPR as well as having managed both Fulham and Portsmouth, appeared confident that the Blues' stay in the Second Division would be a short one. "Chelsea have charisma, passion and still great potential," he enthused, shortly before the season began. "It's the Manchester United of the south.'

That confidence was mirrored by the players. "We had, in theory, the best side in the division," says Clive Wilson. "Bobby Campbell managed to keep it together and, on top of that, he bought Graham Roberts and Peter Nicholas. They added that bit of steel which we needed. We had a lot of flair before, but perhaps not enough steel. Those two coming in bolstered the framework of the team. They helped the team to gel."

Chelsea began the season as 5/1 favourites for the Second Division title. Among the other fancied teams were Manchester City, whose better-known players included former Tottenham midfielder Neil McNab, and future England internationals David White and Andy Hinchcliffe; Crystal Palace, whose great strength lay in their exciting forward line of Ian Wright, Mark Bright and John Salako; and Leeds, who had spent most of the Eighties struggling unsuccessfully to return to the top flight.

The Blues may have been heavily backed, but very soon those 5/1 odds were looking far from generous. Compounding the gloom and despondency surrounding the club, Chelsea's season began disastrously. Lacking the injured Kerry Dixon, Mick Hazard and Tony Dorigo, the Blues slumped to a 2-1 opening day defeat against Blackburn in front of under 9,000 all-seated fans at the Bridge. Worse still, skipper Joe McLaughlin responded to jeers from a section of the crowd by throwing his captain's armband to the ground. "I regret it every time I explode, but it is in my nature," he explained afterwards. "Unfortunately, this has been going on for two years since I asked for a transfer."

McLaughlin was promptly dropped by Campbell for the next match, a 1-1 draw at Crystal Palace, and replaced as captain by Graham Roberts. Four days later Chelsea travelled to the south coast for their first ever meeting with Bournemouth. In the local paper Bobby Campbell had been quoted as saying, "Playing teams like Bournemouth this season would be the same as playing clubs from the Fourth Division." The comments, whether reported accurately or not, helped create a cup tie atmosphere at Dean Court – even the local vicar told Harry Redknapp, Bournemouth's manager, "Let's make them eat their words!" Despite the dramatic appearance of Ken Bates on the bench next to Campbell – the Chelsea chairman left his seat in the directors' box because his view was obscured by a pillar – the Blues went down to a dispiriting 1-0 defeat. The players' mood was hardly improved by the gleefully ironic chant, 'We're only Fourth Division!' which greeted the final whistle. Losing to small fry like Luton and Wimbledon in the First Division had been hard to stomach, but this was simply humiliating.

The poor start continued and after six winless games Chelsea were one place clear of the relegation zone. This certainly hadn't been in the script when the campaign began.

The players may not have said so publicly, but the bleak atmosphere at the near-empty Bridge was hardly helping their cause. Players and fans alike were used to seeing the North stand deserted except for a small bunch of away supporters, but the sight of just a couple of ball boys patrolling the Shed end was hard to bear. "It was depressing with all the terraces shut," says Punky Al. "I'd go in the West stand and there would be just 8,000 in the ground. The atmosphere was poor at all the games until the terraces reopened. Mick Greenaway, who had began the 'Zigger Zagger' chant at Chelsea in the Sixties, got arrested at one of those games. He stood up in the West stand to do the chant and he got kicked out by two coppers. We couldn't believe it, because he was just trying to generate a bit of support for the team. Everyone was booing as he was hauled out and walked all round the ground in front of the empty Shed. People were really furious."

"It was a strange situation, with the huge ground empty at both ends," adds Paul Baker, a regular in the West stand. "To be honest, I think there was a bit of kudos among Chelsea fans that the terraces were closed because it hadn't happened to any other club. But the atmosphere at the games was crap, absolutely terrible."

The Blues' desperately disappointing start piled the pressure on Campbell, who was working without a contract, and he received further bad news when Steve Wicks announced his retirement after a recurrence of a serious back injury. The Blues boss badly needed a win, and he finally achieved one with a 2-0 win at Leeds. "If we had lost that game, there would have been a good chance that Bobby Campbell would have got the sack," suggests John Bumstead, who admits that the goal he scored that day was "a real fluke".

Strengthened by the return of Dorigo and Dixon, Chelsea began to rattle up the points. The early autumn, though, also provided another major embarrassment, a 6-3 aggregate League Cup defeat by Fourth Division Scunthorpe. The second leg at Stamford Bridge, the last of the six games to be played with empty terraces attracted a crowd of just 5,814 – one of the lowest in the club's history.

The Scunthorpe game turned out to be Colin Pates' last for Chelsea. "Bobby Campbell and I never saw eye-to-eye," he says. "He was under the impression that I wanted to leave and I didn't. Also I didn't think Bob was the right man for Chelsea. He had experienced pros at the club and, in my opinion, he didn't treat them with respect. I didn't like his manner. Anyway, after the Scunthorpe game Lennie Lawrence was waiting for me. His first words to me were, 'Chelsea want you out of the door. We'd love to have you at Charlton.' When I found out that what he was saying was true, I didn't have to think too hard about making the switch." Pates joined the Addicks for £430,000, while John Coady also moved on, joining Derry City for £10,000. Despite having over two years to run on his contract, Tony Dorigo also wanted to leave and was linked with Rangers, Manchester United and Liverpool.

Campbell, though, was determined to keep his better players, especially as the Blues had at last hit some form in the league. The reopening of the Shed at the end of October was celebrated with a crushing 5-0 victory over Plymouth, a clear sign that the noise generated by the fans on the terraces could influence events on the pitch. "When everyone moved back into the Shed there was a decent atmosphere for the first time that season," says Paul Baker. "That had been lacking before and it was no surprise we had that run of bad results."

A few weeks later goals by Dixon and Durie helped the Blues win 2-1 at Watford, a display which was chosen by England manager Bobby Robson as the Barclays 'Performance of the Week'. The victory at Vicarage Road pushed the Blues up to third place and delighted Bobby Campbell. "If you persist and believe in what you're doing, you'll see the fruits of your hard work," he said afterwards.

Chelsea's fine form continued throughout November and December, during which time the team remained unbeaten. Highlights of this run were excellent wins at Stoke (3-0) and Birmingham (4-1), Durie and Dixon again sharing the goals at St Andrews.

Even the sight of the Blues in a hideous new red-and-white hooped away shirt at Birmingham couldn't wipe the smiles from the travelling fans' faces. After beating the Brummies, Chelsea moved ahead of a tightly-packed field, which included Blackburn, West Brom and Manchester City, to top the table for the first time that season. There was further good news for the fans when Kerry Dixon, who had been the centre of so much transfer speculation over the past two years, announced that he had signed a four-year extension to his contract. "I feel that the club are going in the right direction," he said. "I want to be part of that. Bobby Campbell has made a helluva difference. He and Ian Porterfield are a good partnership. I believe that we are on the way back to the top."

By now it was becoming apparent that Chelsea simply possessed too much all-round quality for most teams in the division. Led by the inspirational Roberts, the back four were solid defensively while the two full backs, Dorigo and Steve Clarke, were both adept going forwards. In midfield, Nicholas, Bumstead and Darren Wood provided the running power, while Clive Wilson or Kevin McAllister complemented the hard-tackling trio with a touch of flair. But, arguably, it was up front that Chelsea's greatest strength lay: the Blues' international strikers Dixon, Durie and Kevin Wilson combined pace, skill, aggression and finishing prowess and were individually and collectively a genuinely intimidating prospect for second-tier defences.

"The three of us formed excellent partnerships together," reflects Kerry Dixon. "Both lads were really good. Gordon's arrival effectively broke up the Dixon–Speedie partnership but Hollins was right in that Gordon Durie was a good player – as was Kevin. The lesson I learned from that, though, was 'If it's not broke, don't fix it' because it was always going to be a problem fitting three into two. As it turned out, however, it worked for Bobby Campbell, because sometimes he played the three of us – with Kevin Wilson wide or Gordon Durie wide, or in a deeper role. It worked well, and I think we scored about 20 goals each that season."

The one area of the team which didn't convince was the goalkeeping position. Kevin Hitchcock had started the season in goal but, after picking up a knee injury in September, lost his place to Roger Freestone. Following a good run of form, Freestone then conceded ten goals in three games in early January as the Blues won 3-2 at Oxford, then crashed out of the FA Cup, losing 4-0 at Barnsley, and the Simod Cup, going down 4-1 at home to Nottingham Forest.

Perhaps because it was the team's first defeat for over two months, the Barnsley match provoked a flare-up in an otherwise harmonious dressing room. "We came in 3-0 down at half-time and Graham Roberts started blaming the strikers for not scoring," recalls Clive Wilson. "Kerry Dixon got the raving hump and went after Robbo. 'How can you be blaming the strikers when we're three-nil down?' he said. It looked like it was about to kick off in the dressing room, but somebody got in between them and it calmed down."

Bobby Campbell was less concerned about the dressing room bust-up between two of his star players than the worrying leakage of goals. The Blues' next match was against high-flying Crystal Palace and their dangerous trio of strikers – could he risk playing a goalkeeper shorn of confidence in such a vital match? Campbell decided he couldn't and instead splashed out a club record £725,000 to bring former Wimbledon keeper Dave Beasant down to London from Newcastle. Nicknamed 'Lurch' for his vague resemblance to the ungainly Addams Family character, Beasant was a tall, strong keeper with a massive kick. Significantly, his capture indicated to their rivals just how determined the Blues were to escape from Division Two. Still on a high after his penalty save in the previous season's FA Cup final, Beasant enjoyed an assured debut for his new club in a 1-0 win against Palace. There were other personnel changes around the same time: Darren Wood move on to Sheffield Wednesday for £350,000, while 26-year-old Australian striker Dave Mitchell arrived from Feyenoord for £150,000.

In February Chelsea and Manchester City began to pull away from the pack of chasing clubs. At the beginning of the month Chelsea travelled to Walsall and thrashed the home side 7-0, the biggest away league win in the club's history. Gordon Durie was the star of the show, scoring five goals, while Graham Roberts rattled in one of his club record 13 penalties. "The team spirit is fantastic," said Roberts afterwards. "Everybody is playing with a lot of confidence and every time we go forward we look like we are going to score. Our pace up the front is electric and everybody is looking forward to playing."

Campbell was equally pleased with the progress the team had made, and like Roberts, pinpointed the growing sense of camaraderie as an important factor in the Blues' revival. "Make no mistake, football is a serious business," he said "But the atmosphere at the club was too tense when I arrived. You've got to have a joke now and again but equally the players have to know when the joking stops."

As Chelsea went through another month unbeaten, promotion became increasingly likely. Altogether less certain was the ultimate destination of the championship trophy, as home draws against Oldham and Watford saw the Blues drop to second place behind Manchester City. In the middle of March, shortly after the team took a break in Marbella, Chelsea visited a packed Maine Road for a game which was billed as an unofficial title decider. Thousands of Chelsea fans made the trip up north and the team rewarded them with a brilliant performance. The Blues, playing some of their best football of the season, cruised into a three-goal lead through Dixon, Kevin Wilson and a fine solo effort by Dorigo before being pegged back to 3-2 in the closing minutes. The final score gave the impression of a close match, but Chelsea had outplayed City for most of the game and returned to top spot full of confidence for the run-in.

The City game turned out to be the second of eight straight wins which took Chelsea to the cusp of promotion. The highlight of this run was an entertaining 5-3 victory over Barnsley at the Bridge, in which Kerry Dixon equalled his best ever haul for the club by scoring four goals. Two weeks later, however, the Blues' club record 27-match unbeaten run came to end at Leicester in a 2-0 defeat. A chance to wrap up promotion had been lost but, as the disappointed Chelsea fans drifted away from Filbert Street, news filtered through that nearly 100 Liverpool fans had been crushed to death during the FA Cup semi-final at Hillsborough. Apart from the terrible tragedy of so many young lives being lost, the disaster was another dreadful blow to the game's image even though, on this occasion, overcrowding rather than hooliganism was the root cause.

The following week Chelsea again had a chance to make their return to the top flight a certainty. By a strange quirk, Leeds were the visitors – just as they had been at the Blues' last promotion party in 1984. Of the team that played that day only McLaughlin, Bumstead and Dixon remained. Fittingly, it was 'Bummers' who scored the only goal of a scrappy game in front of the Bridge's biggest crowd of the season, 30,337, to set the champagne corks popping along the King's Road once again. "I always seemed to score against them and Villa," he says. "We knew we were going to go up, it was just a matter of actually confirming it. Kevin Wilson was screaming for the ball, but I thought I'd have a try myself. Chelsea fans still come up to me to congratulate me on that goal." The victory also guaranteed that Chelsea would be champions, earning the club £35,000 in prize money from league sponsors Barclays.

The championship trophy was presented to Bobby Campbell and his players at the final home game of the season, a 3-1 victory over Bradford. The game was also notable for the debut of Ken Monkou, a stylish central defender and former model signed from Feyenoord for £100,000. The following week, Graeme Le Saux, a young left-side midfielder from Jersey who had been brought over to the club by John Hollins, made his debut as a substitute in the last game of the season, a 3-2 win at Portsmouth. The victory took Chelsea's final points total to 99, setting a new record for the Second Division.

The overall feeling at Stamford Bridge at the end of a record-breaking season was one of delight, mixed with relief that the club's stay in the Second Division had been so brief. Perhaps, too, there was a sense that the Blues were in the 'wrong' division, anyway, and this may have accounted for the slightly lukewarm public response to the team's success. Certainly, the fans did not celebrate as wildly as they had when John Neal's Blues emerged from the doldrums to gain promotion five years earlier. "The 1984 celebrations were a lot better," says Paul Baker. "I think we expected to go back up in 1989 and that had an impact. The fences were up, too, so people couldn't go on the pitch like they had in 1984 against Leeds." The media interest in Chelsea's return to the top flight was also decidedly apathetic. In *The Sun*, for instance, Brian Woolnough's match report of the Blues' promotion-clinching victory over Leeds – an event of some significance, you might have thought – consisted of just 38 words. With the Hillsborough disaster still dominating the daily sports agenda, the press, it seemed, were not especially bothered about the wrapping up of a story which had become wholly predictable months before.

Nonetheless, for one of the survivors from that earlier era, there was the same sense of satisfaction in a job well done. "With the 1989 team we were so professional it got to the stage where it could run itself," says John Bumstead. "It's hard to say which was the better side – '89 or '84 – but maybe the 1989 side was harder to beat and went on a longer unbeaten run. We were very experienced, very efficient and, at times, pretty ruthless." Bobby Campbell's two summer signings, Graham Roberts and Peter Nicholas, provided much of that ruthless streak, yet their team-mates were certainly not complaining. "They both did well for us," says Kerry Dixon. "Roberts, in particular, was an excellent centre back, a great captain and a very good leader."

All in all, Chelsea looked well equipped not only to survive back in the First Division but to prosper. That, certainly, was the view of Ken Bates. "We are not going back to the First Division as supplicants," he informed fans. "We are returning as of right and intend to play a major role in determining the honours list in 1989/90."

One year on from the agony of relegation, Chelsea were once again on the comeback trail. As it turned out, Bates' optimism proved well founded as the Blues finished fifth in 1989/90 to begin a spell in the top flight which remains unbroken to this day. So, promotion in 1989 finally marked an end to those depressing years in the Second Division when Chelsea were seemingly condemned to annual fixtures with the likes of Cambridge, Shrewsbury and Rotherham.

All that remained was for Chelsea to actually win something of note – it was now nearly 20 years since the club had raised a major trophy in triumph, the 1971 European Cup Winners Cup. The fans who had loyally followed the Blues throughout a topsy-turvy decade were desperate to see their heroes repeat their 1986 Full Members Cup celebrations at Wembley, only this time in a competition whose very mention didn't generate snorts of derision from rival supporters. Surely, for a club the size of Chelsea and with its old tradition of success in cup football, that wasn't too much to ask?

CHAPTER EIGHTEEN
THEN AND NOW

Just after Christmas 1980 an advert appeared in the Chelsea programme which would have struck a chord with many Blues fans. "Feeling desperate?" it asked. "Talk to the Samaritans." With the Chelsea team on a long scoreless run at the time some fans might have felt tempted to ring the helpline number at the bottom of the ad – although quite what advice the friendly and understanding voice at the other end of the line would have offered is not clear.

That dire run of games without a goal – 19 blanks in 22 matches during the second half of the 1980/81 season – was one of the low moments of the Eighties for Chelsea fans. Although seeing as how the goal drought stretched to 876 minutes at one stage perhaps 'moment' is the wrong word in this context. Yet, as we've seen, that dismal episode in Chelsea history was only one of a number of equally depressing periods the club went through during the Eighties.

The close flirtation with relegation to the old Third Division two years later, in 1983, was arguably the blackest moment of all. When Nottingham Forest went down into English football's third tier at the end of the 2004/05 season much was made of the fact that the club had won the European Cup 25 years earlier. Yet Chelsea's decline in the early Eighties was much steeper: if the Blues had gone down in 1983 only 12 years would have elapsed between the club's triumph in the European Cup Winners Cup against Real Madrid and a first acquaintance with life among the third-rate also-rans.

And who's to say that Chelsea's spiralling freefall would have stopped there? Wolves, another big club brought to its knees by financial problems in the Eighties, dropped into the very bottom rung at one stage before beginning a slow upwards climb. Conceivably, the Blues' fate might have been similar if Clive Walker hadn't scored that all-important goal at Bolton in May 1983. Even worse, faced at the time with the very real threat of being turfed out of Stamford Bridge by property developers, Chelsea might possibly have gone out of existence altogether.

But the Eighties were not all gloom, doom and despondency for Blues supporters. Far from it. For a few years there was a real sense that Chelsea were going places – and in some style, too. As John Neal's newly-assembled side powered its way to the Second Division title in 1984 fans flocked back to the Bridge, delighting in the club's revival and the enterprising forward play of Pat Nevin, David Speedie and Kerry Dixon. Ably supported by all-action midfielders John Bumstead, Nigel Spackman and Mickey Thomas, and a well-drilled defence featuring the likes of Colin Pates, Joe McLaughlin and goalkeeper Eddie Niedzwiecki, this was probably the classic Chelsea line-up and the most exciting Blues team of the Eighties.

The halcyon days continued as a slightly modified side under new manager John Hollins went close to winning the First Division championship in 1986. The Blues were in the hunt for the title until Easter when a combination of injuries to key players and inadequate replacements effectively ended their challenge. Sadly for Chelsea fans, that title tilt was as good as it got in the league as internal unrest, the loss of form of pivotal players, more injuries and some misguided signings all contributed to the Blues' eventual relegation via the play-offs.

Unlike previous relegations, in 1975 or 1979 for example, Chelsea's drop into the Second Division in 1988 was something of an own goal. With the players at the Blues' disposal – internationals like Tony Dorigo, Kerry Dixon, Gordon Durie, Pat Nevin and Kevin Wilson, to name just five – the team should have been challenging for a place in the top six rather than desperately scrapping for points at the wrong end of the table. Relegation that year was a stunning blow but, happily for Blues supporters, proved to be just a blip as Bobby Campbell's revamped team surged back to the First Division with a record number of points. A fifth place finish the following season – the highest the Blues had achieved since 1970 – began a renewed spell in the top flight which has been unbroken to the present day. Moreover, by then two of the elements of the highly successful Chelsea team of the late Nineties were in place – Steve Clarke and Graeme Le Saux (although he would spend five years away from the club before being re-signed) – while another, Dennis Wise, would arrive at the start of the new decade. By the end of the Eighties, too, future Chelsea medal winners Eddie Newton and Frank Sinclair were also on the club's books, earning good reviews in the youth team. It may not have appeared so at the time, but the building blocks for the cup glory the Blues enjoyed in years to come were gradually being put together.

It is hard to imagine Chelsea ever again experiencing the dramatic changes in fortune which characterised the club's history in the Eighties. In the Abramovich and Mourinho era a poor season would be one which ended without a trophy rather than, as in the Eighties, a brush with relegation; a disastrous season now would involve the club failing to qualify for the Champions League, as opposed to dropping into the second tier. Of course, there will still be ups and downs – but the ups will, like the Blues' title win in 2005, be higher and the downs, like the club's consecutive Champions League semi-final exits at the hands of Monaco and Liverpool, will generally bring with them the promise of future success.

The fact is that Chelsea is a totally different club now from the one that yo-yoed between the old First and Second Divisions during the late Seventies and throughout the Eighties. The players from that era have all long gone – although Steve Clarke, in his role as Mourinho's right-hand man provides an important link with the Chelsea of old; Ken Bates, who successfully fought off the property developer vultures circling over Stamford Bridge, is now attempting to perform a similar rescue act at Leeds; and the ground, apart from the East stand, is now unrecognisable from the days when fans sheltered from the rain under the Shed or poked fun at the cluster of away supporters huddled together in a corner of the vast North stand.

As is always the case at clubs which undergo a radical transformation it is the fans who change the least. True, Chelsea's recent triumphs, roll-call of famous names and glamorous image have attracted a new breed of well-wadded supporters for whom a season-ticket in excess of £1,000 is easily affordable. Inevitably, too, the exorbitant hikes in ticket prices from the days at the end of the Eighties when entry to the Shed cost a mere fiver have seen some supporters from that period become armchair, rather than match-going, fans.

However, many stalwarts from the Shed, the benches and the old West stand remain and - despite the rampant hooliganism, the crumbling stadium and the patchy results - they have a nostalgic affection for the period. "I remember the Eighties as being an era of almost heroic failure," says Tim Harrison, no doubt speaking for many Chelsea fans of the time. "For much of the Eighties, if you were watching a game or waiting for a result, there was a sense of doom and dread. I always think of those times when rival fans come to Stamford Bridge now and chant 'Where were you when you were shit?' and I keep wanting to bellow back, 'I was here, actually standing where you are now, you bastards!' That was the shit era, but there was a heroism about following Chelsea then. It was back to the music hall joke days in a way. Let's be honest, to say that the Full Members Cup final was the highlight of a whole decade is a pretty damning indictment. Yes, there were two Second Division titles as well and the points totals were awesome but, even so, it *was* only the Second." Watching small-to-middling clubs like Wimbledon,

A SERIOUS CASE OF THE BLUES

Coventry, Norwich and Luton lifting major silverware during the Eighties, while the Blues failed to get past the semi-final stage in either the FA Cup or the League Cup, only added to this sense of disappointment around the Bridge.

While recalling the era as a whole with a mixture of fondness and frustration, Blues supporters also remember and venerate their heroes of 20 years ago. During Chelsea's home match with Fulham towards the end of the 2004/05 season, for example, fans in the Matthew Harding stand were momentarily distracted from events on the pitch when they spotted a familiar face in the TV studio built into the corner of the stand. It was Kerry Dixon, working as a pundit for Sky TV. The chant which went up began as a small ripple, gradually gained force and momentum, and ended with the whole stand belting out, 'There's only one Kerry Dixon!' as if it was 1985 again. "It was a lovely moment," says Kerry. "I don't quite know what happened, but I suppose a few fans must have seen me in the box and started the chant off."

Similarly, John Hollins received a tremendous reception from Chelsea fans when he was standing on a TV platform by Eel Brook Common during the Blues' title celebration street party in May 2005. For a long time the circumstances of his dismissal as Chelsea boss meant that Hollins, who served the club as player, coach and manager for 18 years, was reluctant to return to the Bridge. With the change of regime, that has all changed. "It's great to be back," he says. "It's as a football club should be run. Clubs should recognise past players. Whether someone's played a long time or just six months, it should never be forgotten. What typified the spirit of the new Chelsea was John Terry insisting that Roy Bentley came out with the cup they won 50 years ago."

Tommy Langley, Player of the Year in 1979 and the club's leading scorer in two seasons at the end of the Seventies, is another former star who is revelling in the golden era Chelsea are currently enjoying. "My family and I have been fans all our lives," says Tommy, who can often be found mingling with fellow supporters in The Imperial pub on the King's Road after games at Stamford Bridge. "Just being around the club is lovely, doing spots on Chelsea TV and so on. This is the best we've experienced for a long, long time and, please God, it can only get better. This is what we always envisaged the club being; it's just taken us a long time to get there."

The path from cash-strapped Second Division strugglers to cash-rich champions of England has, certainly, been a lengthy and incident-packed one. The problems Chelsea were confronted with during the early Eighties – huge debts, a rapacious landlord and a hardcore minority of hooligan supporters – could conceivably have killed off the club for good. There are no such worries now as, backed by Roman Abramovich's mega-millions, the Blues look set to dominate English football for years to come. And, while the critics may carp about Chelsea's free-spending policy, there will be no complaints from the fans – particularly those who followed the Blues in 'The Gloomy Years' of the late Seventies and early Eighties when the club could barely afford to pay its own players, let alone buy new ones. For those fans who have known the bad times as well as the good at the Bridge, the glory days to come will taste sweet indeed.

WHERE ARE THEY NOW?

Ian Britton
After leaving Chelsea, Ian won a Scottish championship medal with Dundee United in 1983. In May 1987 later he scored the goal which preserved Burnley's 99-year league status on the last day of the season. He now works as the manager of a sports centre in Nelson, Lancashire.

John Bumstead
One of the highest appearance makers in Chelsea history, 'Bummers' now works as a taxi driver in London. He also does matchday corporate hospitality for Charlton, the club he joined when he left Chelsea in 1991.

Gary Chivers
'Chiv' is the player/manager of the Chelsea Old Boys, a team of ex-Blues who play charity matches on a regular basis (check out their website chelseaoldboys.co.uk for details of future fixtures). He works as a London taxi driver, and also reports on Premiership matches for the PFA and coaches youngsters both here and abroad.

Kerry Dixon
The second highest goalscorer in Chelsea history, Kerry now works as a pundit for Smooth FM and for Sky Sports. Since retiring from the pro game he has also managed Doncaster, Letchworth and Hitchin Town.

Mickey Droy
Owner of a successful electrical import business in Kilburn, Mickey is now 'virtually retired'. He is currently planning to move to St Petersburg, Florida, where he owns property.

Steve Finnieston
Steve has recently returned to his job selling building supplies after a spell as a postman in his home town, Ascot. He is another regular member of the Chelsea Old Boys team, along with his son John.

A SERIOUS CASE OF THE BLUES

John Hollins
Since leaving Chelsea in 1988, John has managed two other league clubs: Swansea and Rochdale. In 2004 he had a spell in China, coaching Stockport County's sister club and in November 2005 he was appointed manager of Vauxhall Conference side Crawley Town.

Tommy Langley
Tommy now works as a football agent, representing a number of players including Charlton's Talal El Karkouri and Youssef Safri of Norwich. For the past few years he has also been a regular presenter on Chelsea TV.

Colin Lee
Colin was appointed manager of Millwall at the start of the 2005/06 season. In December 2005 he became the club's Director of Football but left the Den two months later. He had previously been in charge at Watford, Wolves and Walsall. While out of the game during the 2004/05 season he regularly worked as a match analyst for Chelsea's official radio station, Big Blue.

Ray Lewington
Despite having led Watford to an FA Cup semi-final (2003) and a Carling Cup semi-final (2005), Ray was dismissed as Hornets manager in March 2005. He is now reserve team coach at Fulham, a club he previously managed between 1986 and 1990.

Pat Nevin
From 1998 until 2002 Pat was chief executive at Motherwell, a role he originally combined with playing before hanging up his boots in 2000. He is now a pundit with Channel Five and Radio Five Live.

Colin Pates
Since finishing his playing career with Brighton in 1995, Colin has worked as a PE instructor at the Whitgift School in South Croydon.

David Speedie
Now living in Doncaster, 'Speedo' is the director of his own recruitment company, has interests in overseas properties with the Royal Group and also works as a football agent.

Garry Stanley
Still a mainstay of the Chelsea Old Boys team at the age of 52, Garry now works as a pharmaceutical rep in Hampshire.

David Stride

Now working as a painter and decorator in Hampshire, David is another regular face at Chelsea Old Boys matches.

Clive Walker

Clive's long career saw him play for a host of clubs in league and non-league football. After a brief spell as Brentford's assistant manager, he later managed Ryman League side Molesey. He now runs a print business near Woking and also works as a pundit for Sky and BBC London.

Graham Wilkins

Despite having endured a dozen operations on his knees since retiring from football, Graham only called it a day with the Chelsea Old Boys team in 2005. He works as a travel service agent at Heathrow Airport.

Ray Wilkins

After enjoying an illustrious career with Chelsea, Manchester United, Milan, Rangers, QPR and England Ray moved into management, taking over the reigns at Loftus Road. In 1999 he returned to Stamford Bridge as a coach under Gianluca Vialli. More recently he was Dennis Wise's right-hand man at Millwall between 2003 and 2005. A regular face on Sky Sports, his autobiography is due out in 2006.

Clive Wilson

After leaving Chelsea in 1990, Clive went on to play for QPR, Tottenham and Cambridge United before becoming player/coach at Wingate and Finchley. He has recently completed a university degree in Sports Science at the University of Roehampton, in south-west London.

STATS
1975-89

SEASON 1975/76
LEAGUE DIVISION 2

	P	W	D	L	F	A	W	D	L	F	A	Pts
1. Sunderland	42	19	2	0	48	10	5	6	10	19	26	56
2. Bristol City	42	11	7	3	34	14	8	8	5	25	21	53
3. West Brom	42	10	9	2	29	12	10	4	7	21	21	53
4. Bolton Wanderers	42	12	5	4	36	14	8	7	6	28	24	52
5. Notts County	42	11	6	4	33	13	8	5	8	27	28	49
6. Southampton	42	18	2	1	49	16	3	5	13	17	34	49
7. Luton Town	42	13	6	2	38	15	6	4	11	23	36	48
8. Nottm Forest	42	13	1	7	34	18	4	11	6	21	22	46
9. Charlton Athletic	42	11	5	5	40	34	4	7	10	21	38	42
10. Blackpool	42	9	9	3	26	22	5	5	11	14	27	42
11. CHELSEA	**42**	**7**	**9**	**5**	**25**	**20**	**5**	**7**	**9**	**28**	**34**	**40**
12. Fulham	42	9	8	4	27	14	4	6	11	18	33	40
13. Orient	42	10	6	5	21	12	3	8	10	16	27	40
14. Hull City	42	9	5	7	29	23	5	6	11	16	26	39
15. Blackburn Rovers	42	8	6	7	27	22	4	8	9	18	28	38
16. Plymouth Argyle	42	13	4	4	36	20	0	8	13	12	34	38
17. Oldham Athletic	42	11	8	2	37	24	2	4	15	20	44	38
18. Bristol Rovers	42	7	9	5	20	15	4	7	10	18	35	38
19. Carlisle United	42	9	8	4	9	22	3	5	13	16	37	37
20. Oxford United	42	7	7	7	23	25	4	4	13	16	34	33
21. York City	42	8	3	10	28	34	2	5	14	11	37	28
22. Portsmouth	42	4	6	11	15	23	5	1	15	17	38	25

Top League scorer: Ray Wilkins, 11 goals
Average home attendance: 18,956
Player of the Year: Ray Wilkins

FA CUP

(3)	Bristol Rovers (H)	D1-1
(Rep)	Bristol Rovers (A)	W1-0
(4)	York City (A) W2-0	
(5)	Crystal Palace (H)	L2-3

LEAGUE CUP

(2)	Crewe (A)	L0-1

SEASON 1976/77
LEAGUE DIVISION 2

	P	W	D	L	F	A	W	D	L	F	A	Pts
1. Wolves	42	15	3	3	48	21	7	10	4	36	24	57
2. CHELSEA	**42**	**15**	**6**	**0**	**51**	**22**	**6**	**7**	**8**	**22**	**31**	**55**
3. Nottm Forest	42	14	3	4	53	22	7	7	7	24	21	52
4. Bolton Wanderers	42	15	2	4	46	21	5	9	7	29	33	51
5. Blackpool	42	15	2	4	46	21	5	9	7	29	33	51
6. Luton Town	42	13	5	3	39	17	8	1	12	28	31	48
7. Charlton Athletic	42	14	5	2	52	27	2	11	8	19	31	48
8. Notts County	42	11	5	5	29	20	8	5	8	36	40	48
9. Southampton	42	12	6	3	40	24	5	4	12	32	43	44
10. Millwall	42	9	6	6	31	22	6	7	8	26	31	43
11. Sheffield United	42	9	8	4	32	25	5	4	12	22	38	40
12. Blackburn Rovers	42	12	4	5	31	18	3	5	13	11	36	39
13. Oldham Athletic	42	11	6	4	37	23	3	4	14	15	41	38
14. Hull City	42	9	8	4	31	17	1	9	11	14	36	37
15. Bristol Rovers	42	8	9	4	32	27	4	4	13	21	41	37
16. Burnley	42	8	9	4	27	20	3	5	13	19	44	36
17. Fulham	42	9	7	5	39	25	2	6	13	15	36	35
18. Cardiff City	42	7	6	8	30	30	5	4	12	26	37	34
19. Orient	42	4	8	9	18	23	5	8	8	19	32	34
20. Carlisle United	42	7	7	7	31	33	4	5	12	18	42	34
21. Plymouth Argyle	42	5	9	7	27	25	3	7	11	19	40	32
22. Hereford United	42	6	9	6	28	30	2	6	13	29	48	31

Top League scorer: Steve Finnieston, 24 goals
Average home attendance: 30,633
Player of the Year: Ray Wilkins

FA CUP
(2)	Southampton (A)	D1-1
(Rep)	Southampton (H)	L0-3 (aet)

LEAGUE CUP
(2)	Sheffield United (H)	W3-1
(3)	Huddersfield Town (H)	W2-0
(4)	Arsenal (A)	L1-2

SEASON 1977/78 LEAGUE DIVISION 1

	P	W	D	L	F	A	W	D	L	F	A	Pts
1. Nottm Forest	42	15	6	0	37	8	8	10	3	32	16	64
2. Liverpool	42	15	4	2	37	11	9	5	7	28	23	57
3. Everton	42	14	4	3	47	22	8	7	6	29	23	55
4. Manchester City	42	14	4	3	46	21	6	8	7	28	30	52
5. Arsenal	42	14	5	2	38	12	7	5	9	22	25	52
6. West Brom	42	13	5	3	35	18	5	9	7	27	35	50
7. Coventry City	42	13	5	3	48	23	5	7	9	27	39	48
8. Aston Villa	42	11	4	6	33	18	7	6	8	24	24	46
9. Leeds United	42	12	4	5	39	21	6	6	9	24	32	46
10. Manchester United	42	9	6	6	32	23	7	4	10	35	40	42
11. Birmingham City	42	8	5	8	32	30	8	4	9	23	30	41
12. Derby County	42	10	7	4	37	24	4	6	11	17	35	41
13. Norwich City	42	10	8	3	28	30	1	10	10	24	46	40
14. Middlesbrough	42	8	8	5	25	19	4	7	10	17	35	39
15. Wolves	42	7	8	6	30	27	5	4	12	21	37	36
16. CHELSEA	**42**	**7**	**11**	**3**	**28**	**20**	**4**	**3**	**14**	**18**	**49**	**36**
17. Bristol City	42	9	6	6	37	26	2	7	12	12	27	35
18. Ipswich Town	42	10	5	6	32	24	1	8	12	15	37	35
19. QPR	42	8	8	5	27	26	1	7	13	20	38	33
20. West Ham United	42	8	6	7	31	28	4	2	15	21	41	32
21. Newcastle United	42	4	6	11	26	37	2	4	15	16	41	22
22. Leicester City	42	4	7	10	16	32	1	5	15	10	38	22

Top League scorer: Tommy Langley, 11 goals
Average home attendance: 28,734
Player of the Year: Mickey Droy

FA CUP

(3)	Liverpool (H)	W4-2
(4)	Burnley (H)	W6-2
(5)	Orient (A)	D0-0
(Rep)	Orient (H)	L1-2

LEAGUE CUP

(2)	Crewe (A)	L0-1

SEASON 1978/79
LEAGUE DIVISION 1

	P	W	D	L	F	A	W	D	L	F	A	Pts
1. Liverpool	42	19	2	0	51	4	11	6	4	34	12	68
2. Nottm Forest	42	11	10	0	34	10	10	8	3	27	16	60
3. West Brom	42	13	5	3	38	15	11	6	4	34	20	59
4. Everton	42	12	7	2	32	17	5	10	6	20	23	51
5. Leeds United	42	11	4	6	41	25	7	10	4	29	27	50
6. Ipswich Town	42	11	4	6	34	21	9	5	7	29	28	49
7. Arsenal	42	11	8	2	37	18	6	6	9	24	30	48
8. Aston Villa	42	8	9	4	37	26	7	7	7	22	23	46
9. Manchester United	42	9	7	5	29	25	6	8	7	31	38	45
10. Coventry City	42	11	7	3	41	29	3	9	9	17	39	44
11. Tottenham	42	7	8	6	19	25	6	7	8	29	36	41
12. Middlesbrough	42	10	5	6	33	21	5	5	11	24	29	40
13. Bristol City	42	11	6	4	34	19	4	4	13	13	32	40
14. Southampton	42	9	10	2	35	20	3	6	12	12	33	40
15. Manchester City	42	9	5	7	34	28	4	8	9	24	28	39
16. Norwich City	42	7	10	4	29	19	0	1	8	22	38	37
17. Bolton Wanderers	42	10	5	6	36	28	2	6	13	18	47	35
18. Wolves	42	10	4	7	26	26	3	4	14	18	42	34
19. Derby County	42	8	5	8	25	25	2	6	13	19	46	31
20. QPR	42	4	9	8	24	33	2	4	15	21	40	25
21. Birmingham	42	5	9	7	24	25	1	1	19	13	39	22
22. CHELSEA	**42**	**3**	**5**	**13**	**23**	**42**	**2**	**5**	**14**	**21**	**50**	**20**

Top League scorer: Tommy Langley, 15 goals
Average home attendance: 24,782
Player of the Year: Tommy Langley

FA CUP
(3) Manchester United (A)   L0-3

LEAGUE CUP
(2) Bolton Wanderers (A)   L1-2

SEASON 1979/80
LEAGUE DIVISION 2

	P	W	D	L	F	A	W	D	L	F	A	Pts
1. Leicester City	42	12	5	4	32	19	9	8	4	26	19	55
2. Sunderland	42	16	5	0	47	13	5	7	9	22	29	54
3. Birmingham City	42	14	5	2	37	16	7	6	8	21	22	53
4. CHELSEA	**42**	**14**	**3**	**4**	**34**	**16**	**9**	**4**	**8**	**32**	**36**	**53**
5. QPR	42	10	9	2	46	25	8	4	9	29	28	49
6. Luton Town	42	9	10	2	36	17	7	7	7	30	28	49
7. West Ham United	42	13	2	6	37	21	7	5	9	17	22	47
8. Cambridge United	42	11	6	4	40	23	3	10	8	21	30	44
9. Newcastle United	42	13	6	2	35	19	2	8	11	18	30	44
10. Preston	42	8	10	3	30	23	4	9	8	26	29	43
11. Oldham Athletic	42	12	5	4	30	21	4	6	11	19	32	43
12. Swansea	42	13	1	7	31	20	4	8	9	17	33	43
13. Shrewsbury	42	12	3	6	41	23	6	2	13	19	30	41
14. Orient	42	7	9	5	29	31	5	8	8	19	23	41
15. Cardiff City	42	11	4	6	21	16	5	4	12	20	32	40
16. Wrexham	42	13	2	6	26	15	3	4	14	14	34	38
17. Notts County	42	4	11	6	24	22	7	4	10	27	30	37
18. Watford	42	9	6	6	27	18	3	7	11	12	28	37
19. Bristol Rovers	42	9	8	4	33	23	2	5	14	17	41	35
20. Fulham	42	6	4	11	19	28	5	3	13	23	46	29
21. Burnley	42	5	9	7	19	23	1	6	14	20	50	27
22. Charlton Athletic	42	6	6	9	25	31	0	4	17	14	47	22

Top League scorer: Clive Walker, 13 goals
Average home attendance: 22,929
Player of the Year: Clive Walker

FA CUP

(3) Wigan Athletic (H)	L0-1

LEAGUE CUP

(2) Plymouth Argyle (A)	D2-2
(2) Plymouth Argyle (H)	L1-2

SEASON 1980/81
LEAGUE DIVISION 2

	P	W	D	L	F	A	W	D	L	F	A	Pts
1. West Ham United	42	19	1	1	53	12	9	9	3	26	17	66
2. Notts County	42	10	8	3	26	15	8	9	4	23	23	53
3. Swansea	42	12	5	4	39	19	6	9	6	25	25	50
4. Blackburn Rovers	42	12	8	1	28	7	4	10	7	14	22	50
5. Luton Town	42	10	6	5	35	23	8	6	7	26	23	48
6. Derby County	42	9	8	4	34	26	6	7	8	23	26	45
7. Grimsby	42	10	8	3	21	10	5	7	9	23	32	45
8. QPR	42	11	7	3	36	12	4	6	11	20	34	43
9. Watford	42	13	5	3	34	18	3	6	12	16	27	43
10. Sheffield Wed	42	14	4	3	38	14	3	4	14	15	37	42
11. Newcastle United	42	11	7	3	22	13	3	7	11	8	32	42
12. CHELSEA	**42**	**8**	**6**	**7**	**27**	**15**	**6**	**6**	**9**	**19**	**26**	**40**
13. Cambridge United	42	13	1	7	36	23	4	5	12	17	42	40
14. Shrewsbury	42	9	7	5	33	22	2	10	9	13	25	39
15. Oldham Athletic	42	7	9	5	19	16	5	6	10	20	32	39
16. Wrexham	42	5	8	8	22	24	7	6	8	21	21	38
17. Orient	42	9	8	4	34	20	4	4	13	18	36	38
18. Bolton Wanderers	42	10	5	6	40	27	4	5	12	21	39	38
19. Cardiff City	42	7	7	7	23	24	5	5	11	21	36	36
20. Preston	42	8	7	6	28	26	3	7	11	13	36	36
21. Bristol City	42	6	10	5	19	15	1	6	14	10	36	30
22. Bristol Rovers	42	4	9	8	21	24	1	4	16	13	41	23

Top League scorer: Colin Lee, 15 goals
Average home attendance: 17,896
Player of the Year: Petar Borota

FA CUP
(3)	Southampton (A)	L1-3

LEAGUE CUP
(2)	Cardiff City (A)	L0-1
(2)	Cardiff City(H)	D1-1

SEASON 1981/82
LEAGUE DIVISION 2

	P	W	D	L	F	A	W	D	L	F	A	Pts
1. Luton Town	42	16	3	2	48	19	9	10	2	38	27	88
2. Watford	42	13	6	2	46	16	10	5	6	30	26	80
3. Norwich City	42	14	3	4	41	19	8	2	11	23	31	71
4. Sheffield Wed	42	10	8	3	31	23	10	2	9	24	28	70
5. QPR	42	15	4	2	40	9	6	2	13	25	34	69
6. Barnsley	42	13	4	4	33	14	6	6	9	26	27	67
7. Rotherham	42	13	5	3	42	19	7	2	12	24	35	67
8. Leicester City	42	12	5	4	31	19	6	7	8	25	29	66
9. Newcastle United	42	14	4	3	30	14	4	4	13	22	36	62
10. Blackburn Rovers	42	11	4	6	26	15	5	7	9	21	28	59
11. Oldham Athletic	42	9	9	3	28	23	6	5	10	22	28	59
12. CHELSEA	**42**	**10**	**5**	**6**	**37**	**30**	**5**	**7**	**9**	**23**	**30**	**57**
13. Charlton Athletic	42	11	5	5	33	22	2	7	12	17	43	51
14. Cambridge United	42	11	4	6	31	19	2	5	14	17	34	48
15. Crystal Palace	42	9	2	10	25	26	4	7	10	9	19	48
16. Derby County	42	9	8	4	32	23	3	4	14	21	45	48
17. Grimsby	42	5	8	8	29	30	6	5	10	24	35	46
18. Shrewsbury	42	10	6	5	26	19	1	7	13	11	38	46
19. Bolton Wanderers	42	10	4	7	28	24	3	3	15	11	37	46
20. Cardiff City	42	9	2	10	28	32	3	6	12	17	29	44
21. Wrexham	42	9	4	8	22	22	2	7	12	18	34	44
22. Orient	42	6	8	7	23	24	4	1	16	13	37	39

Top League scorer: Clive Walker, 16 goals
Average home attendance: 13,133
Player of the Year: Mike Fillery

FA CUP

(3)	Hull City (H)	D0-0
(Rep)	Hull City (A)	W2-0
(4)	Wrexham (H)	D0-0
(Rep)	Wrexham (A)	D1-1 (aet)
(Rep)	Wrexham (A)	W2-1
(5)	Liverpool (H)	W2-0
(6)	Tottenham (H)	L2-3

LEAGUE CUP

(2)	Southampton (A)	D1-1
(2)	Southampton (H)	W2-1 (aet)
(3)	Wigan (A)	L2-4

SEASON 1982/83
LEAGUE DIVISION 2

	P	W	D	L	F	A	W	D	L	F	A	Pts
1. QPR	42	16	3	2	51	16	10	4	7	26	20	85
2. Wolves	42	14	5	2	42	16	6	10	5	26	28	75
3. Leicester City	42	11	4	6	36	15	9	6	6	36	29	70
4. Fulham	42	13	5	3	36	20	7	4	10	28	27	69
5. Newcastle United	42	13	6	2	43	21	5	7	9	32	32	67
6. Sheffield Weds	42	9	8	4	33	23	7	7	7	27	24	63
7. Oldham Athletic	42	8	10	3	38	24	6	9	6	26	23	61
8. Leeds United	42	7	11	3	28	22	6	10	5	23	24	60
9. Shrewsbury	42	8	9	4	20	15	7	5	9	28	33	59
10. Barnsley	42	9	8	4	37	28	5	7	9	20	27	57
11. Blackburn Rovers	42	11	7	3	38	21	4	5	12	20	37	57
12. Cambridge United	42	11	7	3	26	17	2	5	14	16	43	51
13. Derby County	42	7	10	4	27	24	3	9	9	22	34	49
14. Carlisle	42	10	6	5	44	28	2	6	13	24	42	48
15. Crystal Palace	42	11	7	3	31	17	1	5	15	12	35	48
16. Middlesbrough	42	8	7	6	27	29	3	8	10	19	38	48
17. Charlton Athletic	42	11	7	3	40	31	2	6	13	23	55	48
18. CHELSEA	**42**	**8**	**8**	**5**	**31**	**22**	**3**	**6**	**12**	**20**	**39**	**47**
19. Grimsby	42	9	7	5	32	26	3	4	14	13	44	47
20. Rotherham	42	6	7	8	22	29	4	8	9	23	39	45
21. Burnley	42	10	4	7	38	24	2	4	15	18	42	44
22. Bolton Wdrs	42	10	2	9	30	26	1	9	11	12	35	44

Top League scorer: Mike Fillery, 9 goals
Average home attendance: 12,737
Player of the Year: Joey Jones

FA CUP

(3)	Huddersfield Town (A)	D1-1
(Rep)	Huddersfield Town (H)	W2-0
(4)	Derby County (A)	L1-2

LEAGUE CUP

(2)	Tranmere Rovers (H)	W3-1
(2)	Tranmere Rovers (A)	W2-1
(3)	Notts County (A)	L0-2

SEASON 1983/84
LEAGUE DIVISION 2

	P	W	D	L	F	A	W	D	L	F	A	Pts
1. CHELSEA	**42**	**15**	**4**	**2**	**55**	**17**	**10**	**9**	**2**	**35**	**3**	**88**
2. Sheffield Weds	42	16	4	1	47	16	10	6	5	25	18	88
3. Newcastle United	42	16	2	3	51	18	8	6	7	34	35	80
4. Manchester City	42	13	3	5	43	21	7	7	7	23	27	70
5. Grimsby	42	13	6	2	36	15	6	7	8	24	32	70
6. Blackburn Rovers	42	9	11	1	35	19	8	5	8	22	27	67
7. Carlisle United	42	10	9	2	29	1	6	7	8	19	28	64
8. Shrewsbury	42	13	5	3	34	8	4	5	12	15	35	61
9. Brighton	42	11	6	4	42	17	6	3	12	27	43	60
10. Leeds United	42	13	4	4	33	16	3	8	10	22	40	60
11. Fulham	42	9	6	6	35	24	6	6	9	25	29	57
12. Huddersfield	42	8	6	7	27	20	6	9	6	29	29	57
13. Charlton Athletic	42	13	4	4	40	26	3	5	13	13	38	57
14. Barnsley	42	9	6	6	33	23	6	1	14	24	30	52
15. Cardiff City	42	11	3	7	32	27	4	3	14	21	39	51
16. Portsmouth	42	8	3	10	46	32	6	4	11	27	32	49
17. Middlesbrough	42	9	8	4	26	18	3	5	13	15	29	49
18. Crystal Palace	42	8	5	8	18	18	4	6	11	24	34	47
19. Oldham Athletic	42	10	6	5	33	27	3	2	16	23	39	47
20. Derby County	42	9	5	7	26	26	2	4	15	10	46	42
21. Swansea	42	7	4	10	20	28	0	4	17	16	57	29
22. Cambridge United	42	4	7	10	20	33	0	5	16	8	44	24

Top League scorer: Kerry Dixon, 28 goals
Average home attendance: 21,079
Player of the Year: Pat Nevin

FA CUP

(3)	Blackburn Rovers (A)	L0-1

LEAGUE CUP

(1)	Gillingham (A)	W2-1
(1)	Gillingham (H)	W4-0
(2)	Leicester City (A)	W2-0
(2)	Leicester City (H)	L0-2 (aet, won 6-5 on pens)
(3)	WBA (H)	L0-1

SEASON 1984/85
LEAGUE DIVISION 1

	P	W	D	L	F	A	W	D	L	F	A	Pts
1.Everton	42	16	3	2	58	17	12	3	6	30	26	90
2.Liverpool	42	12	4	5	36	19	10	7	4	32	16	77
3.Tottenham	42	11	3	7	46	31	12	5	4	32	20	77
4.Man Utd	42	13	6	2	47	13	9	4	8	30	34	76
5.Southampton	42	13	4	4	29	18	6	7	8	27	29	68
6. CHELSEA	**42**	**13**	**3**	**5**	**38**	**20**	**5**	**9**	**7**	**25**	**28**	**66**
7.Arsenal	42	14	5	2	37	14	5	4	12	24	35	66
8.Sheffield Weds	42	12	7	2	39	21	5	7	9	19	24	65
9.Nottm Forest	42	13	4	4	35	18	6	3	12	21	30	64
10.Aston Villa	42	10	7	4	34	20	5	4	12	26	40	56
11.Watford	42	10	5	6	48	30	4	8	9	33	41	55
12. West Brom	42	11	4	6	36	23	5	31	3	22	39	55
13.Luton Town	42	12	5	4	40	22	3	4	14	17	39	54
14.Newcastle Utd	42	11	4	6	33	26	2	9	10	22	44	52
15.Leicester City	42	10	4	7	39	25	5	2	14	28	48	51
16.West Ham Utd	42	7	8	6	27	23	6	4	11	24	45	51
17. Ipswich Town	42	8	7	6	27	20	5	4	12	19	37	50
18.Coventry City	42	11	3	7	29	22	4	2	15	18	42	50
19.QPR	42	11	6	4	41	30	2	5	14	12	42	50
20.Norwich City	42	9	6	6	28	24	4	4	13	18	40	49
21.Sunderland	42	7	6	8	20	26	3	4	14	20	36	40
22.Stoke City	42	3	3	15	18	41	0	5	16	6	50	17

Top League scorer: Kerry Dixon, 24 goals
Average home attendance: 23,061
Player of the Year: David Speedie

FA CUP
(3) Wigan (H) D2-2
(Rep) Wigan (A) W5-0
(4 Millwall (H) L2-3

LEAGUE CUP
(2) Millwall (H) W3-1
(2) Millwall (A) D1-1
(3) Walsall (A) D2-2
(Rep) Walsall (H) W3-0
(4) Manchester City (H) W4-1
(5) Sheffield Wednesday (H) D1-1
(Rep) Sheffield Wednesday (A) D4-4 (aet)
(Rep) Sheffield Wednesday (H) W2-1
(SF) (1) Sunderland (A) L0-2
(SF) (2) Sunderland (H) L2-3

SEASON 1985/86
LEAGUE DIVISION 1

	P	W	D	L	F	A	W	D	L	F	A	Pts
1. Liverpool	42	16	4	1	58	14	10	6	5	31	23	88
2. Everton	42	16	3	2	54	18	10	5	6	33	23	86
3. West Ham United	42	17	2	2	48	16	9	4	8	26	24	84
4. Manchester United	42	12	5	4	35	12	10	5	6	35	24	76
5. Sheffield Wed	42	13	6	2	36	23	8	4	9	27	31	73
6. CHELSEA	**42**	**12**	**4**	**5**	**32**	**27**	**8**	**7**	**6**	**25**	**29**	**71**
7. Arsenal	42	13	5	3	29	15	7	4	10	20	32	69
8. Nottm Forest	42	11	5	5	38	25	8	6	7	31	28	68
9. Luton Town	42	12	6	3	37	15	6	6	9	24	29	66
10. Tottenham	42	12	2	7	47	25	7	6	8	27	27	65
11. Newcastle United	42	12	5	4	46	31	5	7	9	21	41	63
12. Watford	42	11	6	4	40	22	5	5	11	29	40	59
13. QPR	42	12	3	6	33	22	3	4	14	20	44	52
14. Southampton	42	10	6	5	32	18	2	4	15	19	44	46
15. Manchester City	42	7	7	7	25	26	4	5	12	18	31	45
16. Aston Villa	42	7	6	8	27	28	3	8	10	24	39	44
17. Coventry City	42	6	5	10	31	35	5	5	11	17	36	43
18. Oxford United	42	7	7	7	34	27	3	5	13	28	53	42
19. Leicester City	42	7	8	6	35	35	3	4	14	19	41	42
20. Ipswich Town	42	8	5	8	20	24	3	3	15	12	31	41
21. Birmingham City	42	5	2	14	13	25	3	3	15	17	48	29
22. West Brom	42	3	8	10	21	36	1	4	16	14	53	24

Top League scorer: Kerry Dixon and David Speedie, 14 goals
Average home attendance: 21,985
Player of the Year: Eddie Niedzwiecki

FA CUP

(3)	Shrewsbury Town (A) W1-0	
(4)	Liverpool (H)	L1-2

LEAGUE CUP

(2)	Mansfield Town (A)	D2-2
(2)	Mansfield Town (H)	W2-0
(3)	Fulham (H)	D1-1
(Rep)	Fulham (A)	W1-0
(4)	Everton (H)	D2-2
(Rep)	Everton (A)	W2-1
(5)	QPR (A)	D1-1
(Rep)	QPR (H)	L0-2 (aet)

FULL MEMBERS CUP

(1)	Portsmouth (H)	W3-0
(1)	Charlton (A)	W3-1
(Area S/f)	West Brom (A)	D2-2 (Won 5-4 on pens)
(Area final)	Oxford United (A)	W4-1
(Area final)	Oxford United (H)	L0-1
(Final) (Wembley)	Manchester City	W5-4

Full Members Cup final team: Francis, Wood, Rougvie, Pates, McLaughlin, Bumstead, Nevin, Spackman, Lee, Speedie, McAllister

Scorers: Speedie 3, Lee 2

SEASON 1986/87
LEAGUE DIVISION 1

	P	W	D	L	F	A	W	D	L	F	A	Pts
1. Everton	42	16	4	1	49	11	10	4	7	27	20	86
2. Liverpool	42	15	3	3	43	16	8	5	8	29	26	77
3. Tottenham	42	14	3	4	40	14	7	5	9	28	29	71
4. Arsenal	42	12	5	4	31	12	8	5	8	27	23	70
5. Norwich City	42	9	10	2	27	20	8	7	6	26	31	68
6. Wimbledon	42	11	5	5	32	22	8	4	9	25	28	66
7. Luton Town	42	14	5	2	29	13	4	7	10	18	32	66
8. Nottm Forest	42	12	8	1	36	14	6	3	12	28	37	65
9. Watford	42	12	5	4	38	20	6	4	11	29	34	63
10. Coventry City	42	14	4	3	35	17	3	8	10	15	28	63
11. Manchester United	42	13	3	5	38	18	1	11	9	14	27	56
12. Southampton	42	11	5	5	44	24	3	5	13	25	44	52
13. Sheffield Wed	42	9	7	5	39	24	4	6	11	19	35	52
14. CHELSEA	42	8	6	7	30	30	5	7	9	23	34	52
15. West Ham United	42	10	4	7	33	28	4	6	11	19	39	52
16. QPR	42	9	7	5	31	27	4	4	13	17	37	50
17. Newcastle United	42	10	4	7	33	29	2	7	12	14	36	47
18. Oxford United	42	8	8	5	30	25	3	5	13	14	44	46
19. Charlton Athletic	42	7	7	7	26	22	4	4	13	19	33	44
20. Leicester City	42	9	7	5	39	24	2	2	17	15	52	42
21. Manchester City	42	8	6	7	28	24	0	9	12	8	33	39
22. Aston Villa	42	7	7	7	25	25	1	5	15	20	54	37

Average home attendance: 17,694
Player of the Year: Pat Nevin

FA CUP

(3	Aston Villa (A)	D2-2
(Rep)	Aston Villa (H)	W2-1
(4)	Watford (A)	L0-1

LEAGUE CUP

(2)	York City (A)	L0-1
(2)	York City (H)	W3-0
(3)	Cardiff City (A)	L1-2

FULL MEMBERS CUP

(3)	West Ham United (A)	W2-1
(4)	Blackburn Rovers (A)	L0-3

SEASON 1987/88
LEAGUE DIVISION 1

	P	W	D	L	F	A	W	D	L	F	A	Pts
1. Liverpool	40	15	5	0	49	9	11	7	2	38	15	90
2. Manchester United	40	14	5	1	41	17	9	7	4	30	21	81
3. Nottm Forest	40	11	7	2	40	17	9	6	5	27	22	73
4. Everton	40	14	4	2	34	11	5	9	6	19	16	70
5. QPR	40	12	4	4	30	14	7	6	7	18	24	67
6. Arsenal	40	11	4	5	35	16	7	8	5	23	23	66
7. Wimbledon	40	8	9	3	32	20	6	6	8	26	27	57
8. Newcastle United	40	9	6	5	32	23	5	8	7	23	30	56
9. Luton Town	40	11	6	3	40	21	3	5	12	17	37	53
10. Coventry City	40	6	8	6	23	25	7	6	7	23	28	53
11. Sheffield Wed	40	10	2	8	27	30	5	6	9	25	36	53
12. Southampton	40	6	8	6	27	26	6	6	8	22	27	50
13. Tottenham	40	9	5	6	26	23	3	6	11	12	25	47
14. Norwich	40	7	5	8	26	26	5	4	11	14	26	45
15. Derby County	40	6	7	7	18	17	4	6	10	17	28	43
16. West Ham United	40	6	9	5	23	21	3	6	11	17	31	42
17. Charlton Athletic	40	7	7	6	23	21	2	8	10	15	31	42
18. CHELSEA	**40**	**7**	**11**	**2**	**24**	**17**	**2**	**4**	**14**	**26**	**51**	**42**
19. Portsmouth	40	4	8	8	21	27	3	6	11	15	39	35
20. Watford	40	4	5	11	15	24	3	6	11	12	27	32
21. Oxford United	40	5	7	8	24	34	1	6	13	20	46	31

Top League scorer: Kerry Dixon, 25 goals
Average home attendance: 15, 957
Player of the Year: Graham Roberts

FA CUP
(3)   Derby County (A)   W3-1
(4)   Manchester United (A) L0-2

LEAGUE CUP
(2)   Reading (A)   L1-3
(2)   Reading (H)   W3-2

FULL MEMBERS CUP
(1)   Barnsley (H)   W2-1
(2)   Manchester City (A)   W2-0
(3)   Swindon Town (A)   L0-4

SEASON 1988/89
LEAGUE DIVISION 2

	P	W	D	L	F	A	W	D	L	F	A	Pts
1. CHELSEA	**46**	**15**	**6**	**2**	**50**	**25**	**14**	**6**	**3**	**46**	**25**	**99**
2. Manchester City	46	12	8	3	48	28	11	5	7	29	25	82
3. Crystal Palace	46	15	6	2	42	17	8	6	9	29	32	81
4. Watford	46	14	5	2	41	18	8	7	8	33	30	78
5. Blackburn Rovers	46	16	4	3	50	22	6	7	10	24	37	77
6. Swindon Town	46	13	7	2	35	15	7	8	8	33	38	76
7. Barnsley	46	12	8	3	37	21	8	6	9	29	37	74
8. Ipswich Town	46	13	3	7	42	23	9	4	10	29	38	73
9. West Brom	46	13	7	3	43	18	5	11	7	22	23	72
10. Leeds United	46	12	6	5	34	20	5	10	8	25	30	67
11. Sunderland	46	12	8	3	40	23	4	7	12	20	37	63
12. Bournemouth	46	13	3	7	32	20	5	5	13	21	42	62
13. Stoke City	46	10	9	4	33	25	5	5	13	24	47	59
14. Bradford City	46	8	11	4	29	22	5	6	12	23	37	56
15. Leicester City	46	11	6	6	31	20	2	10	11	25	43	55
16. Oldham Athletic	46	9	10	4	49	32	2	11	10	26	40	54
17. Oxford United	46	11	6	6	40	34	3	6	14	22	36	54
18. Plymouth	46	11	4	8	35	22	3	8	12	20	44	54
19. Brighton	46	11	5	7	36	24	3	4	16	21	42	51
20. Portsmouth	46	10	6	7	33	21	3	6	14	20	41	51
21. Hull City	46	7	9	7	31	25	4	5	14	21	43	47
22. Shrewsbury	46	4	11	8	25	31	4	7	12	15	36	42
23. Birmingham City	46	6	4	13	21	33	2	7	14	10	43	35
24. Walsall	46	3	10	10	27	42	2	6	15	14	38	31

Top League scorer: Kerry Dixon, 25 goals
Average home attendance: 15, 957
Player of the Year: Graham Roberts

FA CUP

(3)   Barnsley (A)   L0-4

LEAGUE CUP

(2)   Scunthorpe United (A) L1-4
(2)   Scunthorpe United (H) D2-2

FULL MEMBERS CUP

(1)	Plymouth Argyle (H)	W6-2
(2)	Bradford City (A)	W3-2
(3)	Nottm Forest (H)	L1-4
		(aet)

Also from Vision Sports Publishing

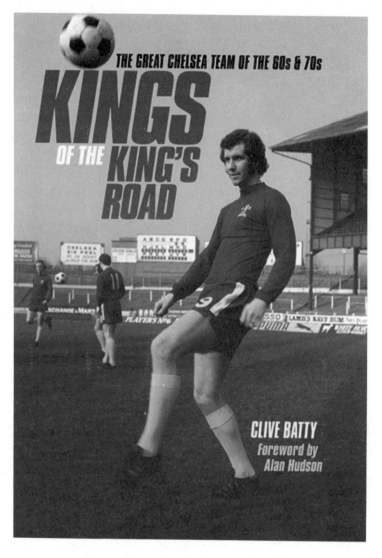

ISBN: 0-954642-81-3

"Kings of the King's Road is a must for all serious Chelsea supporters."
Blue and White Army fanzine

Buy online at **www.visionsp.co.uk**

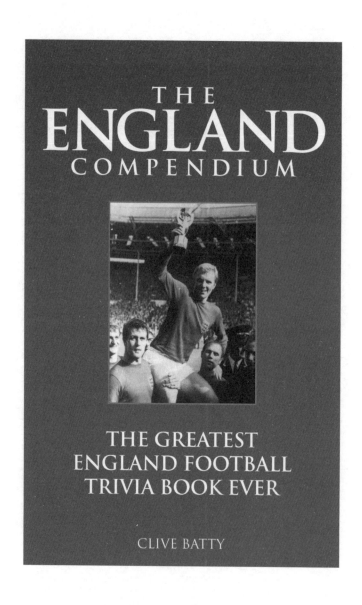

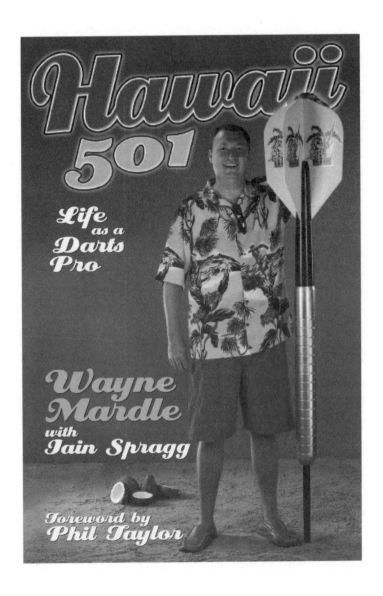

ISBN: 1-905326-06-8

"If there is a funnier sports book published this year I'll eat one of his shirts, flamingoes and all."
Andrew Baker, *The Daily Telegraph*

Buy online at **www.visionsp.co.uk**

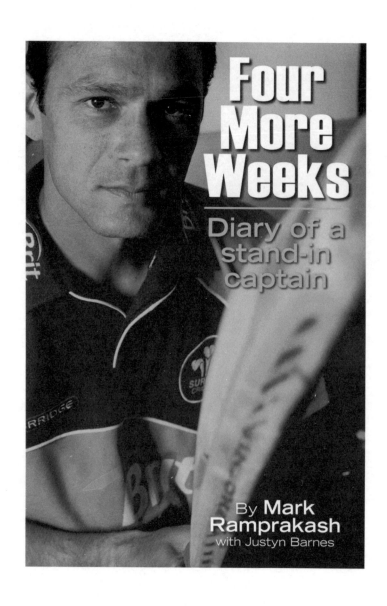

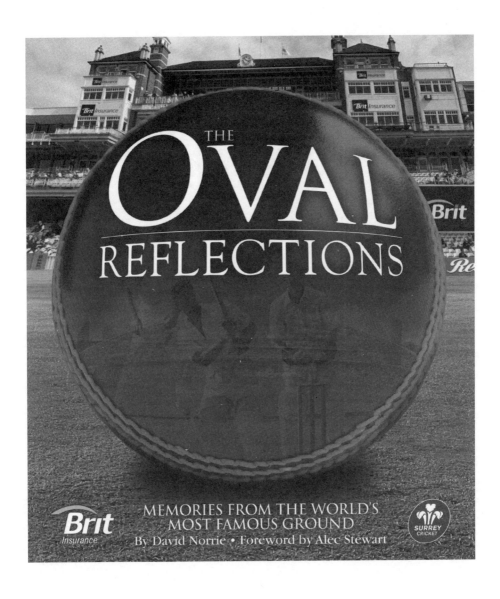

The
ASHES
Miscellany

The greatest England v Australia
cricket trivia book ever

CLIVE BATTY

ISBN: 1-905326-13-0

Publication: October 16th 2006